WRITE PORTABLE CODE

WRITE PORTABLE CODE

An Introduction to Developing Software for Multiple Platforms

by Brian Hook

NO STARCH PRESS

San Francisco

Printed on recycled paper in the United States of America

1 2 3 4 5 6 7 8 9 10 – 07 06 05

No Starch Press and the No Starch Press logo are registered trademarks of No Starch Press, Inc. Other product and company names mentioned herein may be the trademarks of their respective owners. Rather than use a trademark symbol with every occurrence of a trademarked name, we are using the names only in an editorial fashion and to the benefit of the trademark owner, with no intention of infringement of the trademark.

Publisher: William Pollock
Managing Editor: Karol Jurado
Production Manager: Susan Berge
Cover and Interior Design: Octopod Studios
Developmental Editors: William Pollock, Elizabeth Zinkann
Technical Reviewer: Tom Forsyth
Copyeditor: Marilyn Smith
Compositor: Riley Hoffman
Proofreader: Stephanie Provines
Indexer: Kevin Broccoli

For information on book distributors or translations, please contact No Starch Press, Inc. directly:

No Starch Press, Inc.
555 De Haro Street, Suite 250, San Francisco, CA 94107
phone: 415.863.9900; fax: 415.863.9950; info@nostarch.com; http://www.nostarch.com

The information in this book is distributed on an "As Is" basis, without warranty. While every precaution has been taken in the preparation of this work, neither the author nor No Starch Press, Inc. shall have any liability to any person or entity with respect to any loss or damage caused or alleged to be caused directly or indirectly by the information contained in it.

Library of Congress Cataloging-in-Publication Data

Hook, Brian, 1971-
   Write portable code : an introduction to developing software for multiple platforms / Brian Hook.--
1st ed.
        p. cm.
   Includes bibliographical references and index.
   ISBN 1-59327-056-9
1. Software compatibility. 2. Computer software--Development. I. Title.
   QA76.76.C64H66 2005
   005.1--dc22
                                        2005012981

For my wife, Jennifer

BRIEF CONTENTS

CONTENTS IN DETAIL

3
TECHNIQUES FOR PORTABILITY   25

4
EDITING AND SOURCE CONTROL   63

5
PROCESSOR DIFFERENCES   77

6
FLOATING POINT   91

7
PREPROCESSOR   109

8
COMPILERS   119

9
USER INTERACTION

10
NETWORKING

11
OPERATING SYSTEMS

12
DYNAMIC LIBRARIES   175

13
FILESYSTEMS   187

14
SCALABILITY   197

15
PORTABILITY AND DATA   201

16
INTERNATIONALIZATION AND LOCALIZATION   207

17
SCRIPTING LANGUAGES   213

PREFACE

I was having a conversation one day with a programmer colleague of mine about the headache of moving software from one platform to another. While complaining about the headaches of byte ordering, alignment restrictions, and compiler quirks, this friend asked an innocent but important question: "What book should I get if I want to write portable code?"

And the answer was startling: there were none.

With the hundreds of books on topics such as Java, C#, .NET, game programming, DirectX, extreme programming, and agile development, not a single modern book on cross-platform software development existed! This astounded me, especially given the recent flurry of new or different operating systems running on servers, desktops, handhelds, and even cell phones. Shouldn't there be at least one book that talks about the principles of portable software development? Of course, there should be, but there wasn't.

So, that's how this book got its start.

There have been few times in my life when I felt I just *needed* to do something—a compulsion strong enough that I devoted a good chunk of a year to researching and writing about cross-platform software development. I had a very strong vision for how to approach the book, and what you are holding is the end result.

This Book's Audience

I wasn't sure about my intended audience when I first came up with the concept for *Write Portable Code*, but after finishing the book, my "typical" reader became clear: an intermediate to advanced programmer interested in writing software for different platforms. Here are some examples of readers who will benefit from this book:

- A Windows programmer who wants to experiment with Linux at home
- A Mac OS X developer who needs to move her software to Windows to gain access to a wider market
- A Sony PlayStation 2 game developer who must write the Solaris server application for his game's multiplayer component
- A Palm OS developer who has been contracted to port his software to the Windows Mobile platform
- A large vertical integrator vendor that has just discovered its traditional deployment platform has been discontinued and must now move its products to a new system

There are countless reasons why developers may find themselves needing or wanting to port to a new platform, but thankfully, most of the same principles apply, regardless of the specific details. This book discusses and teaches those universal principles of portable software development.

Write Portable Code is written with the intermediate to advanced programmer in mind. However, I suspect that a lot of my readers may be newer to programming, and thus have only heard about portability in the abstract and aren't quite sure how it affects them. In fact, they may not understand what the problem *is*, since they haven't run into it yet. This may also be the case with more experienced programmers who have been working with the same system for a while and have not needed to deal with portability issues.

To help those of you who haven't yet stubbed your toes on the portability speed bump, I'll list a couple theoretical programmers and their situations. If you can identify with any of them, you should be alarmed enough that portability will elevate itself on your list of "Things to Be Concerned About."

Bob, the Java programmer

Bob has been developing applications for Windows the past three years using Borland's JBuilder environment. He has been using the Sun provided Java Runtime Environment (JRE) and happily writing productive, high-quality code. He is confident in his abilities as a Java programmer.

Then, one day, he is informed that his employer will be targeting IBM AIX. He originally thinks that since Java is "high-level" and "portable" and, infamously, "write once, run anywhere," there shouldn't be any real problems with the transition—copy the code to a new machine and run it, right?

Bob quickly finds that JBuilder is not available on AIX, some features on the Windows JRE don't behave the same with the AIX JRE, and some packages that were available on Windows aren't available on AIX. He scrambles to identify the differences in features, performance characteristics, bugs, and packages, and then must learn a whole new set of development tools such as Eclipse. What was originally taken for granted as "easy" has rapidly turned into a nightmare.

Janice, the Visual Basic programmer

Janice has been writing Visual Basic (VB) software for many years, providing forms that interact with Microsoft's Access database. Portability is not even a concept she's aware of, since she has never considered the world outside Microsoft Windows (or Microsoft products, period).

She has been asked to migrate her software to Mac OS X . Unfortunately, she has been living a pretty insulated life as a Microsoft-centric developer. She is alarmed to find that Mac OS X lacks both VB and Access, and she is unsure how to get her software up and running on that platform. Needless to say, the next few months are going to be very difficult for Janice as she learns the ins and outs of cross-platform development the hard way.

Reese, the user interface programmer

Reese has designed and implemented many user interfaces on Microsoft Windows using Visual C++ and Microsoft Foundation Classes (MFC). He has been using these tools and frameworks to rapidly prototype almost any type of application requested.

One of his company's biggest customers has decided to target developing economies that prefer the low cost of Linux, so Reese has been asked to move the suite of applications he has developed to that platform. Reese has never had to work outside the Windows world, and assumes that, given MFC's popularity, a reasonably compatible clone exists on Linux. After some basic research, he finds that this is not true. He must now learn a new development environment, operating system, and variants of the C++ language. Of course, he also must find and migrate to a replacement for MFC on Linux.

Jordan, the Linux/PPC developer

Jordan specializes in the development of server software. She has been asked to port her suite of server applications to Windows, which she initially thinks should be easy, since her applications don't even have user interfaces.

She discovers that almost every major API she uses—sockets, file I/O, security, memory mapping, threading, and so on—looks and acts completely differently on Windows. She is stunned to learn this, having originally thought that, since her applications were simple and used GCC (which is available on Windows as well), a port would take only a day or two.

She then finds that Windows and Linux/PPC don't even represent data the same way in memory, and huge chunks of her code that rely on memory-mapped file input fail on Windows. What was supposed to be pretty simple is now looking like a line-by-line audit of her entire code base.

In each of these cases, competent, talented programmers are suddenly put in the position of feeling not so competent or talented, primarily due to a lack of experience across multiple platforms. A common mistake is to catastrophically underestimate the amount of work required to perform a "simple" task requested by management.

In this book, I don't cover specifics of Java or VB, but many of the concepts hold true regardless of the language in question. This book reveals the issues and obstacles related to porting software. Armed with this information, those of you who are happily working in a single-platform world won't be so shocked when you're forced to move outside your area of immediate expertise.

Online Resources

The following book-related resources are available:

- Information about this book can be found at my website at http://www.writeportablecode.com.
- The Simple Audio Library (SAL) is available from http://www.bookofhook.com/sal.
- The Portable Open Source Harness (POSH) is available from http://www.poshlib.org.

ACKNOWLEDGMENTS

This book is the culmination of a lot of hard work and a lot of research. I would like to thank Bill Pollock and the staff of No Starch Press for answering my questions and giving me guidance even though they had no idea who I was or whether I would even end up selecting them as my publisher. They were very open and responsive about the entire publishing process.

Numerous friends and colleagues helped with the theme and content—too many to list comprehensively, but I would like to point out a few important ones. Casey Muratori, for being a good friend and letting me know when I say or do something stupid. John Hall, for writing *Programming Linux Games* and giving me good advice and feedback about the book writing process (and introducing me to No Starch). David Hedbor, Joe Valenzuela, and Ryan C. Gordon for providing valuable technical advice. The denizens of #icculus.org (irc.freenode.net), gamedevlists-general@lists.sourceforge.net, and the Book of Hook forums for providing answers, questions, opinions, and intelligent discussion. Tom Forsyth for providing astute technical review.

Of course, in this day and age, the online resources at our disposal are vast beyond imagination, including many software development–oriented websites, forums, and mailing lists, along with the general power of search engines. This book could not have been made in such a timely fashion without the general contribution to global knowledge that is the Web and the Internet. To anyone who has ever contributed their knowledge to the world at large—be it in the form of a blog entry, website article, or simply an answer to someone's question on a list archive—thank you.

This book was written using Open Office 1.*x* and Subversion (for revision control), both solid examples of high-quality open-source and cross-platform software development.

I'd also like to thank Starbucks—specifically Dawn Lokey, Jena Kelly, April Gresham, Eric Nyeste, and all the baristas at the Dallas Highway and Powder Springs Road Starbucks locations—for giving me a comfortable environment in which to work.

But most of all, I would like to thank my beautiful wife, Jennifer, for supporting me and our family while I worked on yet another random project to satisfy my own intellectual needs. I could not hope for a more supportive and tolerant spouse. This book was for me, but I'm dedicating it to her.

THE ART OF PORTABLE
SOFTWARE DEVELOPMENT

There is a strong emphasis within the software industry on getting things done as quickly as possible (though indeed, it's the rare project that makes it out the door on time). Emphasizing productivity and product delivery is surely a good thing, but spending a bit more time on that nebulous concept of portability has its advantages.

When we talk about writing portable software, we're referring to the ability to move our software between different platforms. This is a challenging task, since unlike many other aspects of computer science, portable software development relies heavily on experience and anecdotal data. My goal is to assist you, the reader, by providing a single resource that covers the art of portable software development.

The Benefits of Portability

Developing portable software may sound like a lot of work, and it can be. So why is portable software even desirable? Here are some of the main reasons:

Portability expands your market

If you can get your code to run on Linux as well as Windows, you may increase sales by some reasonable percentage. Not only that, but sometimes buyers have heterogeneous computing requirements, and the ability to support all of a customer's systems provides you a considerable advantage over competitors that support a fraction of those systems. For example, if a company runs a combination of Macintosh- and Windows-based computers, that company will likely prefer software that can run on both systems, as opposed to just one or the other.

Portable software is more robust

Aside from the sales and marketing advantages reaped by your ability to support new platforms, portable code has a major technical advantage: it leads to better software. By revealing sloppy assumptions and lazy coding habits, dormant bugs are exposed much faster. Often, serious bugs are discovered very early in the process of moving to a new platform.

Portable software provides freedom

If your company has the ability to switch to a new platform at will, then external forces that exert control over your platforms have a much dampened effect on your own fortunes. If a new platform must be targeted or a new tool suite used, the migration will be lubricated by portable coding habits.

Portability is sometimes necessary

Sometimes portability is not a luxury but rather a necessity. As the computing landscape changes, new technologies arrive and demand their support and attention. Consider moving from DOS to Windows, from Mac OS to System X, from Macintosh to PC, and especially today, the migration from 32-bit processors to 64-bit processors. The latter is a slow but steady movement that most software developers must undertake in the near future if they wish to remain competitive.

Portability provides options

You may find that a particular tool is absolutely essential to your development process, but that it is not available on your preferred host platform. I remember using OS/2 for DOS development because I needed to use Emacs as my text editor, and the DOS version of Emacs wasn't as full featured or robust as the OS/2 version. Currently, some developers are finding it worthwhile to port to Linux because of the Valgrind code-analysis tool.

Some programmers like to write portable software since it appeals to the geek elegance gene we carry, but there are also many practical reasons to do so. Very rarely does someone invest in the effort to develop portable software and wind up regretting it. Larger markets, better software quality, and more options are very powerful incentives to write cross-platform software.

A TALE OF TWO COMPANIES

Joe's company has been using Uberwhack C/C++ for a year now, and the developers have finally grown tired of the compiler's penchant for generating incorrect code and poor adherence to standards. Because they've minimized their dependency on Uberwhack's proprietary libraries and compiler-specific extensions, migrating to the Muchgood C++ Development System is painless and easy. As a result, the developers at Joe's company save months in otherwise lost development time looking for bugs that aren't theirs.

Jane's company, unfortunately, committed to using Uberwhack's proprietary class library, StraitJacket Foundation Classes. The developers also used a few ill-advised extensions to the C++ language that Uberwhack created, and now that their software has become so entwined with the Uberwhack system, it simply isn't feasible to move to a different development system in the near future. This costs them months in development time as they waste time looking for bugs that are the result of the Uberwhack compiler's faulty code generator.

Joe is working on a vertical market hardware device currently based on the Motorola 68000 CPU and OS 9 operating system. Because his code was written in a portable, abstracted manner, when his manager asks how long it will take to migrate the existing code to an Intel StrongArm processor running the Microsoft Pocket PC 2003 operating system, Joe can truthfully answer, "A couple of months."

Jane's company has heard rumors that Joe's company will be switching to the StrongArm/Pocket PC 2003 platform and opts to follow suit. Unfortunately, she has told management that migrating their existing code will be extremely difficult, since it is hard-wired to their current platform. She estimates that it will take the better part of a year before her software is running on the new target system.

Finally, Joe's hardware group doesn't have working systems yet, but Joe has been asked to start developing immediately anyway. Since Joe's code is abstracted at a high level, he can use a target system emulator, making his code ready for testing and debugging even before the hardware group delivers the first prototype, saving valuable months of development time.

While this may seem like an overly contrived example, situations like this arise all the time in many industries. Portable software that avoids tying itself to a single platform provides valuable agility to a software developer, allowing rapid shifts to new platforms as circumstances dictate.

Elements of the Platform

So, portability is the ability to move software between platforms—the environments required to build and run your code.

Porting between platforms involves dealing with some combination of the following platform elements:

- Build tools, such as compiler, linker, and build/project management tools
- Support tools, such as source control, profiler, and debugger tools
- Target processor

- Target operating system
- Libraries and APIs

Each of these has a significant impact on your ability to execute or build software on a new platform. Compiler vendors may have proprietary class libraries and language extensions. Build tools may not work on different platforms. Operating systems may have radically different capabilities. Libraries may not be available on all systems.

The Problem with Assumptions

With few exceptions, the root cause of the majority of problems encountered when porting software is invalid implicit assumptions. These are assumptions that are made for one platform that become invalid once the software is moved to another platform. These assumptions include the following:

- Compile-time assumptions ("All integers are 32 bits")
- Resource assumptions ("I'll be able to make 8 MB arrays on the stack")
- Performance assumptions ("I can count on having a 3 GHz processor")
- Feature assumptions ("I can use multithreading")
- Implementation assumptions ("My target operating system uses main() as its entry point")

There are an alarmingly large number of ways you can make assumptions that bite you later.

With this in mind, I submit that portable software development is the act of converting implicit assumptions to explicit requirements, coupled with the use of abstractions to isolate the general from the specific. Your goal should be to identify invalid assumptions, convert them to explicit requirements, and, whenever possible, introduce abstractions that isolate your general architecture from specific implementations.

Coding Standards

For reasons I'll explain in Chapter 2, I use ANSI C and C++ as this book's demonstration languages. Portability problems with the C language, particularly problems with different implementations, were well known. In 1989, the ANSI/ISO committees ratified a standard (C89) to address many of these problems. After another decade of use and evaluation, the standard was revised (C99), but its full adoption has been slow. Even though C99 is not a prevalent standard, I'll adopt some of its conventions simply to keep things understandable. I'll use C99's support for exact-sized types in the interest of consistency. Table 1 shows the C99 data types.

Table 1: C99 Standard Data Types

Type	Description
int8_t	Signed 8-bit integer
uint8_t	Unsigned 8-bit integer
int16_t	Signed 16-bit integer
uint16_t	Unsigned 16-bit integer
int32_t	Signed 32-bit integer
uint32_t	Unsigned 32-bit integer
int64_t	Signed 64-bit integer
uint64_t	Unsigned 64-bit integer

I've developed a package, the Portable Open Source Harness (POSH) (see Appendix A), which provides a set of C99-like type definitions (among other things). The source code examples in this book will sometimes use POSH features. A production application will need to come up with something very similar to POSH (or it can just use POSH, as it's open source and freely usable) if it intends to be ported to multiple platforms.

The Framework for Portable Programming

It seems that most computer books live in one of two camps: the theoretical or the practical. Much like advice from your parents, the theoretical books (such as academic texts) have only marginal utility when solving specific problems. A book about three-dimensional computer graphics in general can be useful when you're trying to understand the topic as a whole, but when it comes time to write software, you often would like to see specific examples that apply to your situation.

Books in the practical camp (such as trade books) are often great for solving a problem right now, but (like my wardrobe) suffer from temporal instability—it may look good now, but in a few short years, it's going to be embarrassingly inappropriate. There may not be much demand today for books about IBM OS/2 or the PC BIOS, but in 1989, they were all the rage.

This book attempts to bridge the gap between the two camps by providing a conceptual framework for portable programming, while still giving enough real-world details to provide relevance or, at the very least, context.

Timeliness and timelessness are sometimes at odds. Because of the number of compiler bugs, portability problems, and general system differences, it is pretty much impossible to enumerate all of the different portability "gotchas" that programmers face today. In fact, this book directly addresses only a small fraction of the problems that you might encounter in practice. However, the concepts and strategies discussed will help you to navigate the majority of real-world portability problems you may encounter.

My goal is to separate the theory of portability from specific real-world instances. It is far too easy to get bogged down in the details of a single issue when the focus should be directed at the higher-level problem. For this reason, situations where there is lengthy discussion about concrete problems and their solutions are placed in separate sidebars. These provide context with the chapter's higher-level discussion, but are not the focus of the book.

Along with POSH, mentioned in the previous section, I've written a companion portable software library, the Simple Audio Library (SAL), which illustrates many of the concepts discussed here. Where applicable, I have included examples that illustrate the implementations of SAL or POSH and how they relate to the principles discussed in this book. By providing a functional piece of annotated cross-platform software, I hope to appeal to those who learn by example better than they learn by reading.

1

PORTABILITY CONCEPTS

Before we get into the details of porting, we need to take a step back and focus on the concept of portability itself. Sure, it would be easy to dive in and start showing specific examples of converting a sample piece of Linux software to run on a Windows machine, but then I would have addressed only one problem hot spot.

This chapter discusses the various facets of portable development—principles, techniques, and processes for portability—that will allow you to write programs that easily move from one platform to another, regardless of the specifics of the source and destination environments. I'll address specific problems and their solutions once we lock down the basics.

Portability Is a State of Mind, Not a State

Programming is often a stateful endeavor. Your brain shifts gears as you edit, compile, debug, optimize, document, and test. You may be tempted to make porting a separate stage, just like editing or debugging, but "thinking portably" is not a step—it's an all-encompassing state of mind that should inform each specific task a programmer performs. Somewhere in your brain, between the "make variable names meaningful" and "don't hardcode those constants" rules, the "think portably" action should be active at all times.

Like weeds taking over a garden, portability issues have a habit of infiltrating all aspects of the development process. If coding is the process of coercing a computer into a specific set of actions by speaking a language it understands, and portable software development is the process of avoiding any dependencies or assumptions about a specific computer, then there is an indirect but palpable tension between the two tasks. The requirement to get something working on the current platform competes with the desire to get it working on other platforms as well.

It's important to recognize the difference between porting code and writing code portably. The former is a cure; the latter is prevention. Given a choice, I would rather inoculate a programmer against bad practices now than try to fix the side effects of those practices later. This "vaccination" is achieved by practicing portable coding habits so vigorously that the process becomes second nature—a deeply embedded, intuitive understanding that swims beneath the surface of a programmer's thoughts at all times.

Develop Good Portability Habits

Very often, programmers first introduced to the world of portable software worry too much about specific techniques or problems, but experience teaches them that portability is achieved more easily through habits and philosophies that encourage, if not force, a programmer to write portable code. To develop good portability habits, you must first resist the temptation to stress about details like byte ordering or alignment problems.

No matter how much knowledge you have about portability in theory, very often, the practice of porting will illustrate deficiencies in that theory. Theoretically, writing standards-compliant code should make that code more portable. However, making that assumption without testing it could lead you to experience many different problems. For example, it doesn't matter if the ANSI C specification dictates a certain behavior if an uncooperative or buggy compiler flatly refuses to adhere to that standard. Standards-compliant code isn't really helpful if you're dealing with noncompliant tools.

A classic example of this is Microsoft Visual C++ 6.0, which does not properly support the C++ specification for scoping of variables inside a for statement:

```
for ( int i = 0; i < 100; i++ )
    ;
i = 10; /* With MSVC++ 6.0, this variable still exists...with
           compliant compilers the variable is out of scope
           once the for loop exits and thus this line would
           generate an error */
```

Microsoft developers "fixed" this behavior with version 7.*x* of its C++ compiler; however, this introduced backward-compatibility problems with code written for version 6, so it made noncompliance the default behavior. This means that a programmer can charge ahead writing what he feels is safe, portable code on Microsoft Visual C++, only to find that it breaks when compiled with the GNU Compiler Collection (GCC).

But you can catch problems like this easily if you practice good portability habits, such as frequent testing and developing in multiple environments, as you work. This saves you the trouble of remembering all the specific bugs and standards quirks that you may encounter.

Good Habits Trump Specific Knowledge of Bugs or Standards

So, let's look at just what these good portability habits are.

Port Early and Port Often

No code is portable until it has been ported, so it makes sense to port your code early and often. This avoids the common mistake of writing "portable" code and then testing it late in the development process, only to find all the little portability problems at once. By testing your code's portability early, you can catch problems while you still have time to fix them.

Develop in a Heterogeneous Environment

It's possible to dodge the two-stage write-then-port process by developing in a heterogeneous environment. This habit also minimizes the risk of code base atrophy, whereby one fork of your project evolves while another languishes due to inattention from the developers.

For example, early in a project, you might run on Linux, Mac OS X, and Windows, but due to time pressures, the Linux version is deprecated. Six months later, you need to get your software working on Linux, but you find that many changes that were made never propagated to that platform (for example, due to conditional compilation directives).

The first step to developing in a heterogeneous environment is to make sure that the developers are using as many different host systems and tools as is practical. If you're shipping a project that will deploy on Solaris for Sun Sparc, Microsoft Windows on Intel, and Mac OS X on Macintosh, then ensure that your team members use a mix of those systems as their primary development systems. If they are not required to use these systems as their primary development system, a penchant for the "get it working; we'll port it later" mindset tends to take root.

Even when working on similar systems—Windows PCs, for example—it's often a good idea to have a mix of different hardware (video cards, CPUs, sound chips, network adapters, and so on) and software, so that more configuration bugs can be found earlier than later. This helps to fend off the "Works on my machine!" cry from developers when bugs are later reported in the field.

SAL EXAMPLE: HETEROGENEOUS DEVELOPMENT

I developed the Simple Audio Library (SAL) concurrently on a Windows XP–based laptop using Microsoft Visual C++ 6.0, an Apple G4 Power Mac running OS X 10.3 (using XCode/GCC), an AMD Athlon XP–based Linux (ArkLinux, a Red Hat–based distribution) workstation using GCC, and occasionally using Microsoft Embedded Visual C++ for Pocket PC. The bulk of development occurred on the Windows XP machine, with the occasional port and verification on the other platforms every few days.

I occasionally performed quick verification tests using other compilers such as Metrowerks CodeWarrior and Visual C++ 7.x, and sometimes problems or even bugs would show up as a result.

The code never diverged or atrophied too much. However, the Pocket PC support was introduced fairly late into SAL's development and was the cause of much tedium because so many of SAL's assumptions weren't valid for that platform. Specifically, the test program's reliance on the existence of main() created a problem, because Pocket PC does not have console applications, so you must provide a WinMain() method. Other issues were caused by the Pocket PC's emphasis on wide character strings (for internationalization).

I used several different low-level APIs to implement key features such as thread synchronization. I found common abstractions and then put them into a separate abstraction layer, which, in turn, layered itself on the actual implementation for each platform. This meant that moving from a Win32-based mutex scheme to a POSIX threads (pthreads) mutex scheme was very easy to accomplish, because SAL was not riddled with Win32-specific code.

Use a Variety of Compilers

You will also want to use different compilers as much as possible. Different host systems may often dictate this, but sometimes you can get away with using the same compiler on disparate systems; for example, the GCC compiler is fairly ubiquitous across a wide range of platforms.

By compiling successfully on a wide range of compilers, you can avoid being left stranded if your preferred compiler vendor suddenly disappears. It also ensures that the code base does not rely on new (and unproven) language or compiler-specific features.

Test on Several Platforms

Most projects have a well-defined set of deployment targets determined by market dynamics. This simplifies testing and quality assurance tremendously, but it also starts you down the precarious path of implicit assumptions. Even if you know you'll be running on a single target system, it doesn't hurt to target alternate platforms—processors, RAM, storage devices, operating systems, and so on—strictly for testing.

And if your target system is altered due to marketing requirements or changing business relationships, you'll find comfort knowing that your software isn't hardcoded to a single platform.

Support Multiple Libraries

Much of today's software development is less about writing new code than it is about gluing together big chunks of preexisting pieces. If you are dependent on a group of proprietary libraries or APIs, porting to a new platform will be difficult. However, if you take the time early on to support multiple alternative libraries that accomplish the same results, you will have a lot more options in the event a library vendor goes out of business or refuses to make its software available on another platform. There is also the minor side benefit of being able to license or open source your code without worrying about dependencies on closed-source third-party libraries.

A classic example of this is support for OpenGL versus Direct3D, the two preeminent 3D graphics APIs available today. OpenGL is cross-platform and available on a wide range of systems, including all major PC operating systems. Direct3D, on the other hand, is the official 3D graphics API for Windows and available only for Windows. This puts developers in a touchy situation: do you optimize for Windows, the largest market of users in the world, or do you try to support many platforms at once using OpenGL?

Ideally, you abstract the graphics layer so that it can function well on either API. This can be a lot of work, so the ramifications of the abstraction must be thought through clearly before you dive in. However, when it comes time to move your software to a new platform, the abstraction work will pay for itself many times over.

Plan Portability for a New Project

I derive a certain amount of geeky, purist joy from starting work on a new project. There is a kind of "new car smell" when you create a new directory, waiting to be populated with perfect source code built on years of prior experience.

When you find yourself in that rare position of starting with a clean slate, you have the opportunity to plan how to make your project portable. If you take a few points into consideration before you start, you'll save yourself a lot of time and trouble down the road.

Make Portability Easy

As with many other kinds of good habits, the odds of sticking with good portability habits are directly proportional to how easy it is to use them. If the development methodology in place makes portable software development tedious or inefficient, then it will be dropped faster than you can say "missed milestone."

It is important to create procedures, libraries, and mechanisms so that writing portable code is second nature instead of an arduous, ongoing task. For example, a programmer should not need to deal with byte ordering unless she is actually dealing with things at that level.

Choose a Reasonable Level of Portability

While every attempt can be made to write code that is 100 percent portable, practically speaking, this is nearly impossible to achieve without making significant sacrifices to the software's feature set.

You cannot be dogmatic about portability! Your software should be as portable as is practical, but no more. Sacrificing time and effort in the interest of ensuring portability with marginal utility is analogous to spending a week optimizing a routine that is called only once. It's just not an efficient way to spend your time.

This is why establishing a fundamental and realistic baseline—a set of ground rules that define reasonable portability—is so vital to a project. Without this, a project will be doomed to wishy-washy, inoffensive coding designed to run everywhere . . . poorly.

Every platform has its own set of peculiarities involving machines, compilers, tools, processors, hardware, operating systems, and so on. There are thousands of different ways in which a program can be broken by moving from one platform to another. Thankfully, many of these peculiarities are shared, which eases the task of writing portable software. Defining this common ground is one of the first steps to designing and writing portable code.

As I'll talk about later in Chapter 14, a large part of portability is related to scalability (ability to run on systems with a wide variance in performance and features) within the baseline. Scalability is important, but it must be within well-defined parameters to retain any semblance of relevance.

Aside from raw features, you must make assumptions about the underlying performance of your platforms. It is entirely possible to write software that compiles and operates identically on both an 8 MHz Atmel AVR microcontroller and a 3.2 GHz Intel Pentium 4 processor, but whether the result will be meaningful and interesting in both contexts is questionable. The algorithms and data structures used for a workstation class PC are going to be radically different than those for an embedded microcontroller, and limiting a high-powered machine to operations that are practical on radically different architectures is inefficient.

CASE STUDY: FLOATING-POINT MATH

The ANSI C language supports floating-point, single- and double-precision operations by use of the `float` and `double` keywords, respectively, along with their associated mathematical operators. Most programmers take this support as a given. Unfortunately, some devices today, and many devices not too long ago, have extremely poor floating-point math support. For example, the processors used in most personal digital assistants (PDAs) are unable to execute floating-point instructions natively, so significantly slower emulation libraries must be used.

Now, it's entirely possible that very slow floating-point math is acceptable for a particular project because it is used rarely (although even in these cases, an executable may grow in size if a floating-point emulation library must be linked in even if it's used a handful of times). But for projects where strong floating-point performance is assumed, things can get ugly in a hurry when that code must be ported to a system without intrinsic floating-point support.

One common method to address this dichotomy is to write all math operations using special macros that call fixed-point routines instead of floating-point routines on devices without native floating-point support. Here is an example:

```
#if defined NO_FLOAT
typedef int32_t real_t;
extern real_t FixedMul( real_t a, real_t b );
extern real_t FixedAdd( real_t a, real_t b );
#define R_MUL( a, b ) FixedMul( (a),(b))
#define R_ADD( a, b ) FixedAdd( (a),(b))
#else
typedef float real_t;
#define R_MUL( a, b ) ((a)*(b))
#define R_ADD( a, b ) ((a)+(b))
#endif /* NO_FLOAT */
```

A three-element dot product would then be written as follows:

```
real_t R_Dot3( const real_t a[ 3 ], const real_t b[ 3 ] )
{
   real_t x = R_MUL( a[ 0 ], b[ 0 ] );
   real_t y = R_MUL( a[ 1 ], b[ 1 ] );
   real_t z = R_MUL( a[ 2 ], b[ 2 ] );
   return R_ADD( R_ADD( x, y ), z );
}
```

However, the pure floating-point version is significantly easier to read and understand:

```
float R_Dot3( const float a[ 3 ], const float b[ 3 ] )
{
   return a[ 0 ] * b[ 0 ] + a[ 1 ] * b[ 1 ] + a[ 2 ] * b[ 2 ];
}
```

If you must support systems without floating-point capabilities, or if you feel there is a very good chance that this will be necessary, then using the macros is probably a good idea. But if you have the ability to specify native floating-point support as part of your baseline, you would benefit from the increase in code readability and brevity.

Portability is a good idea, and writing portable code is good practice, but if you take it to extremes or write excessively portable code in order to satisfy ideological dogma, your code may suffer as a result. Portability is a means to an end, not an end unto itself.

A network application that predicates its architecture on low-latency, high-bandwidth communication will fail catastrophically when confronted with a modem. So while this application can compile and run anywhere, practically speaking, it is not portable to some classes of networks due to fundamental assumptions made about the networks on which it will reside.

Establishing a baseline is a key element in portable software development, because it creates some assumptions that are perfectly legitimate and allow for the practical development of software effective on a limited class of platforms.

There is a difference between portable to the point of distraction and portable enough. If your project is aimed at a single target platform, but you know you may need to change compilers at some point, then concentrate on keeping your code portable between compilers, and don't worry as much about target systems that you're unlikely to support.

Don't Wed Your Project to Proprietary Products

Modern software development is incredibly complex, and even simple projects may consist of tens of thousands of lines of source code. This complexity often requires the use of (ideally) well-tested and well-documented third-party components such as libraries and tools. Using preexisting components saves time, but it also introduces a host of new portability concerns. Ensuring the portability of your own software is difficult and time-consuming enough, but when you introduce foreign influences, it can be downright daunting. Every time an outsider's component is integrated into a project, flexibility and control are incrementally reduced.

Even with the best-case scenarios—open-source libraries—you must verify that the code compiles and runs everywhere you need it to run. And if you require a platform yet to be supported by the open-source library's contributors, you'll need to do the porting work yourself (which, thankfully, is still an option due to the nature of open source).

Unfortunately, the use of closed-source proprietary libraries removes this alternative. In such a situation, you may find yourself painted into a corner if the provider won't or can't (for instance, if the vendor has gone out of business) support a platform you require. In the worst case, you'll find that you must reimplement the third-party component entirely from scratch for the new platform. Tying your projects to third-party components can be very dangerous in the long run. Many industry veterans can recite stories of projects inexorably linked to an orphaned library or tool set and how that tie affected the entire development process.

For example, many PC developers have used Microsoft's DirectPlay network library because it's free and available, and it claims to provide a large number of features that would take a long time to reinvent. The low-hanging fruit of free and easy technology beckons, but those that grab it run into a mess when trying to port to a non-Microsoft platform such as the Macintosh or a game console. They often find themselves needing to rewrite their entire networking layer from scratch to compensate for their ill-advised commitment to a proprietary technology.

SAL EXAMPLE: THE BASELINE AND USE OF PROPRIETARY APIS

SAL has a fairly modest feature and performance baseline. It is written in ANSI C89 (with the exception of one file written in Objective-C and limited to use on the Mac OS X platform), availing itself to the widest range of platforms possible. The two key technological components are the mixer and assumed threading model.

The mixer is integer-based and assumes that 32-bit integer operations, especially multiplication, will be relatively quick. For this reason, it may not work particularly well on a 16-bit platform such as Palm OS 4.

However, two key parameters—the maximum number of simultaneous voices and the buffer length—are user-definable at run time, allowing SAL to scale cleanly across a wide range of system capabilities. For particularly slow systems, the buffer size can be increased at the cost of more latency. In addition, the number of active voices can be reduced to minimize the amount of work performed in the inner mixing loop. A high-powered system could trivially handle 128-voice polyphony, but in a pinch, you could operate SAL in monaural mode on low-powered devices.

The basic implementation model for SAL creates a separate thread responsible for pulling sample data from active voices. This is the conceptual model used on most of its platforms; however, at least one platform (OS X) uses a callback to the CoreAudio sound API instead. (The callback is called from another thread, so technically another thread *is* used, but SAL does not create it.) Regardless of how the audio system generates mixed data, there is still the underlying assumption that this happens asynchronously, so there is an expectation that synchronization primitives will be provided (in the form of mutexes). A simple single-threaded operating system (such as Mac OS 9 or Microsoft MS-DOS) could, in theory, be supported, but this would require careful planning, since those architectures use interrupts to drive the audio system.

Parts of SAL expect a small amount of memory to be available at all time, although nothing too excessive (by PC standards)—on the order of a few hundred kilobytes. The pulse code modulation (PCM) sample playback implementation assumes that PCM data is resident; however, it is entirely possible to use streaming audio instead, thereby reducing the memory footprint significantly. This requires more work on the part of the application programmer, but the option is there.

The core SAL implementation requires the C standard run-time library (free(), malloc(), vsnprint(), memset(), fprintf(), and so on). However, it could operate effectively in a freestanding (no C run-time library or operating system) environment with minimal modification (primarily consisting of offering replacements for vsnprintf() and memset()).

SAL does not use any proprietary APIs for its core code. However, it does use several platform-specific APIs (Win32, pthreads, CoreAudio, Cocoa, OSS, ALSA, and so on) to implement parts of the architecture. Internal SAL-specific APIs are then layered on top of these APIs. For example, _SAL_lock_mutex() calls WaitForSingleObject() on Win32 and pthread_mutex_lock() on Linux.

There are no core elements to SAL that cannot be ported to a platform within its baseline. However, libraries are often much easier to port than applications.

If you find yourself using a third-party component for a significant portion of your work, you should abstract away from it by at least one level of indirection so that its replacement or augmentation has a reduced impact on the rest of the project. If you find that your project must use a proprietary toolkit or library, look into getting a full source code license or, at the very least, ensuring that the vendor will place the source code under escrow to guard you against that company going out of business.

Port Old Code

Unfortunately, reality rarely allows us the luxury of working on a brand-new project. In many cases, we must deal with portability issues through no fault of our own, as we move someone else's unportable code from one platform to another.

For that situation, some general guidelines and rules can help you manage the process.

Assume Code Is Not Portable Until It Has Been Ported

A lot of programmers think they're good at writing portable code, and many of them are. But the problem is that they'll often claim that their code is portable and should "just compile and run" on a new platform. This is, sadly, rarely the case. No matter how many assurances are given that a code base is portable, always make the assumption that it's not. Until the code has been moved to a new platform and tested, it should be treated with extreme wariness.

During the development of SAL, I constantly ran into portability issues every time I recompiled on another system or switched compilers. There are simply too many things to keep track of mentally, and the proof is in the pudding, as it were. The act of porting is the real litmus test for how portable your code is.

Of course, you can claim that your code is "portability friendly," which is a reasonable description for software written with porting in mind but that has not been ported to a specific platform. There is a large difference between code that is known to be unportable (you tried to port it and couldn't), code that is unknown to be portable (no one has tried to port it), and code that is known to be portable (it has been ported to new platforms).

Modify Only the Bare Essentials

Porting software requires a lot of editing and refactoring, and therefore the possibility of introducing new bugs and breaking the software on its original platform. As tempting as it may be to go through and clean up code unrelated to the port, avoid this at all costs. Keeping a clean source base provides a solid foundation for regression testing.

Working on a large source base that is already functional on one platform can be tricky. Every time you edit a file, there is a small chance that you've just broken something somewhere else. For this reason, extend the rule of "don't touch anything you don't have to" to include "find the path of least resistance."

This means that there is, ideally, some logical division in the software's implementation that will allow you to cleanly delineate your new code from the old code. If you can find this line, it will make porting much easier, since you'll be able to toggle back and forth between your modified code and the "virgin" source.

Plan Your Attack

Before you write or change a single line of code, you must understand exactly what it is you're trying to do. Porting software is different from writing new software, and the approach you take will also be different. Identify the likely portability hot spots so that you know exactly what tasks will be required to move the software onto a new platform. Once you have this itemized list, you can sit down and work out the exact plan of attack you'll use for the porting process.

For example, porting an application from Windows to Linux might have a (very general) checklist like this:

☑ Remove all references to Windows-specific header files.

☑ Update Windows file-handling code to Unix-style file functions.

☑ Isolate and update the entire `CreateWindow` path.

☑ Update resource loading to use Unix-style file-access routines.

☑ Replace registry code with localized file-based preferences.

By having a well-defined checklist ahead of time, you can try to predict what problems you'll encounter later in the porting process and plan accordingly.

Very often, the first instinct is to just get the software moved to the new system and start compiling, fixing errors as the compiler and linker cough them up. Once the progam compiles and links, then you start running it in a debugger until you get it to work. But that's not a very efficient way of handling the porting process. You need to identify all the major areas that need to be touched first to avoid going down one path so far that it interferes with work that must be performed later.

For example, you may find that the first fix that came to mind for one portability problem isn't practical once a later, separate portability problem comes to light. You now need to go back and undo your first set of changes and devise a strategy that solves both portability problems.

Document Everything in Revision Control

In case I haven't made this clear enough already, every change you make is potentially destructive. For this reason, you must document all changes.

Using a revision control system is pretty much mandatory when developing any complex software that will evolve over time. During a port, however, it is even more important, because every change might subtly break something unrelated to your current work, and identifying when this break occurs is much easier if you have clean revision logs.

When starting a port, developers have a strong desire to see things up and running as fast as possible on a new platform. But if you jump into the task without proper planning, you may waste a lot of time exploring dead ends and undoing previous work.

2

ANSI C AND C++

One of the most fundamental choices affecting portability is that of programming language. I use ANSI C and C++ as this book's demonstration languages since they are ubiquitous and tend to contribute to portability problems (without which this book wouldn't have much of a market). ANSI C and C++ are probably the most unportable languages that were still intended to be portable.

Why Not Another Language?

Given that C and C++ suffer from such massive portability problems (we'll get to the specific problems later), it would seem to make sense to migrate to higher-level languages that isolate the user from many cross-platform issues. And today, large classes of applications can and should do this. But there are still many situations where C and C++ are clearly the optimal (or only) choice for development. Why is this so?

C and C++ Provide Low-Level Access

The C programming language was originally designed to untie the Unix operating system from a specific hardware architecture, and so C can probably be considered the first important portable computer programming language. Ratification by a standards body (such as ANSI, ISO, or IEC) and the wide availability of documentation, libraries, compilers, and other development tools have made C (and, later, C++) the prevalent choice for developers that need to write cross-platform, high-performance applications.

C and C++ are the default implementation languages when you need to deal with hardware at a bare-bones level without resorting to assembly code. Higher-level languages have a very hard time letting the programmer work with memory addresses, ports, or DMA buffers directly; in fact, they actively discourage and prevent such manipulation.

ANSI, ISO, IEC—WHAT'S THE DIFFERENCE?

There is some confusion when developers are faced with the difference between an ISO, ANSI, ANSI/ISO, ISO/IEC, and ANSI/ISO/IEC standard. It can be overwhelming when dealing with so many different standards organizations and acronyms, but thankfully it's fairly simple once explained.

ANSI is the American National Standards Institute, and it accredits developers to create standards for use in business and government in the United States. ANSI, in turn, is a member of the International Standards Organization (ISO), so very often, an ANSI standard will be elevated, with some necessary changes, to an ISO standard.

Finally, the IEC (International Electrotechnical Commission) helps prepare and publish the standards that are ratified by ANSI and ISO.

C and C++ Compile to Native Code

Most C and C++ implementations generate native binary code, which is necessary for embedded systems or when code size and performance are of critical importance.

Many languages today compile to a generic, intermediate form (Java bytecodes or early Pascal p-codes are examples), which is a great way to maintain portability. Unfortunately, this has a cost of a significant increase in code size and execution time. Furthermore, such generic codes must be executed by a virtual machine or run-time environment. To compound matters, each implementation of a virtual machine or run-time environment may have subtle bugs or implementation differences, resulting in a portable program that still suffers from platform dependencies.

Very high-level languages make writing portable software significantly easier than C or C++ in the problem domains where they are appropriate. But there will always be a place for low-level languages that offer hardware access and high performance, and those languages still need to support portability.

C and C++ Dialects

The seeds of the C programming language were first planted in the early 1970s by researchers at Bell Labs. At the time, it was developing a new operating system called Unix, and the need for a high-level language for development had been identified.

The researchers involved, including Ken Thompson, Brian Kernighan, and Dennis Ritchie, were used to working with languages such as B, BCPL, PL/I, and Algol-60. However these languages, for various technical reasons, were not practical for the machines they were targeting at the time (DEC PDP-7 and PDP-11).

As a starting point, the researchers took the B language and extended it to provide additional features necessary for their work, and soon the C language was formed. The Unix kernel was then converted to C code.

By 1978, the language had grown considerably in popularity, and Kernighan and Ritchie published their famous *C Programming Language*, which established the first semi-standard dialect of C.

During the next ten years, the C language evolved, outstripping the rapidly out-of-date standard established by Kernighan and Ritchie. It became apparent that the language needed a formal standard, to harness the myriad implementations, and also for the more mundane reason that various organizations and governments were loathe to adopt a computer language that lacked any formal definition.

For this reason, in the early 1980s, the ANSI X3J11 committee was formed to draft and ratify a standard. This work was completed in 1989 as the ANSI X3.159-1989 "C Programming Language," which, in turn, was approved by ISO as ISO/IEC 9899-1990. *ANSI C* is effectively the same as *ISO C*.

Ten years later, the standard was amended and updated to reflect a decade's worth of experience, and thus C99, aka ISO/IEC 9899:1999, was born.

Of course, while C was evolving, other languages (often derived from C) started to appear, most notably C++. C++ began as an experiment in the early 1980s by Bjarne Stroustrup, who was intrigued by the object-oriented capabilities of languages such as Simula and how they might apply to system software development. Much like C, the C++ language's standardization process was somewhat haphazard.

In 1985, Stroustrup published *The C++ Programming Language*, a direct analog to Kernighan and Ritchie's work, which provided the basis for AT&T's first commercial implementation. As the language gained in popularity, the *Annotated Reference Manual* (ARM) by Stroustrup and Margaret Ellis was published in 1990 as a much needed update to Stroustrup's earlier work and, more important, as a complete reference manual for the language itself, not just a particular implementation.

The ARM became the base document for the new ANSI committee, XJ316, which was formed to ratify a standard for C++. It took most of the 1990s before the standard was finally ratified as ISO/IEC 14822:1998.

(Notice that this occurred roughly a year before the revised C99 standard was put in place, which means that some minor but niggling semantic differences between C99 and C++98 exist in the areas they overlap.)

For this book, the focus will be on the 1989 ISO/IEC/ANSI 9899:1999 specification of the C language, which I will refer to as *C89*, since it is by far the most well supported today. Most annotations specific to the C99 specification are presented in the form of sidebars. We'll still have the occasional foray into C++ 98 as relevant or necessary, but when illustrating specific cases that are somewhat independent of language, I'll lean toward C because of its greater ubiquity, clarity, and brevity. In addition, C++ is still a rapidly growing and evolving language, and much of the discussion of various implementation inconsistencies will be obsolete well within the shelf life of this book.

NOTE *I won't address portability to pre-ANSI C ("K&R C"). With the lack of a formal, rigorous standard, the sheer number of differences—major and minor—make it nearly impossible to discuss in a cogent manner.*

Portability and C/C++

There is a broad gap between theoretical portability and practical portability. It is all too easy to fixate on language details instead of writing portable software that happens to use C/C++. The former emphasizes the language itself, concentrating on whether particular constructs are portable, legal, undefined, or implementation-specific. But writing portable software is about architecture, design, and trade-offs when using a particular language; understanding the nuances of a specific language is only a part of the process.

This isn't to devalue in-depth knowledge of a language, but it is important to keep things in perspective and realize that you're trying to write working software, not software that is perfectly portable. Portability is a means to an ends, not an end unto itself.

I set out to write a book about writing portable software using the C and C++ languages, not about writing portable C and C++ code. This is a subtle but important distinction. At times, developers may write code that is technically unportable, but this is unavoidable in the real world. As long as you are aware of and document any nonportable assumptions, you should be fine. The reality is that even a "100 percent portable" program—one that adheres to the letter of the law as defined by a language's standard—can still fail on different platforms due to bugs that are beyond the developer's control. This is why emphasizing structure, design, and process is more important than dogmatically concentrating on language particulars.

For example, converting a pointer to a function to some other representation, such as a pointer to an object or an integer, is pretty much a strict no-no according to the ANSI standard, as the other representation may not be large enough to safely hold a pointer to a function.

Here is an example:

```c
#include <stdio.h>

void foo( void )
{
   printf( "Hello world!\n" );
}
int main( int argc, char *argv[] )
{
   uint32_t f = ( unint32_t ) foo;    /* not guaranteed to work! */
   void (*fnc)() = ( void (*)() ) f; /* also not guaranteed to work */

   /* the following works as you expect on most platforms, even */
      though it's technically "bad" */
   fnc();
   return 0;
}
```

But this type of conversion is something that a lot of real code—even pretty portable code—does. Many event or messaging systems have generic parameter fields that are sometimes filled with pointer data. For example, under Win32, the WM_TIMER message specifies that the LPARAM field of its MSG structure points to a user-defined callback function (as specified with Set-Timer()). That's an integral part of the API, and it's definitely technically not portable, although that's moot given that it's a Windows-specific feature. (The "correct" way to implement this would have to use a union as part of the MSG structure as defined by Microsoft, thereby ensuring the proper size and alignment of any data type stored in the structure's fields.)

The dlsym API returns a pointer to a void that may point to either data or code, depending on the invocation. This technically may fail, but the X/Open System Interface (XSI), which manages the dlfcn APIs, makes the handy caveat that any pointer to data must also be able to contain a pointer to code, neatly sidestepping the problem by using our first rule of portability: convert an implicit assumption to an explicit requirement.

So, while technically there are things you shouldn't do because a language's standard frowns on it, pragmatism may require that you use some nonportable features with the knowledge that your code might break later.

Even though its roots were in portability, C is rife with portability issues. Some of these are due to weak attempts at stricter standardization, and many are due to its focus on being a high-level assembler suitable for writing systems software. But even with these concerns, ANSI C (and to a much lesser extent, ANSI C++) can't be beat as a baseline for writing high-performance, compact, portable code. Therefore, ANSI C and C++ are the languages I'll focus on in this book.

3

TECHNIQUES FOR PORTABILITY

One of my motivations for writing this book was that I encountered so many programmers who had solved portability problems using very similar, but undocumented, techniques. Each of these developers had to discover these approaches independently or by word of mouth, because very few books have been written on the topic of portable software development—a glaring omission in computer literature.

This chapter forms the backbone of this book, as it details various practices and patterns commonly used today for portable software development.

Avoid New Features

Regardless of the language you use, avoid new or experimental language features and libraries. Support for new features tends to be sporadic and buggy, and even when support has spread, there are often corner cases that haven't been properly tested or defined precisely.

Classic cases of this include early implementations of templates, namespaces, and exception handling in C++. Before that, the move from early C to ANSI C felt interminable, since many platforms did not have ANSI C-compatible compilers for quite some time. In some cases, the delay between feature discussion/ratification and widespread implementation can be more than half a decade.

Experience has taught us a reasonable rule of thumb: if a new feature has been implemented for at least five years, it *might* be safe to rely on. Even today, as I write this book, the C99 specification has been around for almost five years, and there is still no fully C99-compliant compiler available.

Deal with Varying Feature Availability

In the world of software development, every time someone writes a portable library designed to run in multiple environments, developers invariably face the philosophical question of how to deal with features available on one platform yet missing on another. For example, consider Mac OS X/Cocoa's column-view data browser, the Windows tree controls and recursive mutexes, the lack of threads on DOS, and the lack of transparent virtual memory on earlier versions of Mac OS. These are typical examples of features available or missing on certain platforms, which a cross-platform library or application will need to reconcile.

One approach maps abstractions directly to the concrete implementation available on each target. For example, feature X on platform A would result in using platform A's implementation of feature X.

But what do you do when platform A doesn't support feature X? An application could query to see if a particular implementation is available and avoid using it if it's not present. However, this approach suffers from numerous drawbacks, such as convoluted conditionals in your application code and poor robustness if a feature you've come to rely on suddenly disappears. The following code snippet illustrates this particular road to madness.

```
api_feature features;
api_get_features( &features );
if ( features.feature_x_present )
{
    /* Do things one way */
}
else if ( features.feature_y_present )
{
```

```
    /* Do things a different way */
}
else if ( features.feature_z_present )
{
    /* Do things yet another way */
}
else
{
    /* Don't do anything at all, possibly warning user */
}
```

This illustrates the conditional execution nightmare that can arise when software tries to deal with widely varying feature availability.

SAL EXAMPLE:

EMULATED VERSUS REQUIRED FEATURES

SAL makes expectations about the underlying implementation in two key areas: recursive mutexes and audio mixing.

Recursive mutexes are a form of mutex (a thread synchronization primitive) that may be locked multiple times by the same thread without deadlocking. Windows has recursive mutexes by default, and the Linux pthreads implementation has them as a type of mutex. OS X provides this facility with its higher-level Cocoa NSRecursiveLock class.

I could have taken a separate approach and implemented my own recursive mutexes on top of nonrecursive mutexes, gaining some generality and, of more direct help, being able to share the pthreads implementation between OS X and Linux. However, this would have required testing and a larger implementation within SAL itself, so I opted not to do that. If I need to support SAL on a platform that does not have recursive mutexes, I will probably end up having to implement them myself in an emulation layer, and then rely only on raw mutexes on the underlying platform.

Audio mixing is sometimes performed as a service by the operating system (waveOut or DirectSound) or a separate audio library (such as SDL_Mixer) within an application. Since mixing is not available on all platforms as a native part of the underlying digital audio subsystem, I felt it was important to implement it directly within SAL, since it's such an important feature.

The downside of reinventing this wheel, surprisingly enough, is not code bloat. SAL would likely be *larger* if it attempted to abstract and support each platform's mixing facilities. The problem is its inability to take advantage of accelerated mixing. Some operating systems and libraries provide accelerated mixing routines in the form of Single Instruction Multiple Data (SIMD) optimizations, and some sound devices have hardware-accelerated mixing, removing the burden entirely from the CPU. But the amount of complexity that abstracting platform-dependent mixing would have entailed would not have been worth it, especially considering that many implementations that should work do not. Many DirectSound drivers are notoriously unreliable when it comes to hardware-accelerated mixing.

SAL takes the easy path. As long as it can send a single buffer of some format to the hardware, everything should work. It removes mixing as a platform responsibility entirely.

CASE STUDY: DIRECT3D AND OPENGL

In the late 1990s, there was a fierce rivalry between two competing 3D graphics APIs: OpenGL and Direct3D. OpenGL had a long history in the Unix workstation market and was generally well thought out and well documented. Direct3D was more ad hoc and shortsighted, a reaction to the need to support consumer-level 3D graphics while understanding that PCs were, by their nature, far more limited than the types of workstations for which OpenGL was designed.

OpenGL has a very rigid and clear policy when it comes to features: any platform that wants to call itself OpenGL must comply completely with the OpenGL standard, *even if that platform cannot provide all those features optimally.* For example, if a particular video card does not support texture-mapped graphics, it must still provide texture-mapped output if requested by the application—meaning that it must emulate this feature entirely in software.

OpenGL extended this philosophy even further by refusing to expose what a platform's underlying feature set might be. In theory, this forced the programmer to write extremely portable code that "just worked," moving the onus of compatibility and performance on each OpenGL implementor.

As you would guess, OpenGL's approach worked a lot better in theory than in practice. It was common for a developer to enable a feature such as texture mapping, only to find that his application had lost 95 percent of its performance. (This is not an exaggeration—it was not uncommon to see frame rates drop from 60 Hz to 1 Hz or even slower.) Users would complain loudly, and the developer would then spend a day or two tracking down the culprit on one particular machine. Finally, some kind of detection code, in the form of querying the OpenGL implementation's GL_RENDERER_STRING, would be wedged into the program to disable any slow features on specific platforms, like this:

```
if ( !strcmp( glGetString( GL_RENDERER ),
            "That Bad Hardware Device Rev 3.0" ) )
{
    features.use_texture_mapping = 0;
}
```

Microsoft approached this problem completely differently with Direct3D by directly exposing each hardware implementation's underlying capabilities through a query mechanism known as *capability bits*, or *cap bits*. A program was expected to query the platform's individual capabilities before making any assumptions about the available feature set.

Unfortunately, Direct3D's approach didn't work very well in practice. For example, drivers would often publish capabilities that they did not accelerate very well, so even though a video card exported "Hey, I support texture mapping," it was no guarantee that its texture-mapping performance was adequate. Sometimes capabilities were mutually exclusive, which is a concept that the capability bits could not convey. Some hardware would claim both trilinear texture mapping and dual texture blending when, in fact, you could enable one or the other, but not both. Probably the most frustrating problem was that a hardware device might provide unique functionality that the DirectX API did not show (unlike OpenGL, which explicitly supported the notion of additional abilities through an extensions mechanism), frustrating developers and hardware manufacturers alike. There was no reward for innovation, since Microsoft completely controlled which features were visible to the developer.

OpenGL allowed expansion from a guaranteed baseline, whereas DirectX allowed variability within a delimited set of features. As a result, OpenGL was considered far more innovation-friendly than DirectX, which was controlled entirely by Microsoft.

Today, the two APIs coexist quietly. Modern 3D acceleration hardware is no longer rife with the hodgepodge of implementations prevalent almost a decade ago, when dozens of products of wildly differing performance and features competed with each other. With the stabilization in the market has come a stabilization in the Direct3D API, but it is still far from perfect. Microsoft's attitude to improving it has been to effectively rewrite it with every new generation of hardware. This is a practical and expedient approach, for sure, but one that leaves developers relearning 3D graphics programming with each new generation.

Which approach is better comes down to philosophy, and both camps have their detractors. At the time of this writing, DirectX is up to version 9 and has stabilized remarkably well. Developers still need to deal with the ins and outs of each hardware accelerator's innate abilities and driver bugs/limitations, but the API itself is reasonably stable. OpenGL has been dying a slow death on the PC, but this has been primarily for political, not technical, reasons. As such, DirectX is the clearly dominant API on Windows, although OpenGL is still the cross-platform 3D graphics API of choice (it's used on Mac OS X and almost every major Unix variant).

Another approach is to completely refuse to use a sporadically available feature, significantly simplifying development, but then you run the risk of your software being inefficient on platforms where that feature is a key aspect of the technology (not to mention catching grief from platform partisans who expect you to support their platform's unique characteristics).

Yet another approach is to factor out as much of each platform's vagaries as possible by implementing everything yourself, effectively allowing the emulation to completely replace any native implementation of a given feature. For example, a cross-platform graphical user interface (GUI) system may eschew any native "widget" functionality and instead handle all widget management internally. This frees the user from worrying about the specifics of each platform, but again there are downsides.

One downside of allowing the emulation to completely replace any native implementation is performance. If everything is being handled by the portability software, then opportunities for using accelerated software or hardware are lost. Another is that the developer has just signed on to tackle the reimplementation of a huge amount of code that is already "done" on each target, which results in duplicated effort, more code to be debugged, and generally a lot more work to be done. Finally, the emulated implementation may lack the expected features or look and feel of a particular target system.

The middle ground uses a native implementation (if available), and only missing features are emulated. This may seem like the best option in most cases (for example, it is not much work to emulate the Windows tree control on the X Window System), but sometimes it can be grossly impractical. For example, enabling a nonaccelerated feature with OpenGL will often drop you down to a "slow path" that is performed completely in software, bypassing any hardware acceleration available. It is highly likely that in a situation like this the user would prefer to run software with a particular feature disabled than suffer a multiple order of magnitude difference in performance.

Use Safe Serialization and Deserialization

One of the most common problem areas with cross-platform is saving (serializing) and loading (deserializing) data in a safe, efficient manner. When working with a single compiler and target, you can always resort to fwrite/fread, but in the cross-platform world, this is not practical, especially when you need to store to a destination other than a file, such as a network buffer.

A portable implementation divides serialization into two parts. The first is converting to a canonical reference format from the underlying platform's in-memory representation of an object. This conversion process should be almost 100 percent portable. For example, suppose you wish to serialize a user record:

```
#define MAX_USER_NAME 30
typedef struct user_record
{
    char name[ MAX_USER_NAME ];
    int16_t priv;

} user_record;
void serialize_user_record( const user_record *ur, void *dst_bytes )
{
    /* production code should have a size tied to
    dst_bytes to prevent buffer overruns */
    /* this section has been omitted for brevity */
    uint8_t *dst = ( uint8_t * ) dst_bytes;

    memcpy( dst, ur->name, MAX_USER_NAME) );
    dst += MAX_USER_NAME;
    dst[ 0 ] = ( uint8_t ) ( ( ur->priv >> 8 ) & 0xFF );
    dst[ 1 ] = ( uint8_t ) ( ur->priv & 0xFF );
}
```

NOTE   *More complete implementations for user record serialization should have buffer over-flow checking and, optionally, the ability to serialize to a text format for printing or human editing.*

The code in serialize_user_record copies the user record into dst_bytes the same way, no matter on which platform you run it. A user_record serialized on a PowerPC running Yellow Dog Linux should create an *identical* set of bytes as a user_record serialized on an Intel xScale running Microsoft Pocket PC 2003.

This would not necessarily hold true if the implementation were the following instead:

```
void serialize_user_record( const user_record *ur, void *dst_bytes )
{
    /* DANGER! DANGER! */
    memcpy( dst_bytes, this, sizeof( *ur ) );
}
```

As I'll discuss in later chapters, a raw structure in memory may have varying alignment, byte ordering, and packing properties, so this alternative implementation would sometimes work and sometimes fail, depending on the compilers used and the platform executing the code. Unfortunately the brevity of the memcpy implementation is incredibly tempting when you're just trying to get something going.

There are different architectural approaches to implementing serialization interfaces. For example, a common idiom uses multiple inheritance so that classes can inherit from input or output archival base classes as necessary. This is an invasive procedure, requiring alteration of the class's basic inheritance structure, which a lot of programmers are loath to do.

Once the data is portably formatted in a buffer, you can then archive it to its final destination. For example, if you're saving to disk, then you might use fwrite; if you're broadcasting over a network, you might call send or sendto, or you may pass it through more processing steps such as compression and encryption before final delivery.

Deserialization operates the same way, but in reverse:

```
void deserialize_user_record( user_record **ur, const void *src_bytes )
{
    /* production code should have a size tied to src_bytes to prevent buffer
overruns */
    /* this has been omitted for brevity */
    const uint8_t *src = ( const uint8_t * ) src_bytes;
    *ur = ( user_record * ) malloc( sizeof( user_record ) );

    memcpy( (*ur)->name, src, MAX_USER_NAME) );
    src += MAX_USER_NAME;
    (*ur)->priv = ( ( ( uint16_t ) src[ 0 ] ) << 8 ) | ( src[ 1 ] );
}
```

Again, there is always the temptation to go with the shortcut, which could be a structure copy through a pointer cast or a memcpy:

```
void deserialize_user_record( user_record **ur, const void *src_bytes )
{
    /* production code should have a size tied to src_bytes to
      prevent buffer overruns */
    /* this segment has been omitted for brevity */
    *ur = ( user_record * ) malloc( sizeof( user_record ) );
```

```
        **ur = * ( user_record * ) src_bytes; /* ouch, bad! */
}
```

As with the serialization example, the preceding code assumes that the in-memory format of a user_record will match that of src_bytes, which is not guaranteed due to alignment, size, and packing considerations.

When the performance of a load operation is a concern, it is reasonable to assert, "I will guarantee that my archival format is byte-for-byte identical to my in memory format," and load straight from storage into preformatted memory structures. If you can enforce appropriate preprocessing (data is platform-specific, for example) and verify it with appropriate run-time checks, then the portability is data-driven instead of code-driven, allowing for faster performance without any real sacrifice in real-world portability.

Integrate Testing

Porting software involves changing and writing a lot of code that may not be tested on another platform for quite some time, which means that many bugs have a lengthy gestation period. For this reason, it is vital that you perform standardized testing to catch bugs as early as possible.

Unit tests are small pieces of code that exercise a particular function or subsystem with known data to ensure that everything behaves as expected. These tests should immediately catch any bugs you've inadvertently introduced during development, and they act as a first line of defense when a particular function works correctly on your Mac but dies a horrible death on Windows. While it may seem like a tedious waste of time to write tests that almost never fail, the few times they do fail, you'll be glad you did.

POSH EXAMPLE: BYTE-ORDER TESTING

The Portable Open Source Harness (POSH) library attempts to determine a target's byte ordering at compile time by inspecting a host of variables. However, it is entirely possible for this guess to be wrong. If POSH then proceeds to act as if the underlying machine uses one byte ordering when the byte ordering is actually very different, things can get ugly in a hurry, since your software is effectively thinking that it's running on the wrong machine!

For this reason, POSH has a quick sanity check for byte ordering:

```
/* This is taken from posh.c */
/* POSH_LITTLE_ENDIAN is defined during compilation by posh.h */
#if defined POSH_LITTLE_ENDIAN
#  define IS_BIG_ENDIAN    0
#  define NATIVE16   POSH_LittleU16
#  define NATIVE32   POSH_LittleU32
#  define NATIVE64   POSH_LittleU64
#  define FOREIGN16 POSH_BigU16
#  define FOREIGN32 POSH_BigU32
#  define FOREIGN64 POSH_BigU64
```

```c
#else
#   define IS_BIG_ENDIAN    1
#   define NATIVE16   POSH_BigU16
#   define NATIVE32   POSH_BigU32
#   define NATIVE64   POSH_BigU64
#   define FOREIGN16 POSH_LittleU16
#   define FOREIGN32 POSH_LittleU32
#   define FOREIGN64 POSH_LittleU64
#endif

static
int
s_testBigEndian( void )
{
   union
   {
posh_byte_t c[ 4 ];
      posh_u32_t  i;
   } u;

   u.i= 1;

   if ( u.c[ 0 ] == 1 )
   {
      return 0;
   }
   return 1;
}
static
const char *
s_testEndianess( void )
{
/* check endianess */
   if ( s_testBigEndian() != IS_BIG_ENDIAN )
   {
return "*ERROR: POSH compile time endianess does not
            match run-time endianess verification.\n";
}

/* make sure our endian swap routines work */
   if ( ( NATIVE32( 0x11223344L ) != 0x11223344L ) ||
        ( FOREIGN32( 0x11223344L ) != 0x44332211L ) ||
        ( NATIVE16( 0x1234 ) != 0x1234 ) ||
        ( FOREIGN16( 0x1234 ) != 0x3412 ) )
{
    return "*ERROR: POSH endianess macro selection failed.
            Please report this to poshlib@poshlib.org!\n";
}
```

```
    /* test serialization routines */

    return 0;
}
```

The preceding code verifies that the compile-time environment's endianess guess matches what the run-time environment discovers. A mismatch should never happen in practice, but every now and then, a particular configuration or situation creeps through, and the sanity check will fail.

Use Compilation Options

It's always nicer if we can force our tools to do the hard work for us, and as luck would have it, our most common tool—the compiler—often provides features that help us find questionable code in the way of warnings and error messages.

Compile-Time Assertions

The art of portable programming is not about avoiding assumptions, but rather about avoiding unreasonable or inaccurate assumptions. Once you do make some assumptions, you need to verify that these assumptions are valid as early as possible. Many assumptions, thankfully, can be validated at compile time using a *compile-time assertion.*

I've seen numerous ways of implementing a compile-time assertion, but I like the following:

```
#define CASSERT( exp, name ) typedef int dummy##name [ (exp) ? 1 : -1 ];
```

This attempts to create a new type of the given name as an array of integers. If the expression passed is false, then it will attempt to define a type consisting an array of size –1, which is illegal and generates an error.

For example, if you entered the following:

```
CASSERT( sizeof( int ) == sizeof( char ), int_as_char )
```

it would expand to:

```
typedef int dummyint_as_char[ -1 ];
```

which generates a compile-time error, just as you would expect. On GCC, the error would be:

```
temp.c:3: error: size of array `dummyint_as_char' is negative
```

Microsoft Visual C++ reports:

```
temp.c(3) : error C2118: negative subscript or subscript is too large
```

And Metrowerks CodeWarrior reports:

```
### mwcc.exe Compiler:
#    File: temp.c
# --------------
#        3: of(int)==sizeof(char)) ? 1 : -1 ];;
#    Error:                                  ^
#    illegal constant expression
```

The error messages don't tell you which assertion failed, but at the very least, you'll have a file and line number to investigate when your code mysteriously stops compiling—a much more desirable situation than if your code compiled and then you ran into mysterious bugs and crashes.

The name parameter is required to avoid triggering a redefinition error (the result of defining the same type multiple times), since under the C language, multiple (even identical) type definitions of the same type are illegal. With C++, this is not the case. If you are compiling only for C++, then the name parameter may be omitted.

Strict Compilation

Many compilers provide a strict or ANSI-only compilation option that reports questionable code. For example GCC has the -ansi and -pedantic parameters, and Microsoft Visual C++ provides the /Xa switch. (Unfortunately, many Windows applications cannot be compiled with /Xa since <windows.h> violates the ANSI standard in countless places.)

When strict compilation is enabled, a compiler will issue either warnings and/or errors when a compiler-specific or compiler-dependent feature is used. This can assist portability greatly. It is also a good idea to enable as many warnings of all types as possible.

Segregate Platform-Dependent Files from Portable Files

A simple technique to make porting and writing portable code much easier is to segregate files based on their platform dependencies. This streamlines the porting process by defining clear landmarks and platform "templates" for programmers working on other platforms.

In addition, by enforcing this separation, you can quickly spot when non-portable code sneaks into a project. If someone puts an #include <windows.h> into SAL_linux.c, it will almost assuredly break the next time it is compiled under Linux, sending up a red flag immediately.

Write Straightforward Code

Programmers, as a breed, enjoy being cute with their code. When something can be written in a clear, concise manner or a slightly cooler but infinitely more obtuse way, all too often, programmers will choose the latter to demonstrate their language prowess. Aside from general maintenance and debugging problems, such cute programming tricks often cause headaches when it comes to portability.

Cute programming tricks often rely on compiler-specific features or aspects of a language that may not be widely implemented. This aside, by obfuscating the intent of a piece of code, someone trying to port to a new platform may not be able to discern what the code does.

Use Unique Names

By definition, portable software often finds itself running in new, unfamiliar environments. Sometimes it will need to be modified to call support libraries and operating system APIs that were heretofore unknown, which means that portable software must play nicely with other software packages.

A common source of conflict is identifiers. For example, when developers ported their DOS applications to Windows, they suddenly found themselves with strange compiler or linker errors having to do with `CreateWindow`, a common function name that happened to collide with Windows' own function of the same name.

In a perfect world, Microsoft would have prefixed its entire Windows API with something like `Win` or `GDI` or `MSW`. The odds of `MSW_CreateWindow` colliding with some random developer's internal libraries are much lower.

But since developers have little say over the naming conventions of libraries and operating systems, the onus is on us to avoid these collisions. In C, this means prefixing everything as much as possible with a somewhat unique identifier. Just keep in mind that certain prefixes are very popular (`x_`, `z_`, `gr_`, and `Gr` are a few examples), so the longer your identifier, the lower your chances of a collision. In years past, long identifiers were frowned upon, since the linkers prevalent at the time often truncated identifiers after a handful of characters (often as few as six!). For example, `Graphics_OpenWindow` and `Graphics_CloseWindow` might both end up as `Graphi` and clash at link time. Thankfully, this is not as much of a problem today, as the C99 specification allows 32 significant characters for identifiers with external linkage.

In C++, you can enclose all global functions as static functions inside a pure static class:

```
class MyLibrary
{
  private:
    virtual ~MyLibrary() = 0; // prevent instantiation
    MyLibrary() {}
  public:
    static void foo( void );
}
```

Then the `foo` function can be called automatically using the appropriate prefix:

```
void func()
{
    MyLibrary::foo();
}
```

Does this buy you anything over just calling it MyLibrary_foo()? Not really, other than appeasing C++ purists. (Well, to be honest, you get one tiny benefit, which is that you can drop the prefix when calling other functions from within the same static class, but some would argue that's a bad thing.)

Or if you want to go nuts with C++, you can use a namespace:

```
namespace MyLibrary
{
    void foo( void );
}
```

But this pretty much does the same thing as the static class, albeit in a more C++-ish fashion.

```
#define SAL_VOLUME_MAX        65535
typedef struct SAL_DeviceInfo_s
{
    sal_i32_t    di_size;
    sal_i32_t    di_channels;
    sal_i32_t    di_bits;
    sal_i32_t    di_sample_rate;
    sal_i32_t    di_bytes_per_sample;
    sal_i32_t    di_bytes_per_frame;
    char         di_name[ SAL_DEVICEINFO_MAX_NAME ];
} SAL_DeviceInfo;
SAL_PUBLIC_API( sal_error_e )  SAL_create_device(
SAL_Device **pp_device,
    const SAL_Callbacks *kp_cb,
    const SAL_SystemParameters *kp_sp,
    sal_u32_t desired_channels,
    sal_u32_t desired_bits,
    sal_u32_t desired_sample_rate,
    sal_u32_t num_voices );
SAL_PUBLIC_API( sal_error_e )  SAL_destroy_device( SAL_Device *p_device );
SAL_PUBLIC_API( sal_error_e )  SAL_get_device_info( SAL_Device *p_device,
                                        SAL_DeviceInfo *p_info );
```

Almost everything has an appropriate prefix to minimize the odds of collision with another library or API. A function name like destroy_device or a constant such as UNKNOWN or INVALIDFORMAT has a dangerously high chance of being defined in another package.

Implement Abstraction

The primary tool you'll use in your quest for portability is *abstraction*. This is the process of isolating system specific elements from your more general architecture. Abstraction allows you to write your mainline code in a clean, system-independent manner.

Abstractions are a trade-off between power and ease of use. Abstractions, by their nature, must take a lot of different implementations and present a lowest common denominator. This makes programmers' lives easier, but since they no longer have access to the underlying implementation's extra features, they may find that their power is limited.

For example, the SAL audio API assumes 8- or 16-bit PCM data, since that is prevalent on almost every major operating system and sound driver. However, Apple's OS X CoreAudio API supports 32-bit floating-point audio formats, which are very powerful. Unfortunately, there is no clean way for SAL to offer this without incurring significant overhead and complexity (via emulating 32-bit floating-point formats on systems that don't support it, or alternatively by allowing that form only on OS X).

Throughout this section I'll be using examples from both SAL and POSH to illustrate the power of abstraction.

Dispatch Abstraction

One of the areas where programmers often use conditional compilation inappropriately is when selecting appropriate functions to execute on different operating systems. Let's use a simple example of emitting a beep from a computer system's speaker.

Under Windows, this is accomplished using the Beep() API. On systems that support ANSI escape sequences, you can print a CTRL-G to the console.

Unfortunately, too many programs would do a conditional at every point a beep is needed:

```
#ifdef _WIN32
    Beep( 440, 100 );  /* 440Hz, 100 ms */
#else
    printf( "\a" );  /* use ANSI "bel" character */
#endif
```

It doesn't take too much imagination to realize that this is a recipe for ugly code if beeping must happen frequently. Ideally, you would like a system where you have a single call within your mainline code, and that call automatically goes to the proper underlying routine—what I refer to as *dispatch abstraction.*

Three common mechanisms for dispatch abstraction are link resolution, function pointer tables, and C++ virtual functions.

Link Resolution

As its name implies, *link resolution* relies on the linker to resolve abstractions statically, most likely through conditional compilation. A function is referred to by the same name across multiple platforms, but its implementation is provided by only a single platform. This is effective only when a single resolution is possible on a specific platform.

For example, SAL uses this technique to abstract the creation and initialization of device-specific data with SAL_create_device, which is a cross-platform function.

```
/* NOTE: This creates a device, but is a non-system-specific
function since the abstraction is handled by the link-resolved
call to _SAL_create_device_data */
sal_error_e
SAL_create_device( SAL_Device **pp_device,
                   const SAL_Callbacks *kp_cb,
                   const SAL_SystemParameters *kp_sp,
                   sal_u32_t desired_channels,
                   sal_u32_t desired_bits,
```

```c
                sal_u32_t desired_sample_rate,
                sal_u32_t num_voices )
{
    sal_error_e err;
    SAL_Device *p_device = 0;

    if ( pp_device == 0 || kp_sp == 0 || num_voices <= 0 )
    {
        return SALERR_INVALIDPARAM;
    }

    if ( kp_cb == 0)
    {
        p_device = ( struct SAL_Device_s * )
            malloc( sizeof( struct SAL_Device_s ) );
        memset( p_device, 0, sizeof( *p_device ) );

        p_device->device_callbacks.alloc   = s_alloc;
        p_device->device_callbacks.free    = s_free;
        p_device->device_callbacks.warning = s_print;
        p_device->device_callbacks.error   = s_error;
    }
    else
    {
        if ( kp_cb->cb_size != sizeof( SAL_Callbacks ) )
        {
            return SALERR_WRONGVERSION;
        }

        if ( ( kp_cb->alloc == 0 ) != ( kp_cb->free == 0 ) )
        {
            return SALERR_INVALIDPARAM;
        }

        *pp_device = ( struct SAL_Device_s * )
            kp_cb->alloc( sizeof( *pp_device ) );
        memset( *pp_device, 0, sizeof( **pp_device ) );
    }

    /* allocate voices */
    p_device->device_voices = ( struct SAL_Voice_s * )
        p_device->device_callbacks.alloc(
            sizeof( struct SAL_Voice_s ) * num_voices );
    memset( ( *pp_device)->device_voices, 0,
        sizeof( struct SAL_Voice_s ) * num_voices );
    p_device->device_max_voices = num_voices;

    /* this will properly dispatch to the _SAL_create_device_data
    implemented by a given platform */
    if ( ( err = _SAL_create_device_data(
```

```
                                *pp_device,
                                kp_sp,
                                desired_channels,
                                desired_bits,
                                desired_sample_rate ) ) != SALERR_OK )
        {
            p_device->device_callbacks.free( p_device->device_voices );
            p_device->device_callbacks.free( *pp_device );
            return err;
        }
        /* Dispatches through a function table */
        _SAL_create_mutex( *pp_device, &(p_device->device_mutex));

        p_device->device_info.di_bytes_per_sample =
            p_device->device_info.di_bits / 8;
        p_device->device_info.di_bytes_per_frame  =
            p_device->device_info.di_bytes_per_sample *
            p_device->device_info.di_channels;

        *pp_device = p_device;

        return SALERR_OK;
    }
```

The call to _SAL_create_device_data is resolved at link time, since it will be defined only one time on any given platform (the other implementations are protected by #ifdef guards). For example, on Windows, _SAL_create_device_data is defined in sal_win32.c and is found only if POSH_OS_WIN32 is defined.

Link resolution provides good performance and robustness. (If the function name cannot be resolved, it is caught at build time, not when the program is being run.) However, it does not offer much flexibility if you would like to resolve the abstraction at run time; that is, if you need to select different implementations dynamically. For example, SAL supports the waveOut and DirectSound audio APIs on Windows, and if you wanted to select which subsystem to use at run time, static link resolution would not be effective. (You could, however, ship two separate executables to resolve this.)

Function Tables

When you need to switch between implementations dynamically, a *function pointer table* is a better solution than static link resolution. A function pointer table consists of an array or a structure containing a set of pointers to functions, which is used to provide a layer of indirection between the portable and nonportable segments of a program.

SAL uses this technique for its core abstraction layer. Inside the SAL_Device structure (in sal_private.h), you'll see this:

```
typedef struct SAL_Device_s
{
    SAL_Callbacks    device_callbacks;
```

```
    sal_mutex_t     device_mutex;
    void            *device_data;
    SAL_DeviceInfo  device_info;

    struct SAL_Voice_s  *device_voices;
    int                 device_max_voices;

    /* implementation callbacks */
    sal_error_e  (*device_fnc_create_mutex)
        ( struct SAL_Device_s *device, sal_mutex_t *p_mtx );
    sal_error_e  (*device_fnc_destroy_mutex)
        ( struct SAL_Device_s *device, sal_mutex_t mtx );
    sal_error_e  (*device_fnc_lock_mutex)
        ( struct SAL_Device_s *device, sal_mutex_t mtx );
    sal_error_e  (*device_fnc_unlock_mutex)
        ( struct SAL_Device_s *device, sal_mutex_t mtx );
    sal_error_e  (*device_fnc_create_thread)
        ( struct SAL_Device_s *device,
          void (*fnc)(void *args), void *targs );
    sal_error_e  (*device_fnc_sleep)
        ( struct SAL_Device_s *device, sal_u32_t duration );
    void         (*device_fnc_destroy)( struct SAL_Device_s *d );
} SAL_Device;
```

Each implementation is responsible for pointing the implementation callbacks at the necessary functions. For example, the Win32 implementation of _SAL_create_device_data looks like this:

```
sal_error_e
_SAL_create_device_data( SAL_Device *device,
                         const SAL_SystemParameters *kp_sp,
                         sal_u32_t desired_channels,
                         sal_u32_t desired_bits,
                         sal_u32_t desired_sample_rate )
{
    device->device_fnc_create_thread = _SAL_create_thread_win32;
    device->device_fnc_create_mutex  = _SAL_create_mutex_win32;
    device->device_fnc_lock_mutex    = _SAL_lock_mutex_win32;
    device->device_fnc_unlock_mutex  = _SAL_unlock_mutex_win32;
    device->device_fnc_destroy_mutex = _SAL_destroy_mutex_win32;
    device->device_fnc_sleep         = _SAL_sleep_win32;

    if ( kp_sp->sp_flags & SAL_SPF_WAVEOUT )
    {
#ifdef SAL_SUPPORT_WAVEOUT
        return _SAL_create_device_data_waveout(
                    device,
                    kp_sp,
                    desired_channels,
                    desired_bits,
```

```
                    desired_sample_rate );
#endif
    }
    else
    {
#ifdef SAL_SUPPORT_DIRECTSOUND
        return _SAL_create_device_data_dsound(
                device,
                kp_sp,
                desired_channels,
                desired_bits,
                desired_sample_rate );
#endif
    }
    return SALERR_UNIMPLEMENTED;
}
```

There is a single statically resolved function, _SAL_create_device_data, which dynamically resolves the remainder of the implementation-specific functions. In the case of SAL, this doesn't buy anything, since most of these functions could have been resolved statically. The exception is the device destruction function, which needs to be dynamically selected.

In this particular case, SAL uses a function pointer table because it provides flexibility for the future. For example, it would be very easy to change it to use pthreads mutexes on OS X instead of the NSRecursiveLocks in use right now. Also, multiple documentation for the same function signature interfered with the documentation tool's ability to mark up each function for each platform uniquely. (The documentation tool is Doxygen, available from http://www.doxygen.org.)

Although SAL uses a function pointer table, I would like to avoid calling through it directly as much as possible. For example, SAL_sleep() is a public function that I would like clients of the library to access, but I would prefer not to expose the innards of the SAL_Device structure unnecessarily. So, I use yet another layer of indirection by dereferencing the function pointers with wrapper functions:

```
sal_error_e
SAL_sleep( SAL_Device *device, sal_u32_t duration )
{
    if ( device == 0 || device->device_fnc_sleep == 0 )
    {
        return SALERR_INVALIDPARAM;
    }
    return device->device_fnc_sleep( device, duration );
}
```

Now both SAL users and SAL itself can call system-specific functions without being exposed to the underlying implementation details or the function table itself.

While SAL gained some flexibility, it also lost a small bit of performance and robustness in the process. Indirect function calls are moderately more expensive than direct calls, but on modern computers, this will hardly be measurable. The other potential problem is that the function pointer table may end up in an invalid state by having NULL or illegal entries, but this is easy enough to test during development.

Virtual Functions

C++ provides support for *polymorphism* through virtual functions. Polymorphism is the ability to perform different actions through a single interface, where the function to be performed is determined by, say, an object's type. This is precisely what you want in an abstraction mechanism.

SAL is not written in C++, but it's easy to conceive an inheritance hierarchy where polymorphism would be used:

```
class SAL_Device
{
private:
    virtual sal_error_e  create_mutex( sal_mutex_t *p_mtx ) = 0;
    virtual sal_error_e  destroy_mutex( sal_mutex_t mtx ) = 0;
    virtual sal_error_e  lock_mutex( sal_mutex_t mtx ) = 0;
    virtual sal_error_e  unlock_mutex( sal_mutex_t mtx ) = 0;
    virtual sal_error_e  create_thread( void (*fnc)(void *args),
                                        void *targs ) = 0;
    virtual sal_error_e  sleep( sal_u32_t duration ) = 0;
    virtual void destroy( void ) = 0;
public:
    static sal_error_e create_device( SAL_Device **pp_device,
                                      const SAL_Callbacks *kp_cb,
                                      const SAL_SystemParameters *kp_sp,
                                      sal_u32_t desired_channels,
                                      sal_u32_t desired_bits,
                                      sal_u32_t desired_sample_rate,
                                      sal_u32_t num_voices );
};
```

Where SAL previously used function pointers, it now defines pure virtual functions in the private portion of the base class. To instantiate a SAL_Device, you would need to call the static SAL_Device::create_device function (a factory function), which would provide a pointer to some (unknown) subclass of SAL_Device.

You define specific implementations by creating a new, concrete class that inherits from SAL_Device. For example, you might define SAL_DeviceWin32, which would implement the required pure virtual functions except for the specific device creation/destruction functions, which would then be provided by yet another child class, SAL_DeviceDirectSound or SAL_DeviceWAVEOUT. SAL and any clients would see only the interface presented by SAL_Device, preserving the abstraction.

There are a couple minor problems associated with virtual function dispatch. Compared with statically resolving abstractions, virtual functions incur a slight performance hit since the appropriate function must be looked up at run time. As with function pointers, this is not a major consideration on modern computers. However, it still may be a concern with embedded or purpose-built devices such as appliances, gaming consoles, and cell phones.

Another problem is that virtual functions are difficult to cleanly alter after an object has been created. If you wanted to change a specific function on the fly, you would need to use a "letter-envelope" idiom (which adds complexity), re-create the object, or pass parameters to all the functions to represent any dynamic information necessary. With a function pointer table, it's as simple as updating a variable.

Abstract Data Types (typedef)

Data types can be abstracted cleanly through the use of typedef. For example, instead of blithely assuming that an integer has 32 bits, you can roll this assumption into a type definition on platforms where this assumption is valid:

```
#if PLATFORM_HAS_32BIT_INT
typedef int int32;
typedef unsigned int uint32;
#endif
```

While the ANSI/ISO C99 specification has introduced standard definitions for sized types through <inttypes.h>, many compilers at the time of this writing still do not fully support C99 and its associated features.

POSH provides these types in a portable manner even on non–C99-compliant systems, either using the C89+ standard <limits.h> or by inference of the compilation environment:

```
#if defined POSH_USE_LIMITS_H
#   if CHAR_BITS > 8
#     error This machine uses 9-bit characters. This is a warning,\
        you can comment this out now.
#   endif /* CHAR_BITS > 8 */

/* 16-bit */
#   if ( USHRT_MAX == 65535 )
      typedef unsigned short posh_u16_t;
      typedef short          posh_i16_t;
#   else
      /* In theory there could still be a 16-bit character type and shorts are
         32-bits in size */
#     error No 16-bit type found
#   endif

/* 32-bit */
#   if ( INT_MAX == 2147483647 )
```

```
  typedef unsigned        posh_u32_t;
  typedef int             posh_i32_t;
# elif ( LONG_MAX == 2147483647 )
  typedef unsigned long  posh_u32_t;
  typedef long           posh_i32_t;
# else
    error No 32-bit type found
# endif

#else /* POSH_USE_LIMITS_H */

  /* This makes fairly major assumptions */
  typedef unsigned short posh_u16_t;
  typedef short          posh_i16_t;

# if !defined POSH_OS_PALM
  typedef unsigned        posh_u32_t;
  typedef int             posh_i32_t;
# else
  typedef unsigned long  posh_u32_t;
  typedef long           posh_i32_t;
# endif
#endif

/* Verify we made the right guesses! */
POSH_COMPILE_TIME_ASSERT(posh_byte_t, sizeof(posh_byte_t) == 1);
POSH_COMPILE_TIME_ASSERT(posh_u8_t, sizeof(posh_u8_t) == 1);
POSH_COMPILE_TIME_ASSERT(posh_i8_t, sizeof(posh_i8_t) == 1);
POSH_COMPILE_TIME_ASSERT(posh_u16_t, sizeof(posh_u16_t) == 2);
POSH_COMPILE_TIME_ASSERT(posh_i16_t, sizeof(posh_i16_t) == 2);
POSH_COMPILE_TIME_ASSERT(posh_u32_t, sizeof(posh_u32_t) == 4);
POSH_COMPILE_TIME_ASSERT(posh_i32_t, sizeof(posh_i32_t) == 4);
```

POSH uses the values defined by <limits.h> to determine the appropriate native types that correspond to POSH's sized types. If <limits.h> is unreliable or unavailable, it will instead blindly assume some characteristics of the underlying system, with the exception of the Palm architecture. After the types are defined, POSH uses compile-time assertions to ensure that the assumptions are valid.

Use the C Preprocessor

While the C preprocessor is much maligned by purists, the fact remains that it is a simple yet powerful tool for managing source code. Two lines of preprocessor code can blank out entire swaths of code, without worrying about comment nesting rules. The preprocessor's arbitrary substitution capability means that minor syntactic differences between platforms can be abstracted trivially.

For example, a case-insensitive string comparison function is available on a wide variety of platforms under the name strcmpi, stricmp, or strcasecmp.

There are many different ways you can encapsulate this difference, but often the simplest is straight macro replacement, as follows:

```
#ifdef _MSC_VER
#define strcasecmp stricmp
#else
... etc. etc.
#endif
```

Granted, this is a rudimentary case that probably warrants just writing and using your own version, but the idea still applies.

The preprocessor causes problems when overzealous programmers go a little overboard with multiline macros that incorporate scoping, local variables, reference global variables, and other such nonintuitive things. In other words, don't do this:

```
#ifdef POSH_OS_WIN32
#define SYS_INIT() { \
extern HWND g_hWnd; \
    char oldtitle[ 1024 ];\
    char newtitle[ 1024 ];\
    \
    GetConsoleTitle( oldtitle, sizeof( oldtitle ) );\
    \
    sprintf( newtitle, "SAL Test - %d:%d", GetCurrentProcessId(),
GetTickCount() );\
    \
    SetConsoleTitle( newtitle );\
    \
    Sleep( 100 );\
    \
    g_hWnd = FindWindow( NULL, newtitle );\
    \
    if ( g_hWnd == 0 )\
    {\
        fprintf( stderr, "Could not find window\n" );\
        exit( 1 );\
    }\
    \
    p_sp->sp_buffer_length_ms = 100;\
    p_sp->sp_hWnd = g_hWnd; }
#endif /* POSH_OS_WIN32 */
.
.
.
int main( int argc, char *argv[] )
{
    SYS_INIT();
}
```

Be Prepared for the Unforseen

As careful, thoughtful, and forward thinking as we may be when defining a reasonable baseline, inevitably one of our requirements will change due to unforeseen consequences. This is not necessarily due to bad planning or foresight, but instead is an unfortunate side effect of our lack of omniscience (at least, that's how I've rationalized it in the past).

Here are some common assumptions that many programmers don't realize are *not* true:

malloc and new are always available

PC developers especially tend to make this assumption, but some systems, like early Mac OS, 16-bit Windows, and Palm OS, don't use malloc/new. Instead, they require you to allocate memory and reference it indirectly using handles that are locked for use, and then unlocked when you're not using them. This was a common architecture on systems without virtual memory, where heap fragmentation was a constant worry. So, this can be a dangerous assumption, especially if you need to target embedded systems based on low-end microcontrollers where memory management is often hardcoded.

stdio file management is available and complete

File input/output presumes the existence of both the stdio subsystem and a filesystem. On embedded devices and many handheld devices, neither is guaranteed to exist.

Graphics output will always be regular RGB (no palettes)

Modern graphics subsystems have been using RGB (red/green/blue) output for years now, and even high-end handheld devices support this. When designing a graphical application, it is *much* easier to support RGB than it is to deal with the older palettized display formats (where a pixel on the display contains a value that indexes into a separate table of colors). When designing even a simple graphics application for a PC, you can safely use the RGB format, but if you find yourself migrating to a handheld or wireless format, you may need to refactor your entire graphics back end to support palettized graphics (which consume much less memory and thus are more popular on low-end hardware).

Networking will be done with TCP/IP

TCP/IP has been the de facto networking standard for a decade, and other network protocols such as NetBEUI, IPX/SPX, and DECNet have fallen by the wayside. When writing an application that requires network communication, it is common to assume TCP/IP support. This is often valid, since even very low-end devices will have working TCP/IP network stacks, but there are many devices that may support only serial or parallel port communications or a custom wire protocol. While this is uncommon, you may find yourself scrambling to abstract your network protocol implementation if your software needs to run on such a system.

Each of these is a reasonable assumption, but all it takes is one platform that doesn't work on that assumption to require a redesign, which can have an exorbitant cost. However, there is little fault in this situation, since at the time of development, the design requirements seemed completely reasonable and, more important, abstracting those subsystems "just because" would have introduced a lot of indirection and extra code for no quantifiable reason.

Sometimes even what seem to be the sanest, safest assumptions can end up proving incorrect. You can't predict the future, so just be aware of *every* assumption you make.

Communicating System-Dependent Information

One complicating factor when trying to design clean, cross-platform programming APIs is communicating system-dependent information from the application to your own code. The DirectSound subsystem in SAL, for example, requires the application's window handle when it calls IDirect-Sound::SetCooperativeLevel(). Since SAL is not responsible for creating or managing an application's window, it must have that information passed in somehow. There are several different ways to handle this in a semi-portable manner.

NOTE *In theory, it would be possible to infer the window bound to the current thread, but there are a lot of corner cases where this might fail. Additionally, while it's tempting to use* NULL *or* GetDesktopWindow() *as the parameter, that is a very bad practice, since Direct-Sound really does want to bind itself to your window, not just any window.*

The first way to handle this communication is to register this information using a separate API call available on only one platform, guarding with appropriate compilation directives, as follows:

```
#ifdef POSH_OS_WIN32
SAL_register_HWND( hWnd ); /* only on Windows */
#endif
SAL_create_device( ... ); /* portable portion */
```

While a bit cumbersome, a separate interface is workable and avoids polluting your core APIs with system-dependent information (in exchange for polluting the calling program with conditional code).

Of course, you can pollute your core APIs if you like. By adding every possible system-dependent variable to various initialization routines, you can fix it all at once, like this:

```
void create_device( void *hwnd_for_win32,
                     void *something_for_OSX,
                     int some_flag_for_linux );
```

While functional, this is a fragile strategy, since the API changes every time a new parameter is added. For example, you may find later that you need to support Palm OS, and it, too, has its own special parameter supplied by the application. This means a new version of the API call with some appropriate suffix must be introduced:

```
void create_device_ex( void *hwnd_for_win32,
                       void *something_for_OSX,
                       int flag_for_linux,
                       short palm_os_thing );
```

Then later on, you add support for Solaris, and now you have create_device_ex_ex, and on it goes.

Another problem with this approach is that sometimes a particular parameter may not be available at the time of the function call; for example, the value for palm_os_thing may not be configured until after you call create_device_ex.

A slightly cleaner method is to encapsulate all your system-dependent information into a structure that is passed to your API call. SAL uses this technique:

```
struct SAL_SystemParametersWin32
{
    sal_i32_t   sp_size; /* size of this data structure */
    sal_u32_t   sp_flags; /* flags for the API call */
    sal_i32_t   sp_buffer_length_ms; /* sound buffer len */

    void        *sp_hWnd; /* HWND */
};

struct SAL_SystemParametersDefault
{
    sal_i32_t   sp_size;
    sal_u32_t   sp_flags;
    sal_i32_t   sp_buffer_length_ms;
};

#ifdef POSH_OS_WIN32
typedef struct SAL_SystemParametersWin32 SAL_SystemParameters;
#else
typedef struct SAL_SystemParametersDefault SAL_SystemParameters;
#endif
```

The sp_size member allows revisions to the system parameters structure later without breaking backward compatibility. By initializing the sp_size variable before calling the API entry point, the API can deduce which version of the SAL_SystemParameters structure was used by the client and react accordingly; for example, by returning an error or performing a conversion to the newer format. The net effect is that you can keep a single API point without continually having to add new entry points to reflect changes to various data structures.

There remains a chance that there is an order dependency, where some information that the API needs is not available until *after* you pass in the system parameters structure. When dealing with this situation, you must either use a separate entry point (as in the `SAL_register_HWND()` example earlier), or you must find a different communication vector.

Function calls are only one kind of communication system that a program can employ. Other, more indirect, mechanisms are possible. Scripting languages, registry/preference systems, and good, old-fashioned global variables can function as well, without polluting your core API.

Regardless of the specific mechanism, the fact remains that there is an exposed system dependency. This is often unavoidable; you can dress this up to minimize the impact on the rest of your code, but it's still there in one form or another.

Bridge Functions

A common pattern for portable programs is partitioning a program into system-dependent and system-independent portions, and then creating bridge (or "glue") functions that connect the two. This subtype of abstraction is analogous to GUIs that follow the model-view-controller (MVC) paradigm, where user-interface independent code (the model) is isolated from the display code (the view) and connected with a controller that acts as a bridge between the two.

The primary purpose of a bridge function is to transform system-dependent data or formats into system-independent data (or the converse), which is then fed into the portable layer (see Figure 3-1).

Low-Level Programming

Even though high-level languages have become dominant for application development, there are still occasions when a programmer needs to get down and talk to a machine in its native language. Sometimes a higher-level language, even one that is fairly close to the metal such as C, doesn't expose core hardware functionality such as the following:

- CPU instruction flags (carry bit, zero flag)
- New instruction sets like Intel MMX/SSE/SSE-2, AMD 3DNow, and Motorola AltiVec
- The results of extended operations such as a 32-bit multiply, which on some architectures will leave a 64-bit result that cannot be easily or quickly retrieved by a high-level language

So, there are legitimate reasons for programming at a lower level. And you'll want to ensure that whenever you write at a lower level you do so as portably as possible.

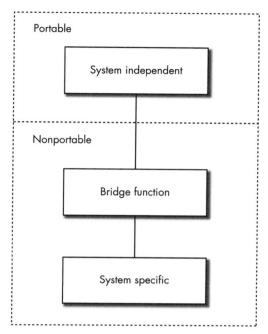

Figure 3-1: Bridge function

Avoid Self-Modifying/Dynamically Generated Code When Possible

Early microcomputers had only a handful of registers, and register access was many times faster than working with main memory. For this reason, registers were valuable but scarce commodities, leading to developers using a lot of interesting tricks in order to give themselves a bit more breathing room.

Imagine having a limited CPU architecture with only four general-purpose registers and trying to write a loop like this:

```
mov d, object_size ; size of an array element in bytes
mov c, num_objects ; number of objects in array
mov b, 0           ; initialize 'b' to 0
mov a, array       ; 'a' will point to the current object
top:
...                ; do some operations
add a, d           ; increment 'a' by size of object
sub c, 1           ; decrement 'c'
jg top             ; continue loop if 'c' is greater than 0
```

'b' is the only register available as a scratch variable, meaning that the inner loop must access memory for storing any intermediate results. Particularly frustrating is that 'd' is effectively a constant which, if known ahead of time, could be substituted into the instruction stream, thereby giving you an extra register.

SAL EXAMPLE: BRIDGE FUNCTIONS

Multithreading APIs for various operating systems expect slightly different signatures for their thread functions. The pthreads API, as implemented by Linux, Mac OS X, and other Unix-based APIs, creates a thread using this function:

```
int pthread_create( pthread_t *thread,
                    const pthread_attr_t *attr,
                    void *(*start_routine)(void *),
                    void *arg );
```

Standard Win32, however, uses this function:

```
uintptr_t _beginthread( void( __cdecl *start_address )( void * ),
                        unsigned stack_size,
                        void *arglist );
```

And Windows CE/Pocket PC prefers the Windows CreateThread API:

```
typedef DWORD (WINAPI *PTHREAD_START_ROUTINE)(LPVOID lpThreadParameter);
typedef PTHREAD_START_ROUTINE LPTHREAD_START_ROUTINE;
HANDLE CreateThread( LPSECURITY_ATTRIBUTES lpThreadAttributes,
                     SIZE_T dwStackSize,
                     LPTHREAD_START_ROUTINE lpStartAddress,
                     LPVOID lpParameter,
                     DWORD dwCreationFlags,
                     LPDWORD lpThreadId );
```

There are three distinct thread functions expected, depending on the operating system:

```
/* return a void pointer, accept a void pointer,
default calling convention */
void *(*start_routine)(void *);
/* return nothing, accept a void pointer, cdecl calling convention */
void (__cdecl *start_routine)(void *);
/* return a DWORD, accept a void pointer, WINAPI calling convention */
DWORD ( WINAPI *start_routine)(void *);
```

A developer cannot be expected to provide three variations of the same thread function, since this violates the principle of abstraction (and is a pain in the butt as well). The bridge function can come to your rescue here.

Each thread function accepts a pointer to void for its parameters and may return something different on each platform, so the lowest common denominator is a function that returns void and accepts a void pointer, with a calling convention that you define (so that it is consistent for the user). SAL defines the thread start function, as passed to _SAL_create_thread(), as follows:

```
typedef void ( POSH_CDECL *SAL_THREAD_FUNC)(void *args);
sal_error_ _SAL_create_thread( SAL_Device *device,
                               SAL_THREAD_FUNC func,
                               void *targs );
```

Regardless of the platform, any user of SAL (in this case, SAL itself, since _SAL_create_thread() is not exported for public use) can provide a thread start function of the type SAL_THREAD_FUNC and not worry about the underlying implementation. This is achieved by each implementation providing a bridge thread start function that dispatches to your generic one.

As an example let's look at _SAL_create_thread_wince:

```
typedef struct _SAL_WinCEBridgeFunctionParameters_s
{
    SAL_THREAD_FUNC bfp_fnc;      /**< thread function */
    void           *bfp_targs;    /**< pointer to thread arguments */
} _SAL_WinCEBridgeFunctionParameters;

static
sal_error_e
_SAL_create_thread_wince( SAL_Device *device,
                          SAL_THREAD_FUNC fnc,
                          void *targs )
{
    HANDLE hThread;
    _SAL_WinCEBridgeFunctionParameters bfp;

    bfp.bfp_fnc   = fnc;
bfp.bfp_targs = targs;
    if ( device == 0 || fnc == 0 )
{
        return SALERR_INVALIDPARAM;
    }

    if ( ( hThread = CreateThread(
                        /* lpThreadAttributes, ignored on WinCE */
                        NULL,
                        /* stack size, ignored on WinCE */
                        0,
                        /* thread start function */
                        s_bridge_function,
                        /* lpParameter */
                        &bfp,
                        /* creation flags */
0,
                        NULL ) ) == (HANDLE)-1 )
    {
return SALERR_SYSTEMFAILURE;}

    SetThreadPriority( hThread, THREAD_PRIORITY_HIGHEST );

    return SALERR_OK;
}
```

This demonstrates two important elements. The first is that the call to Create-Thread dispatches to s_bridge_function, *not* to the user's thread function, since the function signatures don't match, whereas s_bridge_function is in a form that CreateThread expects. The second is that the parameter passed to s_bridge_function contains the user's thread function and the user's thread function parameters.

s_bridge_function is trivially simple. It just unbundles the bridge parameters and calls the user's function directly:

```
static
DWORD WINAPI
s_bridge_function( LPVOID lpParameter )
{
    _SAL_WinCEBridgeFunctionParameters *bfp =
        ( _SAL_WinCEBridgeFunctionParameters * ) lpParameter;

    bfp->bfp_fnc( bfp->bfp_targs );

    return 1;
}
```

Assembly language programmers recognized this and used a technique called *self-modifying code.* The programmer would assemble the instructions and then look for, in this case, the add a, d instruction and note the address. Then he would go back and patch the code in question in place with the appropriate constant for that particular invocation, freeing up a register.

Aside from the obvious problem that this is tied directly to a particularly CPU implementation, it brings up other issues. The main one is security. Most operating systems won't allow a program to write willy-nilly into its own code, since this is the result of a bug in the vast majority of cases (for example, writing through an uninitialized pointer). Of course, you can work around this (with sufficient security privileges) using operating system calls such as VirtualProtect() (Windows) and mprotect (Linux), but now you're getting deeper into the portability hole.

An extreme form of this is *dynamically generated code.* As the name implies, dynamically generated code is created and assembled at run time by filling a buffer of data with processor instructions, flagging the memory as executable, assigning a function pointer to it, and then executing it. Here is an example under the Windows operating system:

```
unsigned char *add_two;
float (*fnc_add_two)( float, float );

void test()
{
    DWORD old_protect; /* Windows-ism */
    float c;

    add_two = VirtualAlloc( NULL, 32, MEM_COMMIT, PAGE_READWRITE );
```

```
/* initialize to NOP */
memset( add_two, 0x90, 32 );

/* The first four instructions equate to 'fld [esp+4] */
add_two[ 0 ] = 0xD9; /* co-processor escape */
add_two[ 1 ] = 0x44; /* mod r/m byte */
add_two[ 2 ] = 0x24; /* SIB */
add_two[ 3 ] = 0x04; /* index */

/* the next four bytes equate to 'fadd [esp+8]' */
add_two[ 4 ] = 0xD8; /* co-processor escape */
add_two[ 5 ] = 0x44; /* mod r/m byte */
add_two[ 6 ] = 0x24; /* SIB */
add_two[ 7 ] = 0x08; /* index */

/* this is a one-opcode RET instruction */
add_two[ 8 ] = 0xC3;

/* on Linux you would use mprotect */
VirtualProtect( add_two, 32, PAGE_EXECUTE, &old_protect );
fnc_add_two = ( float (*)(float,float)) add_two;

/* this should now work */
c = fnc_add_two( 1, 2 );
printf( "c = %f\n", c );
}
```

Not only is this pretty scary stuff, but it's also not portable for a host of reasons.

You can also load executable code as data, using the same dynamically generated code technique. Instead of filling in the buffer with constant data, you load its contents from disk and mark it as executable. This can be extremely dangerous, but it's also a practical solution if you want to load code on a host that may not support dynamic libraries (DLLs or shared objects).

Needless to say, this is all hacky and not very portable, but at times, it's necessary when trying to obtain maximum performance from limited resources.

So even though it's obvious, it's still worth stating that if you can avoid doing stuff like this, then you should.

Keep a High-Level Fallback

When using any type of assembly language, dynamically generated or statically linked, retaining a high-level *fallback* version is vital. A fallback is a default, working implementation of a feature, suitable for use as a reference or checkpoint when working on a different implementation of that feature. For example, if you're writing an optimized platform-specific memory-copying routine, you might use `memcpy` as a fallback for testing or when bringing up your code on a new target. Without this, you have no way to perform regression tests to ensure that your low-level code is not subtly diverging from your high-level implementation.

Assembly language code fragments have a tendency to act a bit differently than their high-level analogs since they don't have to adhere to a high-level language's semantics. For example, you may write a small piece of floating-point assembly to add two numbers and store the result as an integer:

```
; sample code to compute a+b and store the resulting integer version
; into a variable called result. This is Intel 80x87 FPU code.
fld a        ; load 'a' onto floating point stack
fadd b       ; add 'b' to stop of stack
fistp result ; store result as an integer into 'result'
```

This works as you would expect with few surprises, yet it doesn't actually match the following C code:

```
result = ( int ) ( a + b );
```

C imposes its own rules for floating point–to–integer conversion—specifically, the result must be truncated (rounded toward zero). The assembly language version, however, will use the current rounding mode in effect, which is usually round to nearest integer, but may be different depending on the current state of the FPU control register.

This means that the assembly language version might give a result of 6 when adding 4.5 and 1.1 (4.5 + 1.1 = 5.6, rounded to nearest integer is 6), but the C version would produce a value of 5 since the fractional portion is discarded.

With a C fallback, you can ensure that any surprises are caught early by verifying the assembly version against the high-level version with a set of regression tests. Using the prior examples as a sample, you might have something like this:

```
extern int add_two_floats_C( float a, float b );
extern int add_two_floats_asm( float a, float b );
void test_add_two_floats()
{
   int i;

   /* use the same seed so this is reproducible if necessary */
   srand( 3 );
   for ( i = 0; i < TEST_ITERATIONS; i++ )
   {
      /* test using values from -RAND_MAX/2 to +RAND_MAX/2 with
         a random fractional component thrown in */
      float a = ( float ) ( rand() - RAND_MAX/2 ) +
                          ( rand() / ( float ) RAND_MAX );
```

```
        float b = ( float ) ( rand() - RAND_MAX/2 ) +
                          ( rand() / ( float ) RAND_MAX );
        assert( add_two_floats_C( a, b ) == add_two_floats_asm( a, b ) );
    }
}
```

This is a trivial example that isn't particularly robust, but it demonstrates the intent of a regression test. A production implementation would be much more thorough and provide a lot more features, such as logging and the ability to specify tolerances.

Selecting between implementations can be done with conditional compilation, function pointers, or virtual functions in a class hierarchy, as described in the section called "Dispatch Abstraction" earlier in this chapter.

When strange bugs start creeping into a program with a lot of low-level code, having a high-level fallback can save the day, especially for corner cases that verification tests might not catch. When some odd behavior shows up, you can at least discount the low-level implementation by substituting the reference implementation. If the bug goes away, there's a good chance that the culprit lies in the low-level code.

Finally, the high-level reference implementation of equivalent low-level code makes porting much easier when you have a new target. A code base optimized for an Intel CPU that is then moved to a PowerPC architecture will be difficult to bring up without a high-level, portable reference implementation.

High-level reference implementations reduce the effort to move to a new platform considerably, even if you have a large chunk of otherwise unportable low-level source. Without them, you're starting from scratch every time you move to a new architecture.

The register Keyword

C and C++ allow a programmer to hint or request that a variable should be stored in a register, on the assumption that the programmer knows the variable will be used heavily, as follows:

```
register int counter;
for ( counter = 0; counter < SOME_VALUE; counter++ )
{
    /* do something */
}
```

While the rationale for the register storage class was reasonably sound at the time ("please make this fast without making me rewrite this routine in assembly"), the advancement of compiler optimization technology has made this feature somewhat moot for most of today's software. In fact, with many compilers, it is ignored outright (the C/C++ standards do not require that the register keyword be honored), since forcing a variable into a register may interfere with the compiler's optimizer.

The register keyword is an anachronism and is best avoided unless there is a demonstrable increase in performance from its use.

External versus In-Line asm Files

When assembly code must be integrated into a project, it is often placed in separate, external files suitable for processing by a separate tool: the assembler. Doing things this way has traditionally been annoying and tedious, since other tools such as debuggers and profilers often don't know how to handle the assembly files. In addition, the programmer needs to handle mundane details such as calling and naming conventions. To address this, some compilers, including Microsoft Visual C++ and GCC, offer the ability to place assembly language directly inside C/C++ code. For example, on Microsoft Visual C++ you can do this:

```
int add_two_floats_C( float a, float b )
{
    int result;
    __asm fld a
    __asm fadd b
    __asm fistp result
    return result;
}
```

In-lining the assembly directives this way has the advantage of often using an internal assembler and overall tighter integration with the rest of the project. Debuggers and profilers have less difficulty dealing with this than working with separate files, and the compiler handles the tedious entry and exit code associated with different calling conventions.

For example, the previous function would look like this in assembly, much of which is minutiae that most programmers care little for:

```
PUBLIC _add_two_floats
_TEXT SEGMENT
_add_two_floats PROC NEAR
    push ebp
    mov ebp, esp
    fld DWORD PTR [ebp+8]
    fadd DWORD PTR [ebp + 12 ]
    fistp DWORD PTR [ebp - 4 ]
    mov eax, DWORD PTR [ebp - 4 ]
    mov esp, ebp
    pop ebp
    ret 0
_add_two_floats ENDP
_TEXT ENDS
```

The external assembler version is significantly wordier for little in return, and since it is embedded directly into the C code, there are fewer opportunities for things to hiccup. The compiler is responsible for cleaning the stack, allocating variables, locating variables on the stack, and otherwise managing all the other mundane aspects of interfacing. The downside is that now you're dependent on the compiler vendor not messing this up, which is a somewhat iffy proposition, since in-line assembly is one of the more common problem areas for compiler bugs. For example, sometimes in-line assemblers don't support newer instructions or, even worse, silently disable all optimizations when they encounter any in-line assembly.

Low-level system programming is a necessary evil in the real world, but with the proper precautions and abstraction, it's still possible to get at the lowest level of the system without sacrificing ease of portability when moving to a new host.

4

EDITING AND SOURCE CONTROL

Before you even think about the issues related to the code you write, you need to deal with something even more fundamental: getting the files onto your host platform so that you can edit them. This task is often not as simple as you would expect, unless you're lucky enough to be using a single-host, multiple-target environment. This chapter covers the act of editing and managing your source files while writing cross-platform software.

Text File Line Ending Differences

Text files created and edited on different operating systems need to deal with multiple types of line endings (see also Chapter 13, which discusses filesystems). DOS and Windows use carriage return/linefeed pairs (\r\n) to note an end-of-line; Unix uses linefeeds (\n); and the Macintosh, prior to OS X, uses carriage returns (\r).

This becomes a problem when developing source code across a wide variety of host operating systems. If a file is created on Unix, it may not be edited correctly on a Windows machine.

For example, Figure 4-1 shows part of `posh.h` correctly loaded in Windows Notepad.

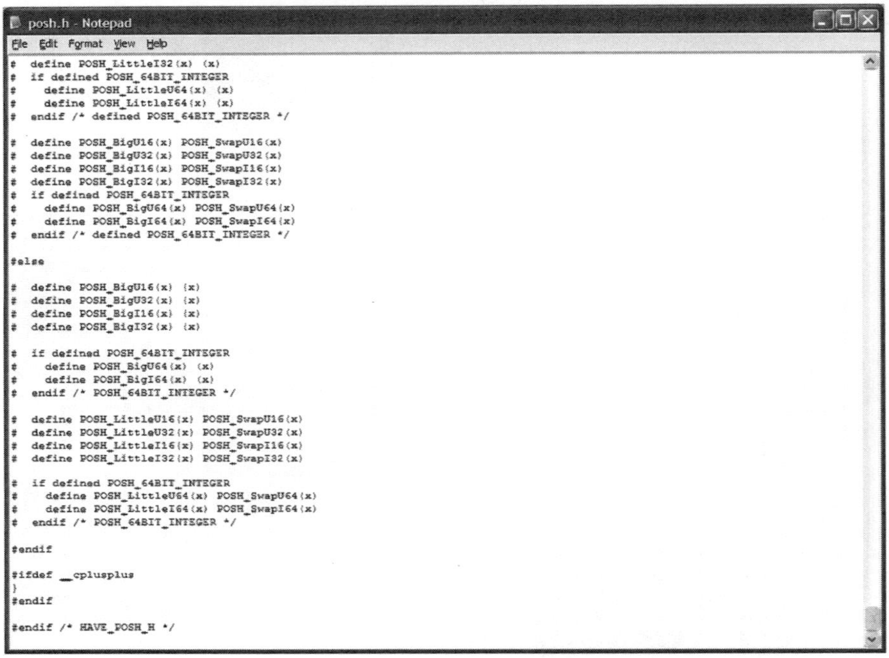

Figure 4-1: Windows Notepad displays `posh.h` *correctly when it has Windows-style line endings.*

Figure 4-2 illustrates what happens when Notepad attempts to load the same file when it has Unix-style line endings.

On Windows, it is up to the application to properly handle different line endings, both for loading and saving. For example, neither Emacs nor Microsoft Visual Studio has any problem loading and displaying the file shown in Figure 4-2.

Revision control systems try to help with this problem by converting to a canonical line-ending format (usually Unix-style linefeeds) in the repository, and then transforming the files back to an operating system native form when they're checked out from the repository. After the file has been edited and checked back in, it is reconverted to the canonical format automatically. This also helps when trying to view differences *(diffs)*, since some diff programs will think two identical files are 100 percent different if they don't use the same line-ending format.

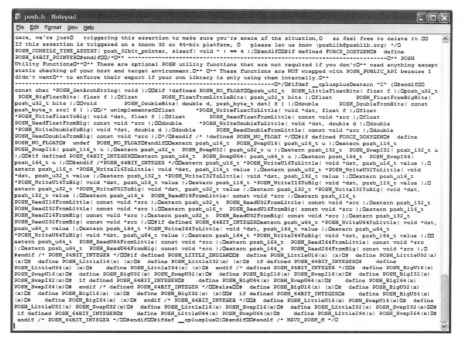

Figure 4-2: Windows Notepad has problems when a file has Unix-style line endings.

Portable Filenames

Every filesystem today has a different idea about what constitutes an acceptable filename. While we're mostly past the dark days of MS-DOS's 8.3 FAT filesystem limitations, there are significant enough differences that you should avoid "exotic" names.

Try to keep the overall name as short as possible. If you want to be totally safe, going with the ancient and crusty 8.3 format won't hurt, but it does lean toward cryptic filenames. A reasonable limit is 31 characters, corresponding to the limit on Mac OS; most other operating systems support much longer filename lengths. Also, consistency about case doesn't hurt, since some operating systems are case-insensitive (DOS), others are case-sensitive (Unix/Linux), and yet others are case-insensitive but case-retentive (Windows). Finally, avoid punctuation characters and spaces. Stick with letters, numbers, and the underscore character if you want maximum compatibility. See the discussion of filesystems in Chapter 13 for more specifics.

Filename extensions are another gotcha. DOS and Windows determine a file's type by its extension, such as .doc, .txt, .html, and so on. Unix and Linux use filename extensions for data types, but differentiate between programs and data with a file attribute. Mac OS 9 ignores a file's extension and instead examines its metadata to determine how to run it. This carries over to source filenames.

For a while, there were a lot of different ways to denote a C++ source file: .C, .cc, .cpp, .c++, and .cxx. Header files had extensions of .h, .hh, .hpp, or .hxx. There is no official standard on this, but today the majority of compilers accept .cpp/.h as the standard. If you're working with an older development environment with its own stubborn idea of acceptable C++ filenames, be prepared to use a script to perform batch renaming or, if your operating system allows it, to create a set of symbolic links with the appropriate extension.

Source Control

As you work on the files on your new host platform, you'll need to track your changes with a revision control system. Every time a file is edited on one system and checked back into the main source code repository, any and all changes *must* be noted, stored, and easily retrieved. This lets you avoid situations where you ask, "Why does the Solaris version of my software think that the database is corrupt after I made this tiny change on my Windows box?"

Source Control Systems

Supposedly, more than 300 different source control systems are out there. However, only a handful are in common use. The ideal revision control system, which often will both manage revisions and handle the task of moving files onto a new platform (as opposed to copying the files manually), should be cross-platform, and thankfully quite a few are.

rcs

The Revision Control System (rcs), originally developed by Walter Tichy in the early 1980s, was the first widely adopted cross-platform source control system. While it was influenced heavily by AT&T's proprietary Source Code Control System (SCCS), which shipped with Unix System V at the time, rcs's price (free) and open nature made it quite a bit more popular. It is still possibly the most popular version control system in use today, primarily because it is the bedrock on which some other higher-level version control systems are founded. By today's standards it's fairly primitive, but its influence and ubiquity are hard to deny.

cvs

The Concurrent Version System (cvs) was originally a front end to rcs that allowed simultaneous (nonexclusive) file editing. Both SCCS and rcs required users to lock source files for exclusive access, so that when a file was locked for writing, no one else could edit that file. (Well, they couldn't edit a locked file without using unsafe workarounds like breaking the lock locally and locking the file later once the current owner relinquished the lock.)

With large projects, this exclusive lock policy became a serious impediment to development. Sometimes a programmer would need to edit many source files at once, and thus would lock all those source files and begin work. Five o'clock would roll around, and the programmer would go home, leaving half the source repository inaccessible to the rest of the team until his return. This type of situation was so common that specific, often draconian, policies would be enacted to limit when and how many locks could be acquired by an individual.

cvs is not without its annoyances. Ask any cvs user about it, and she will probably rant for five minutes nonstop about its shortcomings. Common operations such as file renaming, deletion, merging, branching, movement, and addition are cumbersome and difficult. Updates to the repository are not done atomically, which means backing out an entire set of changes can be a complex task.

Additionally, binary files must be specially flagged, or they'll often end up corrupted. This requirement is a side effect of the way the cvs addresses the problem of multiplatform text-file conversions: by automating the conversion from host to canonical text formats. When cvs adds an unrecognized binary file to a repository and the contributor forgets to specify the -kb flag (for check in as binary), very bad things happen. Any binary values that correspond to the carriage-return or linefeed characters may get tranformed, often rendering the binary file unusable the next time it's checked out. (It is a sad statement when "automatically recognizes binary files" is considered a major selling point for a revision control system.)

Despite these difficulties, cvs is the preeminent version control system for cross-platform and/or open-source developers today. While crude, quirky, problematic, and difficult to use, cvs has sufficient resources, books, front-end user interfaces (TortoiseCVS is a popular example), and experienced users that its integration and use are relatively straightforward for most teams. Its wide availability on a huge number of platforms and its open-source nature are also considerable advantages. cvs is the revision control system of choice for SourceForge.net, the largest community open-source repository in the world.

Perforce

Perforce (also called P4 by many of its users) is a commercial revision control product that is popular with commercial developers due to its robustness, performance, wide availability, and available support (Perforce has a reputation for outstanding technical support). Unlike many commercial applications, Perforce emphasizes portability; it is available on some pretty obscure platforms (IBM OS/390, Amiga, OpenVMS, and so on).

Perforce also provides some features that cvs sorely lacks. It handles binary files far more reliably than cvs, and it supports atomic operations. Groups of files are checked in as a single unit (as a *change set*). If any file cannot be committed to the repository, then all the files are held back, thus preventing unsynchronized check-ins. Perforce also has its own security model, whereas cvs relies on the server's native operating system to provide security. This internal consistency provides a more unified experience for the Perforce user.

Perforce is a commercial tool with dedicated support available. In contrast, cvs requires the generosity of the open-source community or the services of a third-party support group like Ximbiot. Perforce is also available free for use for open-source projects, an admirable move (although largely moot since most open-source projects still prefer noncommercial tools).

All that said, Perforce is not free for closed-source projects, nor is it open software, and those two factors are often enough to dissuade its use by many.

BitKeeper

BitKeeper is another source control tool but with a controversial history stemming from its license. BitMover, the parent company of BitKeeper, made its software "mostly free," meaning that BitKeeper could be used for free but with some restrictions, which annoyed some open-source advocates.

One notable coup for BitKeeper was convincing the Linux kernel maintainers to use it for their source control. Technically speaking, it is superior to cvs in pretty much all ways. As a commercial system (like Perforce), significant resources are available to make it best in class. It supports distributed development (instead of requiring the client/server model that most other systems use), making it easier for remote developers to use. Its peer-to-peer design and replicated database system also ensure a high degree of reliability and performance difficult to achieve with the other, more traditional, systems.

Subversion

Subversion is positioned as "the new cvs." It is superior to cvs in nearly all ways, addressing most of the common complaints users have about cvs, but not taking the "we need to reinvent revision control" attitude that the BitMover folks adopted. Subversion also uses a database back end (BerkeleyDB) instead of the file-oriented back end of cvs. This provides some gains but has the scary side effect that if something happens to the binary database, you may not be able to retrieve its contents.

Subversion has not attained critical mass yet. Because cvs owns such a massive chunk of market share, especially with open-source projects, any project choosing Subversion for source control runs the risk of alienating a significant number of contributors. At the time of this writing, Subversion has just reached 1.0.5 status, hopefully providing momentum and allowing it to overtake cvs in time. I happen to use Subversion, but I'm sure that cvs will continue to live for several more decades, just as SCCS is still in use for legacy projects today.

GNU arch

While Subversion is "the new cvs," the Free Software Foundation is positioning its own new version control system, arch, as the "the new, better cvs." Unlike Subversion, arch is willing to move away from the cvs-like comfort zone.

For example, one of arch's greatest strengths is that it employs a distributed repository model, unlike the single repository model that most other systems use. This is a radical departure from the mainline, and provides a lot of strength to the implementation (similar to BitKeeper). The other advantages of arch are probably considered more esoteric, including entire tree patches, global project names, and a more "assembly of lightweight tools" architecture. However, at the time of this writing, is not considered ready for mass consumption by many developers.

Checkout by Proxy

In a bad situation, you might be faced with a system that simply does not have the source control system you're using or, even worse, you might be forced to use a platform-dependent source control system such as Microsoft's Visual SourceSafe. While this should be a rare instance if you're using one of the major source control systems, it's not completely unheard of. For example, BitKeeper is not available for early versions of Mac OS.

So, if you find yourself in the rather unenviable situation of porting your software to Mac OS 9, and you've been happily using BitKeeper now for your entire project, you might wonder how to tackle the problem. Your first option is to go crazy and move your entire source control system over to a new package that you may not be familiar with, lacks the features you like about BitKeeper, and may end up having its own incompatible systems. That's not very tempting.

If you're lucky, you'll be able to have the Macintosh mount your filesystem remotely using software such as Thursby's DAVE file-sharing system. If you have a PC handy, you then check out your source code to the PC, edit those files directly from the Macintosh, and once everything works, check it back in from the PC. Not all computer systems can mount each other's filesystems, however, which means that you're looking at a rather nasty last resort: checkout by proxy.

If your source control system is not compatible with a particular host and you can't mount the target platform's filesystem (or have it mount another machine's), then you'll need to proxy your files onto the new platform. This involves performing any file locking or checkouts on a system (the proxy) compatible with your source control software, then transferring all the files over to the new host. Ideally, it's on your network, so you can FTP your files over. If not, you need to bundle the files into some archive format (.zip or .tar.gz), and then copy (via tape, floppy disk, CD, or DVD-ROM) the files over.

Once there, you unpack the archive on the target system, get everything working in a marathon coding session, pack it back up, return it to the proxy system, and then check all your files back in, praying that nothing major changed "while you were away." You also must ensure that you don't edit files on the proxy system *and* on the remote system, because if you do, you'll need to merge the remote and proxy system source trees before integrating the changes back into the central repository.

This checkout by proxy method is neither pretty nor easy, but as a last resort, it works. The moral here is to make sure that any revision control system you plan on using supports all the platforms you think you *might* need to support in the future.

Build Tools

Now that you've managed to get your files onto a new system without mangling the line endings or running into case-sensitivity and other file-naming problems, you can ago ahead and start compiling your source code. The choice now is whether to go with platform-specific build tools or portable build tools.

Platform-Specific Build Tools

Platform-specific build tools usually consist of some kind of integrated development environment (IDE) responsible for managing files, projects, and dependencies. IDEs often provide a host of other handy features including integrated help, an API reference, a debugger, and a profiler. Various IDEs are available for different operating systems:

- Windows has development environments from Microsoft (Visual Studio), Metrowerks (CodeWarrior), Borland (C++Builder), and the free environment Dev-C++ (based on GCC using Cygwin and/or MinGW).

- Mac OS X offers the free ProjectBuilder and X-Code environments from Apple (which are just fancy front ends wrapped around modified versions of jam, gdb, and gcc) and Metrowerks CodeWarrior.

- Linux possesses a wide selection of both commercial environments (Borland C++Builder-X, Metrowerks CodeWarrior, and CodeForge) and free environments (Anjuta Dev Studio, Eclipse, and KDevelop).

- Sun features the commercial Sun One Studio for Solaris and Linux.

In other words, there are a lot of options for both commercial and free platform-specific integrated build environments.

IDEs attempt to hide the arcane details of source code dependencies, compiler and linker switches, and debugging commands within a pleasant, easy-to-use interface. For example, Figure 4-3 shows Microsoft Visual C++ 6.0.

Note the multiple panels that provide visual feedback for the build and editing process. The workspace panel (left) has a list of all files in the project, which can be edited by simply double-clicking the filename. The edit window can contain multiple files for editing, and the output window (bottom) shows the results of the build process. Recompiling requires only a single keystroke or button click. Debugging occurs within the editor, so code may be edited in the same environment in which it is debugged. Help is a single keystroke (F1) away. Dependencies between different files are automatically determined without any user intervention.

For developers new to a particular platform or tool chain, this type of environment can be a lifesaver, since all of the gritty details are hidden from view. For example, the compiler command line for this project is:

```
cl /nologo /MTd /W3 /ZI /Od /D "WIN32" /D "_DEBUG" /D "_CONSOLE" /D
"_MBCS" /Fp"Debug/test.pch" /YX /Fo"Debug/" /Fd"Debug/" /FD /GZ /c
```

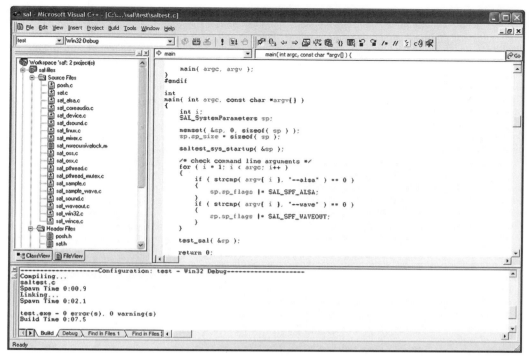

Figure 4-3: Microsoft Visual C++

This is necessary for each file! Most developers would rather not figure that out on their own unless absolutely necessary.

IDEs are not all cookies and milk, however. Here are some of their disadvantages:

- Due to their heavy integration, their use tends to be an all-or-nothing prospect.
- Setting up a build system with each tool requires a lot of learning and maintenance.
- They're often not particularly amenable to automation. Configuring periodic builds across a group of machines can be cumbersome.
- Most of the high-quality IDEs are proprietary and expensive, which makes them impractical for developers on a limited budget.
- Since many of these environments are tied to a specific compiler, migrating between compilers can be overly strenuous for the developer, because it requires changing the build system as well.

Portable Build Tools

Portable build tools solve a lot of the problems associated with the proprietary, host-specific build environments by pushing more of the work onto the developer, thus lessening the burden on the tools. Common examples are scripts (custom programs written in Perl, Python, or a shell language such as sh or REXX) that are processed by specialized build tools such as make and jam.

Assuming that you can execute your script on all your desired host platforms, building on a new platform simply means adding a new entry for that particular host environment and tools. All higher-level dependency checking and project management can then be handled portably.

make

make is the granddaddy of all build-management tools, finding its roots during the early days of Unix development. As the story goes, make's developer, Stuart Feldman of Bell Labs (developers of Unix), found that he and many of his coworkers were running into the same "bug": they would forget to compile some files during development, inadvertently linking older, out-of-date object modules into their binaries. So bugs would be fixed and features added, and yet mysteriously these revisions would not show up in the final executable.

To address this, Stuart wrote a handy little program called *make* that, in theory, was simple enough to understand. It took a set of targets, dependencies, production rules, and macros, defined in a *makefile*, processed them, and made sure that anything that was out-of-date was updated appropriately.

For the relatively small, Unix-only projects of the time, make worked very well. But as software projects have grown, the ability of make to keep up has been limited. Every time a new feature is bolted on, makefiles become increasingly fragile. In fact, if you were to survey most developers that use make, the vast majority of them would probably admit that they don't touch their makefiles except to add files. And when a process gets to the point that it's considered somewhere between black magic and quantum physics, you know things are bad.

As an example of how bad it can get, here's an example from the GNU tutorial on make. This rule is used for generating dependency files from .c files:

```
%.d: %.c
        @set -e; rm -f $@; \
        $(CC) -M $(CPPFLAGS) $< > $@.$$$$; \
        sed 's,\($*\)\.o[ :]*,\1.o $@ : ,g' < $@.$$$$ > $@; \
        rm -f $@.$$$$
```

If that doesn't give you cold shivers, nothing will.

make's inability to keep up with modern software projects led to the arrival of helper utilities such as GNU's automake and autoconf. These tools perform tasks like generating makefiles and configuration scripts that, in theory, make development easier for the programmer. Unfortunately, they trade complexity for more complexity; creating the makefile is no longer difficult, but the programmer now must learn how to edit automake and configuration files.

make's popularity has worked against it as well. The program itself has become popular, and it has also spawned a plethora of make-like clones (GNU make), substitutes (jam and scons, described later), variants (Microsoft NMAKE), and commercial versions (Opus Make).

While make definitely has its faults and quirks, it's still the most widely used build tool today. Its ubiquity, popularity, and user base guarantee that it is available on pretty much every platform under the sun.

SAL EXAMPLE: A SIMPLE MAKEFILE

Here is a very simple makefile that builds the test program included with SAL:

```
# Simple example makefile that uses GCC and builds the SAL test
CC=gcc
CFLAGS=-g -DSAL_SUPPORT_OSS
LDLIBS=-lpthread
saltest: src/sal.o src/posh.o src/sal_device.o src/sal_mixer.o \
    src/sal_sound.o src/sal_sample.o src/os/sal_pthread.o \
    src/os/sal_pthread_mutex.o src/backends/sal_oss.o \
    src/backends/sal_alsa.o src/os/sal_linux.o src/sal_sample_wave.o \
    test/saltest.o
    $(LINK.o) $^ $(LDLIBS) -o $@
```

This makefile says, "Build an executable named saltest, which is dependent on the following object files." The $(LINK.o) $^ ($LDLIBS) -o $@ statement tells make how to build the final executable, using make's rather cryptic syntax for variables, macros, and implicit rules. The first three lines define variables that are automatically plugged into the build process by make. (It implicitly understands that CC is used for compiling C source files, CFLAGS should be passed to the compiler, and LDLIBS are libraries that should be passed to the linker.)

Production makefiles are considerably more complex, spanning multiple files (*recursive makes*) with thousands of lines, multiple dependencies, variables, conditional execution, and implicit and explicit production files for different file types.

---

jam

jam ("just another make") is a highly portable open-source build management tool from Perforce that, as you would guess from the name, has a lot of similarities to make. But since it was developed after make became popular, it has incorporated a slew of improvements and fixes that make it easier to use and more powerful, including the following:

- jamfiles (jam equivalent of makefiles) have a cleaner and simpler syntax.
- Compiler- and platform-specific idiosyncrasies (such as path separators and compiler flags) are kept out of the jamfiles and are instead stored in a platform-specific jambase file.
- It includes automatic dependency checking with header scanning (no more make depend).
- It's very fast.
- It's easy to perform builds in parallel.

The only real downside to using jam is that it isn't as popular as make, so requiring its use can sometimes make other developers balk. That said, it's an integral part of the Mac OS X development tools, free, and gaining popularity.

Scripts and Batch Files

Of course, long before there were build management tools, there were command-line shell scripts (also known as batch files). When it came right down to it, if you really needed to manage a repetitive build, you could write a simple script in your favorite shell language such as csh, sh, DOS BATCH, or VMS DCL.

Slow, inefficient, and nonportable, shell scripts are also almost always available in one form or another on any given platform. They are straightforward to implement, since they typically eschew such advanced notions as dependency checking.

One step beyond basic shell scripts are scripts written in higher-level, dedicated programming languages such as Perl and Python. These support the development of customized build processes that provide more flexibility than the more rigid, predefined rule sets available with make or jam. One tool, scons, is a build management tool written in Python and uses Python as its configuration language.

Whether you use Python, Perl, scons, or some other scripting language, you'll have an immense amount of power and portability on any system that has your scripting language of choice. You'll find Python and Perl on most systems that are even remotely popular today.

Editors

Having a cross-platform editor isn't nearly as important as a cross-platform source control system, but it can help. How important such an editor is really depends on how picky you are about your editing environment.

Some programmers will sit down and use pretty much any editor with minimal complaint. Others spend hours or days configuring their environments precisely, and when forced to edit even a little bit of text on a foreign system will whine and groan that they can't get any work done because they don't have things *just* so.

If you're one of the latter, you should probably look into using a transportable editor that is easy to install and configure in a short amount of time.

The obvious choice here is Emacs, which is jokingly referred to as a "good operating system with a bad editor"—the point being that Emacs has grown into something far more than a simple editor. Emacs is widely available and easy to install, and local configurations are easy to set up by simply copying a customized .emacs file to the new system. Other cross-platform editors do exist, including the minimalist but ubiquitous vi and VIM editors, and of course, larger cross-platform IDEs such as CodeWarrior and Eclipse have editing functionality built in with their project management features.

SAL EXAMPLE: SHELL SCRIPTS

SAL has a very simple shell script, written in sh, that does the same thing as a makefile, although a bit less elegantly.

On the plus side, it's pretty clear what it's doing, since it's just a one command:

```
#/bin/sh
gcc -g src/posh.c src/sal.c src/sal_device.c \
src/sal_mixer.c src/sal_sound.c src/sal_sample.c \
src/os/sal_pthread.c src/os/sal_pthread_mutex.c \
src/backends/sal_oss.c src/backends/sal_alsa.c \
src/os/sal_linux.c src/sal_sample_wave.c test/saltest.c \
-lpthread -o test/test
```

Of course, shell scripts also offer conditionals, flow control, and variables, so it's easy enough to add support for things like command-line arguments:

```
#/bin/sh
if [ "$1" = "cpp" ]; then
    CPPDEF="-x c++"
    CPPLIB=-lstdc++
else
    CPPDEF=
    CPPLIB=
fi

ALSALIB=
ALSADEF=
OSSDEF=

if [ "$2" = "alsa" ] || [ "$3" = "alsa" ] ; then
    ALSALIB=-lasound
ALSADEF=-DSAL_SUPPORT_ALSA
fi

if [ "$2" = "oss" ] || [ "$3" = "oss" ] ; then
    OSSDEF=-DSAL_SUPPORT_OSS
fi

gcc $OSSDEF $ALSADEF $CPPDEF -g src/posh.c src/sal.c src/sal_device.c \
src/sal_mixer.c src/sal_sound.c src/sal_sample.c src/os/sal_pthread.c \
src/os/sal_pthread_mutex.c src/backends/sal_oss.c \
src/backends/sal_alsa.c src/os/sal_linux.c src/sal_sample_wave.c \
test/saltest.c $ALSALIB -lpthread $CPPLIB -o test/test
```

This example supports an optional c or cpp command-line argument that determines whether the source files should be compiled as C or C++ files. It also supports the alsa and oss command-line arguments to determine which audio subsystems should be supported.

Summary

While much of the emphasis on portable software development is on programming and coding habits, the "simple" first step of migrating source code to and editing on a new host platform can be trying by itself. In this chapter we've covered a lot of the issues that can come up during this process, from editing files to working with source control on different systems.

5

PROCESSOR DIFFERENCES

The differences between comparable process architectures, such as desktop RISC chips, can be dramatic, and when moving code between high-end desktop processors such as the IBM G5 and lower-end processors such as the Intel xScale, the amount of work required for a successful transition is often surprising.

Computer processor designs vary radically in their storage requirements (alignment of data and ordering of bytes), data sizes and formats, and, obviously, performance. This chapter covers some of the common issues you'll encounter when moving between processor architectures.

Note that when you're migrating from a high-performance system to a lower-end one, the feature set may be portable, but your chosen algorithms and data structures may not scale down as neatly. This issue is addressed in the discussion of scalability in Chapter 14.

Alignment

Most processors prefer (or even require) that memory accesses be *aligned*. This means that when the processor accesses a chunk of data *n* bytes in length, the chunk's beginning address must be some multiple of *n*. For example, a four-byte variable should be on a four-byte boundary (address is a multiple of four); a two-byte variable should be on a two-byte boundary (address is a multiple of two); and so on.

However, processors often have different requirements for memory accesses. For example, the Intel x86 architecture allows unaligned memory accesses but imposes a significant performance penalty on unaligned operations. A misaligned access on many RISC processors will result in a processor fault, causing either a crash or, if the fault is handled by a software trap, a *very* slow unaligned access (the access is handled entirely in software). And on the ARM line of embedded processors, a misaligned access will result in incorrect data, which is probably the least ideal outcome, since it can result in incorrect behavior that is silently accepted.

NOTE *Certain ARM implementations with memory management units will implement optional alignment checking, but this feature is not ubiquitous across the entire ARM family.*

For maximum portability, alignment should be forced to the highest granularity possible. Any tricks such as pointer manipulation should be avoided, because they might incur unexpected misaligned accesses. One of the more common memory-alignment errors occurs when accessing a memory buffer via an invalid pointer cast.

A union is a handy mechanism that will guarantee alignment between two different types. For example, Motorola's SIMD AltiVec instruction set requires 16-byte alignment when transferring data between the floating-point and vector (SIMD) units:

```
/* Based on code from:
http://developer.apple.com/hardware/ve/alignment.html */
/* NOTE: "vector" is a keyword specific to the
Altivec enabled GCC compilers */
vector float FillVectorFloat( float f1, float f2, float f3, float f4 )
{
    /* this union guarantees that the 'scalars' array will be
    aligned the same as the */
    /* 'vector float v' */
    union
    {
        float scalars[ vec_step( vector float ) ];
        vector float v;
    } buffer;

    /* copy four floating point values into array of scalars */
```

```
        buffer.scalars[0] = f1;
        buffer.scalars[1] = f2;
        buffer.scalars[2] = f3;
        buffer.scalars[3] = f4;

/* return vec float equivalent */
    return buffer.v;
}
```

MISALIGNED ACCESSES THROUGH POINTER CASTING

SAL has a WAVE file-parsing function, _SAL_create_sample_from_wave(), that could have easily taken the buffer and simply cast it to the appropriate structure:

```
typedef struct
{
    char        wh_riff[ 4 ];
    sal_u32_t   wh_size;
    char        wh_wave[ 4 ];
    char        wh_fmt[ 4 ];
    sal_u32_t   wh_chunk_header_size;
} _SAL_WaveHeader;


sal_error_e
SAL_create_sample_from_wav( SAL_Device *device,
                            SAL_Sample **pp_sample,
                            const void *kp_src,
                            int src_size )
{
_SAL_WaveHeader *pwh = ( _SAL_WaveHeader * ) kp_src;
    .
    .
    .
    /* verify that this is a legit WAV file
       NOTE: wf_chunk_header_size might be a misaligned access! */
    if ( strncmp( pwh->wh_riff, "RIFF", 4 ) ||
         strncmp( pwh->wh_wave, "WAVE", 4 ) ||
         pwh->wh_chunk_header_size != 16 )
    {
        return SALERR_INVALIDPARAM;
    }
}
```

Depending on the alignment of kp_src, the comparison statement using pwh->wh_chunk_header_size may result in a misaligned access. While this won't happen in the vast majority of cases, since most buffers are allocated on paragraph or page boundaries, if you've written a naive buffer allocation/free system that works on byte boundaries, this could be a real problem.

The marginally slower, but safer, solution is to copy the incoming data into a structure, which will be aligned correctly by the compiler:

```
sal_error_e
SAL_create_sample_from_wav( SAL_Device *device,
                            SAL_Sample **pp_sample,
                            const void *kp_src,
                            int src_size )
{
    _SAL_WaveHeader wh;
    .
    .
    .
    /* this still makes assumptions about padding, byte ordering, etc. */
    memcpy( &wh, kp_src, sizeof( wh ) );

    /* verify that this is a legit WAV file
       NOTE: wf_chunk_header_size will be aligned correctly */
if ( strncmp( wh.wh_riff, "RIFF", 4 ) ||
        strncmp( wh.wh_wave, "WAVE", 4 ) ||
        wh.wh_chunk_header_size != 16 )
    {
        return SALERR_INVALIDPARAM;
    }
}
```

However, raw copies don't handle byte ordering or padding issues, so often you need to parse the raw memory and transform it into the correct form, like so:

```
const sal_byte_t *kp_bytes = ( const sal_byte_t * ) kp_src;
    .
    .
    .
    /* read out wave header */
    memcpy( wh.wh_riff, kp_bytes, 4 );
    kp_bytes += 4;
    wh.wh_size = POSH_ReadU32FromLittle( kp_bytes );
kp_bytes += 4;
    memcpy( wh.wh_wave, kp_bytes, 4 );
    kp_bytes += 4;
    memcpy( wh.wh_fmt, kp_bytes, 4 );
    kp_bytes += 4;
    wh.wh_chunk_header_size = POSH_ReadU32FromLittle( kp_bytes );
    kp_bytes += 4;

    /* verify that this is a legit WAV file */
    if ( strncmp( wh.wh_riff, "RIFF", 4 ) ||
        strncmp( wh.wh_wave, "WAVE", 4 ) ||
        wh.wh_chunk_header_size != 16 )
    {
        return SALERR_INVALIDPARAM;
    }
```

Byte Ordering and Endianess

Multibyte data types such as integers may be represented in one of two forms: *little-endian* or *big-endian*, indicating the order bytes are represented within the data type. On a little-endian architecture such as the Intel x86, the least significant bytes are placed first (that is, at a lower address). A big-endian architecture, like the Motorola PowerPC, places the most significant bytes first.

There are also mixed-endian and bi-endian machines. For example, the PDP-11 stored 32-bit values as two big-endian shorts (most significant bytes at the lower address), but with the least significant short stored at the lower address (2-3-0-1 where 1 corresponds to the lowest address). Many modern CPUs and coprocessors (network processors, graphics processing units, and sound chips) support bi-endian operation, where they can operate in little-endian or big-endian mode. This ability helps both performance and portability. Unfortunately, rarely can an application control this feature; the operating system or device drivers usually control the endianess mode for specific hardware.

Big-Endian versus Little-Endian Values

Consider the following example:

```
union
{
   long l; /* assuming sizeof( long ) == 4 */
   unsigned char c[ 4 ];
} u;
u.l = 0x12345678;
printf( "c[ 0 ] = 0x%x\n", ( unsigned ) u.c[ 0 ] );
```

Here are the little-endian and big-endian values for this example:

Address	Little-Endian Value	Big-Endian Value
&c[0]	0x78	0x12
&c[1]	0x56	0x34
&c[2]	0x34	0x56
&c[3]	0x12	0x78

When run on a little-endian machine, you would expect the output to be as follows:

```
c[ 0 ] = 0x78
```

And on a big-endian CPU, you would expect to see this output:

```
c[ 0 ] = 0x12
```

This poses a significant problem: multibyte data cannot be shared directly between processors with different byte ordering. For example, if you were to write some multibyte data to a file and then read it back on an architecture of different endianess, the data would be garbled, like so:

```
void write_ulong( FILE *fp, unsigned long u )
{
    /* BAD!  Storing to disk in 'native' format of the current CPU */
    fwrite( &u, sizeof( u ), 1, fp );
}
unsigned long read_ulong( FILE *fp )
{
    unsigned long u;
    /* BAD!  Blithely assuming that the format on disk matches the
    processor's byte ordering! */
    fread( &u, sizeof( u ), 1, fp );
    return u;
}
```

BYTE-ORDERING EXAMPLE:

POWERPC VERSUS INTEL X86

Now let's consider an example to demonstrate the effects of byte ordering. If you were to execute the following on a PowerPC:

```
write_ulong( fp, 0x12345678 );
```

and then run it again on an Intel x86 like this:

```
unsigned long ul = read_ulong( fp );
```

you would be in for a surprise: the variable ul will contain 0x78563412 on the Intel processor. The reason is that the bytes on disk are in "PowerPC format" (stored as 0x12,0x34,0x56,0x78), which will be backward when read and stored into ul (0x12 in the lowest address, 0x34 in the next, and so on). This is probably one of the most common—if not *the* most common—bugs programmers encounter when migrating between platforms.

Standardized Storage Format

A solution to the problem of different byte ordering is to store data in a standardized byte order. Software running on processors that do not match this standardized format must then manually "swizzle" the bytes to convert from the canonical format to the processor's native format. Another option is to store data in the platform's native byte order and then mark what that order is in the file's header. Several file formats, such as TIFF, specify the endianess this way.

NOTE *Some file formats, such as the TIFF graphics format, don't have a fixed endianess. Instead, a program must inspect the TIFF header to determine its byte ordering.*

Now let's assume that a standardized storage format is big-endian. You could then write the code shown at the beginning of this section as follows:

```
void write_ulong( FILE *fp, unsigned long u )
{
    unsigned char c[ 4 ];
    c[ 0 ] = ( unsigned char ) ( u >> 24 );
    c[ 1 ] = ( unsigned char ) ( u >> 16 );
    c[ 2 ] = ( unsigned char ) ( u >> 8 );
    c[ 3 ] = ( unsigned char ) u;
    fwrite( c, sizeof( c ), 1, fp );
}
unsigned long read_ulong( FILE *fp )
{
    unsigned char c[ 4 ];
    unsigned long u = 0;

    fread( c, sizeof( c ), 1, fp );

    u |= ( ( unsigned long ) c[ 0 ] ) << 24;
    u |= ( ( unsigned long ) c[ 1 ] ) << 16;
    u |= ( ( unsigned long ) c[ 2 ] ) << 8;
    u |= ( ( unsigned long ) c[ 3 ] );
    return u;
}
```

This code example makes no assumption regarding the data's organization in memory; instead, it directly extracts the relevant values by shifting and masking. The only complaint with this code is that it exacts a performance toll even when the storage format matches the processor's native format.

To optimize such situations, you can detect byte ordering and perform manual construction/reconstruction only when necessary, as follows:

```
unsigned long read_ulong( FILE *fp )
{
    unsigned char c[ 4 ];
    unsigned long u;

    fread( c, sizeof( c ), 1, fp );

    /* this function is discussed next */
    if ( is_big_endian() )
    {
        /* this is fine, but only on big-endian systems */
        /* Obviously you'd move this conditional outside */
        /* this loop for performance */
```

```
      return * ( unsigned long * ) c;
   }

   u  = ( ( unsigned long ) c[ 0 ] ) << 24;
   u |= ( ( unsigned long ) c[ 1 ] ) << 16;
   u |= ( ( unsigned long ) c[ 2 ] ) << 8;
   u |= ( ( unsigned long ) c[ 3 ] );
   return u;
}
```

Now you simply write your is_big_endian() function, which you can base on the initial code fragment that illustrated the problem:

```
int
is_big_endian( void )
{
   union
   {
      unsigned long l;
      unsigned char c[ 4 ];
   } u;
   u.l = 0xFF000000;
   /* big-endian architectures will have the MSB at
   the lowest address */
   if ( u.c[ 0 ] == 0xFF )
      return 1;
   return 0;
}
```

NOTE   *If you control your storage format, then you can avoid byte-ordering concerns by using a text format for data storage. This is discussed in more detail in Chapter 15.*

Fixed Network Byte Ordering

The TCP/IP network protocol specifies a big-endian network byte order, which means that parameters provided to the network layer (but not the actual data being transmitted) must be in big-endian format.

For example, a 32-bit IPv4 address and 16-bit port specification, such as the ones used in the sockaddr structure, must be in network order. This means that this code:

```
struct sockaddr_in svr;
/* UNPORTABLE: sin_port is expected to be in network byte order! */
svr.sin_port = PORT_NO;
```

will mysteriously fail on little-endian architectures, since PORT_NO is in the incorrect byte order.

In order to fix this, the BSD sockets and Winsock APIs provide helper functions that convert from host to network byte ordering and back:

```
uint32_t htonl( uint32_t hostlong );    /* host to network long */
uint16_t htons( uint16_t hostshort );   /* host to network short */
uint32_t ntohl( uint32_t netlong );     /* network to host long */
uint16_t ntohs( uint16_t netshort );    /* network to host short */
```

The portable version of the port assignment statement would then be:

```
struct sockaddr_in svr;
svr.sin_port = htons( PORT_NO ); /* convert from host to network ordering */
```

Byte ordering should not be a concern for most programs unless they are storing and/or loading binary data or directly extracting bytes by reference from larger multibyte values. As long as you convert to and from a predefined byte-ordering format for storage and avoid directly extracting bytes by reference from larger multibyte values, processor endianess should not be a major issue.

Signed Integer Representation

Many programmers assume that a signed integer is represented in two's complement form, since this is the most common representation on modern computer systems; however, the ANSI C and C++ specifications do not dictate the format of a signed integer. Some processors do use one's complement or even sign-magnitude format. If your code might run on those systems, you should not make assumptions about signed integer ranges and bit formats.

For example, instead of assuming that a 16-bit signed value has a minimum value of −32768, use the preprocessor constant SHRT_MIN defined in <limits.h>. Another common case is the assumption that ~0 == −1, which is not true on a one's complement machine, where −0 == ~0.

Size of Native Types

Processors have a *natural word size*, corresponding to their internal register size, which represents the optimal size of a variable. Originally, there was an expectation that C compilers would make the int type correspond to this word size, allowing a programmer to use int any time optimal performance was desired (assuming no other constraints on the range of the variable in question). This was true for many years; however, at some point, a critical mass of programs made the assumption that sizeof(int)==4.

The assumption about int size played havoc with compiler writers who needed backward compatibility but who were targeting 64-bit platforms.

POSH EXAMPLE: BYTE-ORDERING CAPABILITIES

POSH provides a host of byte-ordering assistance functions and macros. First, it has a slew of byte-swapping functions suitable for converting little-endian to big-endian and back:

```
extern posh_u16_t  POSH_SwapU16( posh_u16_t u );
extern posh_i16_t  POSH_SwapI16( posh_i16_t u );
extern posh_u32_t  POSH_SwapU32( posh_u32_t u );
extern posh_i32_t  POSH_SwapI32( posh_i32_t u );
```

In addition, it has serialization and deserialization functions that automatically convert from the native format to a user-specified destination format:

```
extern posh_u16_t *POSH_WriteU16ToLittle( void *dst, posh_u16_t value );
extern posh_i16_t *POSH_WriteI16ToLittle( void *dst, posh_i16_t value );
extern posh_u32_t *POSH_WriteU32ToLittle( void *dst, posh_u32_t value );
extern posh_i32_t *POSH_WriteI32ToLittle( void *dst, posh_i32_t value );

extern posh_u16_t *POSH_WriteU16ToBig( void *dst, posh_u16_t value );
extern posh_i16_t *POSH_WriteI16ToBig( void *dst, posh_i16_t value );
extern posh_u32_t *POSH_WriteU32ToBig( void *dst, posh_u32_t value );
extern posh_i32_t *POSH_WriteI32ToBig( void *dst, posh_i32_t value );

extern posh_u16_t  POSH_ReadU16FromLittle( const void *src );
extern posh_i16_t  POSH_ReadI16FromLittle( const void *src );
extern posh_u32_t  POSH_ReadU32FromLittle( const void *src );
extern posh_i32_t  POSH_ReadI32FromLittle( const void *src );

extern posh_u16_t  POSH_ReadU16FromBig( const void *src );
extern posh_i16_t  POSH_ReadI16FromBig( const void *src );
extern posh_u32_t  POSH_ReadU32FromBig( const void *src );
extern posh_i32_t  POSH_ReadI32FromBig( const void *src );
```

On top of these are macros that convert a value to native format. These macros are redefined depending on the byte order of the current platform:

```
#if defined POSH_LITTLE_ENDIAN

#   define POSH_LittleU16(x) (x)
#   define POSH_LittleU32(x) (x)
#   define POSH_LittleI16(x) (x)
#   define POSH_LittleI32(x) (x)
#   if defined POSH_64BIT_INTEGER
#     define POSH_LittleU64(x) (x)
#     define POSH_LittleI64(x) (x)
#   endif /* defined POSH_64BIT_INTEGER */

#   define POSH_BigU16(x) POSH_SwapU16(x)
#   define POSH_BigU32(x) POSH_SwapU32(x)
#   define POSH_BigI16(x) POSH_SwapI16(x)
#   define POSH_BigI32(x) POSH_SwapI32(x)
```

```
#  if defined POSH_64BIT_INTEGER
#    define POSH_BigU64(x) POSH_SwapU64(x)
#    define POSH_BigI64(x) POSH_SwapI64(x)
#  endif /* defined POSH_64BIT_INTEGER */

#else

#  define POSH_BigU16(x) (x)
#  define POSH_BigU32(x) (x)
#  define POSH_BigI16(x) (x)
#  define POSH_BigI32(x) (x)

#  if defined POSH_64BIT_INTEGER
#    define POSH_BigU64(x) (x)
#    define POSH_BigI64(x) (x)
#  endif /* POSH_64BIT_INTEGER */

#  define POSH_LittleU16(x) POSH_SwapU16(x)
#  define POSH_LittleU32(x) POSH_SwapU32(x)
#  define POSH_LittleI16(x) POSH_SwapI16(x)
#  define POSH_LittleI32(x) POSH_SwapI32(x)

#  if defined POSH_64BIT_INTEGER
#    define POSH_LittleU64(x) POSH_SwapU64(x)
#    define POSH_LittleI64(x) POSH_SwapI64(x)
#  endif /* POSH_64BIT_INTEGER */

#endif
```

With these macros, an application can trivially convert to and from any byte ordering without needing to explicitly detect the current platform's endianess. The previous function to read an unsigned long value then becomes:

```
unsigned long read_ulong( FILE *fp )
{
    unsigned char c[ 4 ];
    unsigned long u;

    fread( c, sizeof( c ), 1, fp );
    return POSH_ReadU32FromBig( c );
}
or
unsigned long read_ulong( FILE *fp )
{
    unsigned long u;

    fread( u, sizeof( u ), 1, fp );
    return POSH_BigU32( u );
}
```

As a result, numerous models were introduced for 64-bit architectures, with varying emphasis on interoperability with 32-bit platforms versus ideal performance for 64-bit platforms. These models have names like LP64, ILP64, LLP64, ILP32, and LP32, which indicate the size of the core C data types, as shown in Table 5-1. L corresponds to a long, P corresponds to pointer size, I corresponds to int, and LL corresponds to a long long. (Other models exist as well; these are just a few of the more common ones.)

NOTE   long long *is a type specific to a few compilers, notably GCC. Other compilers, such as Microsoft Visual C++, use an* _int64 *type instead.*

Table 5-1: Some Programming Models

Type	LP64	ILP64	LLP64	ILP32	LP32
char	8	8	8	8	8
short	16	16	16	16	16
int	32	64	32	32	16
long	64	64	32	32	32
long long			64		
pointer	64	64	64	32	32

Most programmers are familiar with the traditional 32-bit programming model, ILP32, where integers, longs, and pointers are 32 bits in size. LP32, originally used by the Win16 C API, is an even simpler specification designed around the idiosyncrasies of the Intel 8086 family, which had 16-bit integer registers but 20-bit (8086) or 24-bit (80286) addressing. (And, even more idiosyncratic, the 8086 and 80286 processors used a segmented addressing architecture.)

Since the ILP32 model lacks 64-bit types, it is inappropriate for 64-bit CPUs, which have an address space beyond the 4 GB limit of 32-bit systems. For 64-bit CPUs, you need 64-bit pointers, which all the other models have. All that remains then is to decide what is more important:

- Maintaining the assumption that sizeof(int)==sizeof(long)==sizeof(void *)
- Maintaining the assumption that sizeof(int)==*machine word size*
- Maintaining the assumption that sizeof(int)==4

Since the first two assumptions are mutually exclusive on 64-bit architectures, confusion ensues (thus the proliferation of models).

Regrettably, the ANSI standard does not take a position on this issue, leaving it up to each compiler writer (and compiler user) to deal with this on a case-by-case basis. Sun, SGI, and Compaq/DEC use the LP64 model for their Unix variants, whereas Microsoft uses the LLP64 (or, more accurately, P64) model for 64-bit Windows support.

Microsoft was concerned primarily with a clean, easy, and safe migration to Win64. To ensure this, the Microsoft developers wanted to avoid, as much as possible, breaking assumptions in 32-bit code while still gaining 64-bit pointers. The LLP64 model provides this by creating 64-bit integers only by using the _int64 or long long types. Structures that do not contain pointers retain the exact same size between ILP32 and LLP64, an important consideration for backward-compatibility.

This puts you, the ostensibly portable programmer, in a predicament: you must decide whether to use the C native types (short, int, and long) or a set of sized types like those provided by C99 (inttypes.h), as shown in Table 5-2.

Table 5-2: C99 Sized Types

Type	Description
int8_t	Signed 8-bit integer
uint8_t	Unsigned 8-bit integer
int16_t	Signed 16-bit integer
uint16_t	Unsigned 16-bit integer
int32_t	Signed 32-bit integer
uint32_t	Unsigned 32-bit integer
int64_t	Signed 64-bit integer
uint64_t	Unsigned 64-bit integer

As a rule, if you absolutely must enforce a particular size—for example, when creating a rigidly formatted structure definition or when you require a guaranteed range—use the sized types. If you do not require a specific range, such as when you need an indexing variable that will reach only into the thousands, the C native integer type should allow the compiler to make the right choice for you, but, unfortunately, this is not always the case. Some platforms err on the side of compatibility and provide 32-bit integers when the architecture is natively 64-bit.

A program that requests a particular size variable, such as a 32-bit integer, by using C99's uint32_t type, may find itself suffering from very poor performance when migrating to a lower-end platform that does not support the operations on those sizes natively. For example, the 8086 processor is a 16-bit processor, so 32-bit integer operations often required a function call. Be careful to specify exact sizes only when you truly need them, such as when you have range or packing concerns.

Address Space

One of the major signposts for the advancement of computer architectures has been *address space*, or the total amount of memory a computer system can easily access.

Early computers could access only the tiniest amount of memory due to limitations with both the size of a pointer and the available hardware.

POSH EXAMPLE: SIZED TYPES

POSH supplies analogs to the C99 (inttypes.h) definitions, as follows:

posh_byte_t	Unsigned 8-bit quantity
posh_i8_t	Signed 8-bit integer
posh_u8_t	Unsigned 8-bit integer
posh_i16_t	Signed 16-bit integer
posh_u16_t	Unsigned 16-bit integer
posh_i32_t	Signed 32-bit integer
posh_u32_t	Unsigned 32-bit integer
posh_i64_t	Signed 64-bit integer
posh_u64_t	Unsigned 64-bit integer

As a general, but inaccurate, rule, a computer system may access no more memory than the size of a pointer will allow; that is, addressable bytes are 2-to-the-pointer bits in size. However, there are many exceptions to this, such as systems where pointers are larger than the actual address space. The Motorola 68000 could address only 16 MB, even though it had 32-bit pointer registers, and the Intel 8086 could address only 64 KB easily (with a single pointer access) but up to 1 MB in total using its segmented memory architecture. Today, we're seeing machines with 64-bit pointers; however, even those can access a much smaller range of memory, sometimes as low as 40 bits. Older computer systems used paged, windowed, or banked memory access to reach more memory than was addressable natively.

Programs that work with large arrays or structures need to be aware of any potential limitations as they migrate to lower-end platforms. This is often a surprising gotcha that programmers don't expect. For example, something as innocuous as this:

```
static unsigned char buffer[ 0x20000 ];
```

suddenly stops building when targeting a lower-end system with, say, 16-bit pointers.

Summary

Along with operating system differences, the most fundamental component of a platform is the choice of processor. Processors can differ radically in performance, features, and implementations issues, and this is one of the most common areas during portable software development. This chapter covers the majority of key issues related to architectural differences between processors.

6

FLOATING POINT

The inconsistent performance and accuracy of floating-point calculations, along with their bit-wise representations, have been a source of problems for computer scientists for decades, and it wasn't until the introduction of the various IEEE standards in the early 1980s that they've come under control. This chapter discusses some of the issues facing portable software that relies on floating-point data and computations.

History of Floating Point

Throughout computing's early years, especially from the 1960s onward, nearly every minicomputer and mainframe manufacturer implemented its own proprietary floating-point formats and conventions. Portability—both of code and data—was nearly impossible with that state of events, which was tenable solely because of the proprietary nature of software at the time.

Custom applications for each system were the rule, not the exception, so developers who needed to deal with a platform's idiosyncrasies were not too concerned, as they had little or no expectation of moving their software to a competing machine.

The late 1970s saw the beginning of a steady migration of high-end mini-computer and mainframe features to microcomputers (PCs), and floating point was one of these. At about this same time, the lack of floating-point arithmetic standardization became a serious concern. To address this issue, the IEEE p754 committee was formed. It consisted of a group of engineers from many of the major microprocessor and systems manufacturers of the time, such as Intel, Zilog, and Motorola. This committee went on to define the IEEE 754 floating-point specification, which has acted as the standard for floating-point formats and computations ever since. (The IEEE 754 standard was eventually rolled into the IEC 60559 standard, so the two are basically synonymous; IEC 60559 is also sometimes referred to as IEC 559.)

NOTE *There were still the occasional oddball computers that did floating point their own way, such as some of Cray and DEC's larger machines of the time. Gaming consoles such as Sony's PS2 also have their own proprietary formats, since portability is not a very big concern for these manufacturers (in fact, they prefer to dissuade it).*

The IEEE 754 specification took many years of politicking and compromises to see the light of day, but in retrospect, it has proved to be a well-crafted, precise, practical standard that does not impose any unreasonable constraints. By defining storage formats, mathematical operations, rounding modes, exceptions, and the bit-wise representation of special values, development of portable software that uses floating point has become orders of magnitude simpler.

Standard C and C++ Floating-Point Support

Until recently, the C and C++ languages were agnostic on the issue of floating point, defining the requirements in almost meaninglessly ambiguous terms. The size and format of the basic floating-point types are loosely specified, and the accuracy and operation of floating-point operations (+, -, *, and /) and library functions are implementation-defined. However, starting with C++98 and C99, *optional* support for IEEE 754 has been added (an application can query for the existence of IEEE 754 conformance).

So, as wonderful as the IEEE 754 standard may be, there is a fairly significant stumbling block to its use in portable software: the C and C++ language specifications do not require it. C++98 and C99 provide only optional support for the standard. This is an inconvenient but understandable caveat, since floating-point, and especially IEEE 754-compliant floating-point, support isn't available on many platforms that are otherwise C/C++ compatible.

This means that while float and double will *often* correspond to IEEE 754 single-precision and double-precision formats, respectively, it is not guaranteed. This also applies to the rounding modes, exceptions, and other aspects of the IEEE 754 standard.

Problems with Floating Point

Now that you have an idea of the general issues with floating point and the attempts to standardize it—by both the IEEE and C and C++ standards—let's look at some of the specific problems that applications may encounter with floating point.

Inconsistent Evaluation

With C and C++, there are no hard-and-fast rules regarding the consistency and nature of floating-point expression evaluations. This means you cannot count on:

```
float add( float a, float b )
{
    return a + b;
}
```
returning the same result as:
```
float add2( float a, float b )
{
    float c = a + b;
    return c;
}
```

The Intel x87 FPU architecture stores 80-bit precision intermediate results on the floating-point stack, losing precision only when values are stored to memory. The first function in the preceding example, add(), can generate a sequence of:

```
fld  a   ; load 'a' onto stack
fadd b   ; add 'b' onto stack
```

with the expectation that the caller will pop the resulting value off the stack and into an appropriate variable. If that variable is a double, then it is possible that any extra precision will be retained.

The second function, add2(), stores to an intermediate value locally, which could generate a code sequence such as this:

```
fld a    ; load 'a' onto stack
fadd b   ; add 'b' to top of stack
fstp c   ; store result (and pop stack) to float variable 'c'
fld c    ; load 'c' back onto stack so that caller may retrieve result
```

The fstp/fld instruction pair will strip off any extra precision before returning to the caller.

So a program that used these functions in an equality test:

```
if ( add( x, y ) != add2( x, y ) )
    printf( "Error: this shouldn't happen!" );
```

may unexpectedly encounter unexpected behavior as the code is moved from compiler to compiler, or even as different optimization switches are set.

With GNU GCC, the function add2() will generate different results with optimizations enabled than it will with optimizations disabled:

```
; Optimizations DISABLED
pushl   %ebp
movl    %esp, %ebp
subl    $8, %esp
flds    8(%ebp)
fadds   12(%ebp)
fstps   -4(%ebp)
movl    -4(%ebp), %eax
movl    %eax, -8(%ebp)
flds    -8(%ebp)
leave
ret

; Optimizations ENABLED
pushl   %ebp
movl    %esp, %ebp
flds    12(%ebp)
fadds   8(%ebp)          ; Note that the store/load has been optimized away!
popl    %ebp
ret
```

Programs cannot rely on the consistency and precision of floating-point operations, especially in the context of comparison tests. This may work sometimes on some systems, but it is a very easy area in which to embroil yourself with portability woes and difficult to find bugs.

Floating Point and Networked Applications

Given that floating-point operations are often inconsistent, when two different systems share floating-point data directly, all kinds of bad things can happen.

For example, a worst-case situation often arises when two computers must run parallel simulations in lockstep. Each machine performs simulations internally, occasionally receiving input from the other machine. (Peer-to-peer networked computer games and simulators often operate this way.)

Once input is received, each machine simulates the world for one discrete step and then broadcasts this state to the others.

Given identical input, a fixed update rate, and a known starting state, the machines should have *identical* views of the simulation. Of course, sometimes this isn't the case, so the machines will have state verification checks, where they examine their own simulation and compare it against the simulation results of another machine; if the results don't match, a synchronization error is generated.

With floating-point math, synchronization becomes a very significant issue, since subtle differences in calculations will arise as the result of architectural or compiler differences. Even though the differences may be so small as to be negligible (although, occasionally, even tiny changes may be the difference between "you are behind this wall" and "you are in this wall"), when doing a bit-wise comparison for synchronization checking, these differences become show stoppers. You're either synchronized or you're not, and even a single-bit discrepancy between two floating-point values is enough to cause a synchronization error.

A more robust (but still imperfect) method is to quantize any floating-point numbers to a more limited fixed-point representation that should match between computers with slightly different floating-point evaluation paths, as described in the "Fixed-Point Integer Math" section a little later in this chapter.

Conversions

Under both the C and C++ standards, a floating point–to–integer conversion is handled through truncation (round toward zero), where the fractional portion of the floating-point value is chopped off:

```
float x = 1.33f, y = -1.33f;
/* ix will be 1 and iy will be -1 */
int ix = ( int ) x, iy = ( int ) y;
```

Believe it or not, this has some pretty nasty performance side effects on some systems.

Most modern CPUs have a configurable floating-point rounding mode. The IEEE 754 specification declares four different rounding modes: up (toward positive infinity), down (toward negative infinity), chop (toward 0), and toward nearest representable value. The default rounding mode for most situations is round toward nearest, but this causes problems, since C and C++ require truncation for floating point–to–integer conversion. As a result, it is often necessary for a compiler to generate appropriate floating-point rounding mode changes to the CPU *every time a floating-point value is cast to an integer!*

The simple function:

```
int round( float s )
{
    return ( int ) s;
}
```
generates the following code:
```
_round:
    pushl   %ebp              ; save EBP
    movl    %esp, %ebp        ; put stack pointer into EBP
    subl    $8, %esp          ; allocate space on the stack
    fnstcw  -2(%ebp)          ; store current FPU control word
    movzwl  -2(%ebp), %eax    ; move the FPU control word to EAX
    orw     $3072, %ax        ; or EAX with 3072 (to set rounding mode)
    movw    %ax, -4(%ebp)     ; mov AX into memory EBP[-4]
    flds    8(%ebp)           ; load 's' into the FPU
    fldcw   -4(%ebp)          ; load the control word from  EBP[-4]
    fistpl  -8(%ebp)          ; store 's' as integer back into EBP[-8]
    fldcw   -2(%ebp)          ; reload the old control word
    movl    -8(%ebp), %eax    ; move return value into EAX
    movl    %ebp, %esp        ; restore everything
    popl    %ebp
    ret
```

That is a lot of code for what is a conceptually simple operation, but the C/C++ rounding standards require this every time. Some of those instructions, such as fldcw, are far deadlier than you would expect, since they force a flush of the floating-point unit's (FPU's) entire state, causing a hiccup in its pipeline.

Contrast this with a noncompliant implementation:

```
_round:
    pushl   %ebp              ; save EBP
    movl    %esp, %ebp        ; put stack pointer into EBP
    subl    $4, %esp          ; allocate space on the stack
    flds    4(%ebp)           ; load 's' into the FPU
    fistpl  -4(%ebp)          ; store 's' as integer back into EBP[-8]
    movl    -4(%ebp), %eax    ; move return value into EAX
    movl    %ebp, %esp        ; restore everything
```

```
popl    %ebp
ret
```

Some compilers offer the ability to perform fast but noncompliant floating point–to–integer conversion (by eschewing all control word manipulation and just calling `fistp` immediately with no setup); however, these are proprietary and very nonportable extensions to the standards.

Fixed-Point Integer Math

With all the portability problems that floating point presents, it is sometimes simpler to convert floating-point operations into integer or fixed-point ones. The semantics of integer representations, while not perfect, are still much clearer than that of floating point.

For example, instead of broadcasting a position as raw floating-point values, you could use a quantized fixed-point value instead. The quantization process strips off unneeded precision bits, allowing for "imprecise" comparisons:

```
int snap_to_quarters( float s )
{
    s *= 4.0;
    if ( s >= 0 )
        s = s + 0.5;
    else
        s = s - 0.5;
    return ( int ) s;
}
```

This code snaps a floating-point value to one-quarter precision and returns its fixed-point value (an integer scaled up by a factor of four). So, multiple values near the same quantization value will evaluate to the same fixed-point number, allowing for equality comparisons with a well-defined precision.

However, fixed point is not perfect either. Fixed-point representations have a static range and precision, which is is not nearly as flexible as floating point. In addition, there is no portable way to handle overflow conditions, which are important since common fixed-point operations will frequently overflow as part of their standard operations. For example, a 32-bit fixed-point multiplication requires 64 bits of intermediate storage, which C and C++ do not provide portably (at least until C99 implementations become more popular).

Extraction of Integer Bits from a Float

Occasionally, it is useful or necessary to look at the integer representation of a floating-point value's raw bits. For example, you may wish to display a floating-point value's bits as an integer in a debugger, or you may want to perform a nominally nonportable performance optimization, such as directly manipulating the sign bit or using an integer instead of floating-point comparison.

NOTE   *With IEEE 754 floating-point values, you can directly compare the bits of two floating-point values for a magnitude comparison, as long as both values share the same sign.*

The most straightforward method is to cast the floating-point value's address to an integer pointer (assuming sizeof(int) == sizeof(float)) and then work with those bits directly:

```
uint32_t get_float_bits( float f )
{
    /* this assumes that sizeof(float) == sizeof(int); the conversion */
    /* will not result in a trap representation for an integer, and   */
    /* the alignment properties of int and float are identical        */
    return * ( int * ) &f;
}
```

Unfortunately, there is one problem with this approach: it's technically illegal. According to the C and C++ standards, int and float are considered *incompatible types*, so there is no guarantee that a program won't explode when that line occurs.

But that's the language lawyer in me talking. Realistically, for the *vast* bulk of popular computer architectures, the pointer cast will do the right thing, since a 32-bit value is a 32-bit value. For example, with GCC on Cygwin/x86, the integer representation for the 32-bit floating-point value 1.0 is 0x3f800000. If you write a piece of code that does this:

```
float foo( void )
{
    float f = 1.0;
    return f;
}
```

the actual unoptimized (optimized code simply does an fld1 and returns, but that doesn't really help me make my point) assembly code looks like this:

```
    pushl   %ebp              ; save EBP
    movl    %esp, %ebp        ; move ESP into EBP
    subl    $8, %esp          ; ESP = ESP - 8
    movl    $0x3f800000, %eax ; EAX = 0x3f800000
    movl    %eax, -4(%ebp)    ; EBP[-4] = 0x3f800000
    movl    -4(%ebp), %eax    ; EAX = 0x3f800000
    movl    %eax, -8(%ebp)    ; EBP[-8] = 0x3f800000
    flds    -8(%ebp)          ; top of stack=0x3f800000=1.0f
    leave
    ret
```

Ignoring the inefficiencies, the preceding code fragment clearly illustrates that for this platform, a regular integer value that is interpreted as a 32-bit floating-point value works.

Unfortunately, type incompatibilities aside, there is another problem: some compilers aggressively optimize code by assuming no aliases. When a compiler sees something like this:

```
/* Again, we're assuming that the conversion from float to integer bits */
/* is verified to do "what we expect" on this platform, even though the C */
/* standard says that this might explode */
float f;
int x;
f = 1.0f;
x = * ( int * ) &f;
```

it is free to assume that x is entirely independent of f (that is, any change to x will not affect the value of f and vice versa), since the standard claims they are incompatible types. With this assumption, the compiler might perform the assignment to f after the assignment of x!

You can address the assumption of no aliases in several ways:

- Use a union, which forces many compilers to assume aliasing (GCC has this as an extension). Technically, this is still just as illegal as the pointer cast, but it has a few properties going for it that make it slightly less likely to melt down. First, it will be aligned correctly for any of its members. Second, it will also be large enough to contain its largest member. This means that on a system where you might run into an alignment or overflow issue (for example, floats are 32 bits and integers are 16 bits), instead of *really* bad behavior, you'll just get pretty bad behavior.

- Perform an intermediate cast to a void * or unsigned char * type, which forces the compiler to assume that some type of aliasing might occur. (If this were not allowed, far too many programs today would break.)

- Cast the address of the float to an unsigned char * and read the data directly that way. This is 100 percent legal, but it only tells you what the bits are, not necessarily what they mean (since their meaning is inherently unportable).

- Use the compiler's optimization switches to disable strict aliasing rules or assume no aliasing.

The safest method to extract the bits from a float is to perform an intermediate cast to a void * or unsigned char * type, as follows:

```
/* assumes that dst is at least as large as sizeof(float) */
void float_to_bits( float f, unsigned char dst[] )
{
    int i;
    unsigned char *c = ( unsigned char * ) &f;
```

```
   for ( i = 0; i < sizeof( f ); i++ )
      dst[ i ] = c[ i ];
}
```

This method extracts the raw bits, but does not attempt to reassemble them into a different multibyte value such as an integer. There are no violations of the type incompatibility or aliasing rules.

Using a union looks like this:

```
uint32_t float_to_bits( float f )
{
   union
   {
      int i;        /* again, assuming sizeof(int)==sizeof(float) */
      float f;
   } u;
   u.f = f;
   return u.i;
}
```

According to the C and C++ standards, the results of executing this code are still undefined (there is no guarantee what happens to other members of a union after one member is written to), but at least it's more defined than casting arbitrarily through a pointer.

Additionally, C++ has the reinterpret_cast operator:

```
float f = 1.0f;
int i = reinterpret_cast< float &>( f );
```

While this is very C++ish, it's no safer than just doing a straight cast.

Implementation Queries

You could attempt to cover all your bases when writing floating-point code by including <float.h> and examining the predefined symbols listed in Table 6-1. This way, you could try to support all the different floating-point formats.

Table 6-1: C and C++ Constants for Floating-Point Format

Constant	Meaning
FLT_ROUNDS	Current rounding mode
FLT_RADIX	Radix of the floating-point format's exponent representation
FLT_DIG	Number of decimal digits required to accurately represent a float
DBL_MAX	Maximum value that may be represented by a double

POSH uses the union method to extract the bits from a floating-point value.

```
posh_u32_t
POSH_LittleFloatBits( float f )
{
    union
    {
        float f32;
        posh_u32_t u32;
    } u;

    u.f32 = f;

    return POSH_LittleU32( u.u32 );
}

posh_u32_t
POSH_BigFloatBits( float f )
{
    union
    {
        float f32;
        posh_u32_t u32;
    } u;

    u.f32 = f;

    return POSH_BigU32( u.u32 );
}
```

This is not ideal, but as of this writing, this has not been a problem with any POSH-supported architectures.

Under C++, you can include <numeric_limits> and examine a specifically instantiated template. The template numeric_limits is defined as follows:

```
namespace std
{
    template<class T> class numeric_limits
    {
    public:
        static const bool is_specialized = false;
        static T min() throw();
        static T max() throw();
        static const int digits = 0;
```

```
            static const int digits10 = 0;
            static const bool is_signed = false;
            static const bool is_integer = false;
            static const bool is_exact = false;
            static const int radix = 0;
            static T epsilon() throw();
            static T round_error() throw();
            static const int min_exponent = 0;
            static const int min_exponent10 = 0;
            static const int max_exponent = 0;
            static const int max_exponent10 = 0;
            static const bool has_infinity = false;
            static const bool has_quiet_NaN = false;
            static const bool has_signaling_NaN = false;
            static const float_denorm_style has_denorm = denorm_absent;
            static const bool has_denorm_loss = false;
            static T infinity() throw();
            static T quiet_NaN() throw();
            static T signaling_NaN() throw();
            static T denorm_min() throw();
            static const bool is_iec559 = false;
            static const bool is_bounded = false;
            static const bool is_modulo = false;
            static const bool traps = false;
            static const bool tinyness_before = false;
            static const float_round_style round_style = round_toward_zero;
        };
    };
```

For example, with C, you would look at FLT_ROUNDS in <float.h>; with C++, you could instead inspect numeric_limits<float>::round_style.

NOTE   *C++ still has the equivalent of* <float.h> *in its* <cfloat> *header file.*

We could examine many more constraints, but in practice, any attempt to support any and all conceivable floating-point formats is extremely tedious and error-prone (which is effectively what the C and C++ standards allow). It is much easier (and safer) to establish a baseline that includes only systems with expected floating-point formats and operations or, better yet, to avoid writing code that is dependent on a platform's specific floating-point implementation.

Exceptional Results

Many floating-point operations and functions generate special results—infinity, not a number (NaN), and so on—if given improper inputs. For example, the tangent of 90 degrees or the square root of a negative number cannot return a proper value and may raise an exception as well.

The IEEE 754 specification defines five different kinds of exceptions:

Underflow conditions
Occur when an operation results in a value too small to represent in a normalized floating-point value.

Overflow conditions
The opposite of an underflow condition: an operation occurs where the resulting value is too large to represent in the desired destination format.

Divide-by-zero conditions
Result when a valid, nonzero floating-point value is divided by zero. Note this specifically excludes situations such as NaN/0 and 0/0, which generate invalid operation exceptions instead.

Invalid operation exceptions
Handle most of the illegal operations not covered by the other conditions. These include operations such as infinity minus infinity, using a NaN in a comparison operation, 0 divided by 0, and infinity divided by infinity.

Inexact exceptions
Generated when the result of an operation is not exactly represented by the binary floating-point value. This is very common (for example, 2.0/3.0), and thus this exception is often masked. It is also raised when an overflow condition occurs and no overflow exception is raised.

When these exceptional situations are encountered, a special value is returned and an exception may be generated.

Special Values

Before IEEE 754 support, each compiler and platform could have its own floating-point format, precluding a portable way to check for exceptional values (you can query errno after calling certain standard library functions, but this doesn't help you when dealing with a regular mathematical operation such as division). Each platform provides a set of functions or macros to check for these special cases. Microsoft Visual C++ 6.0 provides functions such as _isnan, _finite, and _fpclass. Other compilers and platforms might provide similar functions such as isnan and fpclassify.

If identifying these different types of special values is important to your application, you'll need to abstract the floating-point identification and error functions, unless you can assume C99 support.

To address the confusion that arose from the plethora of floating-point classification macros and functions, the C99 standard formalized a set of classification routines in <math.h>, along with predefined constants for floating-point value classification, as shown in Table 6-2.

Table 6-2: C99 Floating-Point Classification

Classification Routine	Description
int fpclassify(x)	Classifies the given argument and returns its type, such as FP_NAN, FP_INFINITE, or possibly an implementation-defined value
int isfinite(x)	Returns nonzero if x is finite
int isinf(x)	Returns nonzero if x is +/- infinity
int isnan(x)	Returns nonzero if x is NaN
int isnormal(x)	Returns nonzero if x is normal
int signbit(x)	Returns 1 if x is negative; returns 0 if x is positive
FP_INFINITE	Predefined constant indicates value is +/- infinity
FP_NAN	Predefined constant indicates value is NaN
FP_NORMAL	Predefined constant indicates value is normal
FP_SUBNORMAL	Predefined constant indicates value is subnormal
FP_ZERO	Predefined constant indicates value is +/- 0

Several nonnumeric values must still be represented in a floating-point format. The IEEE 754 specification dictates them as shown in Table 6-3.

Table 6-3: Nonnumeric Values That Must Be Represented as Floating Point

Value	Representation
Positive 0	All zero bits
Negative 0	One bit (sign bit) followed by 31 zero bits
Infinity	Zero bit, followed by 8 one bits, followed by 23 zero bits
-Infinity	One bit, followed by 8 one bits, followed by 23 zero bits
NaN (not a number)	Nonzero fraction with all one bits in the exponent; sign bit determines signaling (0) or quiet (1)
Denormalized	Nonzero fraction with all zero bits in the exponent; any sign

NOTE *The IEEE specification differentiates between* signaling NaNs *and* quiet NaNs. *Signaling NaNs will generate an exception when used in an arithmetic operation. Quiet NaNs will propagate through the chain of most floating-point operations without raising an exception.*

It is generally much safer to use the classification macros available from the language or a vendor than it is to examine a floating-point value's bits directly.

Exceptions

There are numerous situations where the result of a floating-point operation may result in a bad thing happening (the classic example is divide-by-zero). In these situations, an implementation *may* generate an exception (in addition to any special values as a return value) but is not required to do so.

Many (but not all) C and C++ implementations allow the programmer to use the signal() API to install a SIGFPE signal handler; however, this support is neither mandated nor reliable, since it requires cooperation from both the platform's floating-point and its exception-handling implementation. <fenv.h> defines the exceptions FE_OVERFLOW, FE_UNDERFLOW, FE_DIVBYZERO, FE_INVALID, and FE_INEXACT, but *only* if the implementation supports that specific exception.

The C standard requires that floating-point exceptions be masked at program startup, after which an application can enable specific exceptions using either a platform-specific API or through use of the C99 <fenv.h> API. For example, C99 allows a program to mask exceptions temporarily to guarantee nonstop operation through the feholdexcept() function, whereas Microsoft Visual C++ 6.0 on the Intel 80x86 platform has the proprietary _control87() or _controlfp() function.

Floating-Point Environment Access

Prior to C99's standardization of floating-point environment access, each compiler vendor would offer its own set of macros, header files, and APIs to manage this access. This isn't nearly as bad as it sounds, since the number of required functions is reasonably low. For example, Microsoft Visual C++ 6 exports the _controlfp, _statusfp, and _clearfp APIs to interface with the floating-point environment. Even on systems that do not provide this API, it is usually fairly easy to write equivalents with a few lines of assembler.

The C99 specification provides a set of macros and functions defined in <fenv.h> to interact with the floating-point environment, as shown in Table 6-4. Exceptions may be raised, masked, tested, and cleared, and the floating-point rounding mode can be set and retrieved as well.

Table 6-4: C99 Floating-Point Exception Functions

Function	Description
void feclearexcept(int excepts)	Clears the specified floating-point exceptions
void fegetexceptflag(fexcept_t *flagp, int excepts)	Retrieves an implementation-defined representation of the current floating-point state
void feraiseexcept(int excepts)	Raises the specified exceptions
void fesetexceptflag(const fexcept_t *flagp, int excepts);	Sets the current floating-point state
int fetestexcept(int excepts);	Tests the status word to see if any of the given exceptions are raised

Table 6-4: C99 Floating-Point Exception Functions (continued)

Function	Description
`int fegetround(void);`	Gets the current rounding mode
`int fesetround(int round);`	Sets the current rounding mode
`void fegetenv(fenv_t *envp);`	Retrieves the entire floating-point environment (status and control words) with a single function call
`int feholdexcept(fenv_t *envp);`	Retrieves the current environment and stores it in the given parameter, then sets the current state to be "nonstop" so that no exceptions will be raised
`void fesetenv(const fenv_t *envp);`	Sets the current environment, presumably retrieved previously with a call to `fegetenv`/ `feholdexcept`
`void feupdateenv(const fenv_t *envp);`	Saves the currently raised floating-point exceptions locally, installs the floating-point environment specified by `envp`, and then raises the saved floating-point exceptions

Storage Formats

The IEEE 754 specification defines two major storage formats—single precision and double precision—and several optional higher-precision forms, such as extended double precision (`long double` with some compilers) and even quadruple precision.

With most IEEE 754 implementations, the C and C++ `float` type will correspond to a 32-bit value formatted as shown in Table 6-5.

Table 6-5: IEEE 754 Single-Precision Format

Bit	Meaning
31	Sign bit (0=positive, 1=negative)
24–30	Exponent
0–23	Mantissa/fraction (implicit leading one)

Table 6-6 describes the IEEE double-precision format, usually represented as double in C and C++.

Table 6-6: IEEE 754 64-Bit Double-Precision Format

Bit	Meaning
63	Sign (0=positive, 1=negative)
52–62	Exponent
0–51	Mantissa/fraction

Finally, the extended-precision format is 80 bits, as shown in Table 6-7. It is not very common as a storage format. Some compiler implementations support it with the long double type.

Table 6-7: IEEE 754 80-Bit Extended-Precision Format

Bit	Meaning
79	Sign (0=positive, 1=negative)
78–64	Exponent
63	Always 1
0–62	Mantissa/fraction

Summary

The behavior of floating-point operations is one of those things that many programmers give little thought to. They assume that 1.0 is just 1.0 and is represented identically on all computers, but as this chapter demonstrates this is often not the case. The ANSI C and C++ standards don't address the issue of floating-point operations definitively, so any program that must rely on the accuracy of floating-point operations must be very careful.

7

PREPROCESSOR

Probably no single aspect of the C and C++ languages is as maligned by computer language purists as the preprocessor. Preprocessors transform raw source text with little or no regard for a language's syntax or semantics, often leading to difficult to find bugs or compilation errors if (ab)used aggressively. Every new language that comes out seems to make it a point to eschew the preprocessor, and users of those new languages always complain that it's missing. The reality is that preprocessors provide a host of powerful features, such as conditional compilation and raw text substitution, that are often difficult to emulate or implement within a language proper. In this chapter we'll get into the meat of the C/C++ preprocessor and how you can leverage its power to make porting easier, while avoiding some of the pitfalls associated with its use.

Predefined Symbols

Predefined symbols vary between compilers and platforms. For example, every compiler vendor seems to have a need to define something different to represent "generating code for an 80x86 target." Some compilers use i386; others uses __i386__; and Microsoft Visual C++ uses _M_IX86.

The C standard defines only a few required portable preprocessor constants. Table 7-1 lists the definitions as per the C89 language standard.

Table 7-1: C89 Predefined Macro Names

Macro Name	Description
__DATE__	The date of translation of the preprocessing translation unit: a character string literal of the form *mmm dd yyyy*, where the names of the months are the same as those generated by the asctime function, and the first character of *dd* is a space character if the value is less than 10. If the date of translation is not available, an implementation-defined valid date shall be supplied.
__FILE__	The presumed name of the current source file (a character string literal).
__LINE__	The presumed line number (within the current source file) of the current source line (an integer constant).
__STDC__	The integer constant 1, intended to indicate a conforming implementation.
__TIME__	The time of translation of the preprocessing translation unit; a character string literal of the form *hh:mm:ss*, as in the time generated by the asctime function. If the time of translation is not available, an implementation-defined valid time shall be supplied.

C99 introduced several additional predefined constants and identifiers, as shown in Table 7-2.

Table 7-2: Additional C99 Predefined Macro Names and Identifiers

Macro Name	Description
__STDC_IEC_559__	The decimal constant 1, intended to indicate conformance to the specifications in annex F (IEC 60559/IEEE-754 floating-point arithmetic).
__STDC_HOSTED__	The integer constant 1 if the implementation is a hosted implementation or the integer constant 0 if it is not.
__STDC_IEC_559_COMPLEX__	The decimal constant 1, intended to indicate adherence to the specifications in annex G (IEC 60559-compatible complex arithmetic).
__STDC_VERSION__	The specific version of C implemented, such as 199901L for C99.

Table 7-2: Additional C99 Predefined Macro Names and Identifiers (continued)

Macro Name	Description
__STDC_ISO_10646__	A decimal constant of the form *yyyymmL* (for example, 199712L), intended to indicate that values of type wchar_t are the coded representations of the characters defined by ISO/IEC 10646, along with all amendments and technical corrigenda as of the specified year and month.
__func__	A predefined identifier that can be used to discover the unadorned name of the enclosing function; similar in purpose to __FILE__ and __LINE__. One caveat is that this is defined by the compiler, not the preprocessor, since the preprocessor doesn't understand the concept of functions or function names.

In addition, __cplusplus is defined when compiling a C++ source file.

Older compilers may not define __STDC__, indicating that they were developed before the C89 standard was popularized. This is actually nice, since you can immediately bomb out if you find yourself on a compiler that is pre-ANSI (realistically speaking, trying to support both early C and ANSI C is just not worth the trouble).

```
#if !defined __STDC__
#error This source code requires an ANSI compliant compiler
#endif
```

There is one potential hazard with this, and that is the rather haphazard way in which different compilers actually define __STDC__. Here are some of the ways that __STDC__ may be treated:

- Define it, but don't specify a value.
- Set the value to 1.
- Set the value to 0 unless compiling in strict mode; in that case set the value to 1.
- Not set it at all, unless compiling in strict mode.

Admittedly not setting __STDC__ is fairly rare. Today's most popular compilers generally set __STDC__ if they adhere to the ANSI specification *as a minimum,* as opposed to adhering to it slavishly and disallowing extensions.

Header Files

Only a handful of header files are considered standard within the C language. Prior to the C99 standard, you could count on only the header files shown in Table 7-3, and even then, noncompliant implementations would still occasionally omit some.

Table 7-3: Pre-C99 Standard Headers

Header	Description
assert.h	Assertion management
ctype.h	Classification of characters
errno.h	Error numbers and handling
float.h	Floating-point environment
iso646.h	For handling ISO 646 character sets
limits.h	Definition of integer limits
math.h	Standard math functions
string.h	String handling
stdarg.h	Variable argument lists
stdio.h	Standard input/output functions
stdlib.h	Standard library, miscellaneous functions
wctype.h	Wide character analog of <ctype.h>
wchar.h	Wide character string support
signal.h	For managing exceptions/signal handling
stddef.h	Useful macro and type definitions
time.h	Time and date query and conversion
locale.h	Localization support
setjmp.h	setjmp/longjmp (nonlocal goto) support

C99 supports the header files listed in Table 7-3, and it adds those shown in Table 7-4.

Table 7-4: C99 Additional Header Files

Header	Description
complex.h	Complex math support
fenv.h	Floating-point environment
inttypes.h	Functions for manipulating greatest width integers
stdbool.h	Defines bool type and true/false
stdint.h	Defines integer types of specific widths
tgmath.h	Type-generic math macros

Keeping straight which header files are portable, which are vendor-specific, which are library-specific, and which are platform-specific can become confusing. The standard header files <stdio.h>, <stdlib.h>, and <string.h> exist on most platforms with a C compiler, but there are many other header files that are pseudo-standard (commonly found on a particular family of operating systems or in a particular vendor's compiler implementation) but are still nonportable, such as <unistd.h>, <windows.h>, <malloc.h>, <process.h>, ,<sys/stat.h>, and <varargs.h>.

Header File Path Specification

Header files reside in different locations depending on the platform. It is unwise to assume that a particular file is in an absolute location such as:

```
#include "/usr/include/some_project.h"
#include "../src/local_header.h"
```

Use an absolute path only if you can *guarantee* that every source code installation will have header files in the exact same location. Often, it is easier to include the files by name only:

```
#include "some_project.h"
#include "local_header.h"
```

Then specify the location of header files using compiler switches, such as -I/usr/include and -I../src.

At least one compiler (Metrowerks CodeWarrior) has a very idiosyncratic method for finding header files. Suppose you have two files—src/foo.c and src/foo.h—and src/foo.c includes foo.h as such:

```
#include "foo.h"
```

Then CodeWarrior, by default, *will not* be able to find foo.h correctly unless you're compiling from within the src/ directory. You will need to specify a special command-line switch, -cwd source, so that it searches for header files in the same directory as the source file.

Header Filenames

Different operating systems and their filesystems behave differently when it comes to case-sensitivity and path separators. If you compile this statement on a machine running Microsoft Windows:

```
#include <STDIO.H>
```

there is a good chance it will successfully find and load stdio.h (note the lowercase). However, it absolutely will not work on Linux, where filesystems are case-sensitive. The compiler or preprocessor will complain that the file cannot be found.

Similarly, be aware that path separators may change from system to system. On Windows, the preferred separator is the backslash:

```
#include <MyLib\MyHeader.h>
```

On Unix-like systems (including Mac OS X), the forward slash is used:

```
#include <MyLib/MyHeader.h>
```

And, of course, there's always one in a crowd that has to be really different. In this case, it's Mac OS prior to OS X, which uses a colon as a path separator:

```
#include <MyLib:MyHeader.h>
```

Thankfully, the C standard states that the backslash (\) is specifically illegal in header file inclusion statements. Between that stipulation and the huge amount of Unix-centric source code in the world, most compilers will recognize the forward slash (/) separator properly. I would recommend using the forward slash separator at all times.

Additionally, the caveats on acceptable filename length and characters mentioned in Chapter 13 apply here as well.

Configuration Macros

Oftentimes, projects have large-scale configuration changes dictated by a handful of macros. For example, SAL looks for several symbols to determine which audio subsystems to support (for example, SAL_SUPPORT_OSS and SAL_SUPPORT_ALSA on Linux).

Variables such as these can be controlled either at the command line or by simply setting them in a global location such as a common header file. Most compilers support the former, but some compilers support only the latter (Metrowerks CodeWarrior uses prefix files).

Setting the variables at the command line has two major benefits:

- It allows you to build multiple versions of your software without editing the source code.
- You don't need to edit any files if you simply need to change some configuration variables.

This latter benefit is a significant convenience when dealing with source control systems. Needing to check out an important project file simply because you want to comment out a #define is annoying and can lead to errors. For example, programmers can "break the lock" on a file, edit it locally to change some configuration variables, and make significant changes, forgetting that the file isn't really checked out.

Changing the variables through a prefix header or by having a configuration section in a globally included header file has the added advantage of readability and self-documentation. If a programmer is looking at some unknown definition, she can simply search all the project files to find where it's defined and maybe learn about its usage. If its definition is not documented in the source code anywhere, then she may be at a loss when trying to discern its purpose.

Conditional Compilation

One of the reasons that language purists dislike preprocessors is due to the ease with which they can be abused. It's tantalizingly easy to add quick fixes to code that must compile on a wide range platforms. For example, you may have some sockets code that needs WSAStartup() to execute if you're running Windows:

```
void init_sockets()
{
#ifdef _WIN32
WSAStartup();
#endif
}
```

That is innocent enough, except WSAStartup() is a Windows function, so you need to include <windows.h> as well:

```
#ifdef _WIN32
#include <windows.h>
#endif
void init_sockets()
{
#ifdef _WIN32
    WSAStartup();
#endif
}
```

Hmmm, the code is getting a bit uglier. Then as time goes on, the file grows, with things like this:

```
#ifdef _WIN32
    {
        DWORD count, flags = 0;
        extern WSABUF wsabuffers[];
        WSARecv( wsabuffers, 1, &count, &flags, NULL, NULL );
        ... copy out of wsabuffers into buffer ...
    }
#else
    recv( s, buffer, buf_size, 0 );
#endif
```

And it has now spiraled out of control. This is exactly what abuse of conditional compilation can lead to, and for obvious reasons, it's something you want to avoid.

This isn't to say that conditional compilation is worthless. It's incredibly useful when used in moderation. For this particular example, it would be much cleaner and safer to simply have two separate implementations of socket functions: one file for Windows and one for other operating systems. This approach minimizes the amount of #ifdef invasiveness in the core source code without sacrificing portability.

The C/C++ preprocessor is a wonderfully simple yet powerful tool, but it is far too easy to abuse its features, creating code that is difficult to read and maintain. If you find your code riddled with conditional compilation statements, it's probably a good sign that you need to streamline your implementation.

Pragmas

C and C++ compilers provide the pragma facility to communicate directly with the compiler in an implementation-defined manner. For example, on Microsoft Visual C++, you can use #pragma warn(disable: *xxxx*) to disable a particular compiler warning.

By their very nature, pragmas are not particularly portable, but the C standard specifically states that all compilers must ignore pragmas they do not understand. Unfortunately, some compilers will still choke on an unrecognized pragma, so you'll want to use conditional compilation to bracket pragmas:

```
#ifdef _MSC_VER
#pragma warning( disable: 4786 )
#endif /* _MSC_VER */
```

C99 STANDARD PRAGMAS

C99 introduced a set of standard pragmas (a bit of an oxymoron), in the form:

```
#pragma STDC [name] [option]
```

Here is an example:

```
#pragma STDC FP_CONTRACT ON
```

As of this writing, the following are the three ratified standard pragmas:

- FP_CONTRACT controls whether floating-point expressions may be contracted.

- FENV_ACCESS is used to bracket operations that modify the floating-point status or state.

- CX_LIMITED_RANGE tells the compiler that certain assumptions about complex number calculations are safe.

Summary

While often derided as crude, primitive, and unsophisticated, the C/C++ preprocessor is surprisingly effective for assisting cross-platform software development. Conditional compilation, pragmas, raw text substitution, and the availability of predefined symbols can radically ease the burden when moving software from one system to another.

8

COMPILERS

ANSI C and C++ have been around for more than 15 years now, and many different compilers have been written for these languages. ANSI C is inarguably the most popular compiled programming language in the world, and C++ is rapidly approaching C's popularity.

With the number of compilers available, quirks and idiosyncrasies between implementations are inevitable. Some compilers extend the language to support the needs of a particular platform; others simply add features and libraries that the developers felt would be useful to their users. And, of course, there are always differences of opinion when it comes to how a particular code fragment should be compiled.

This chapter examines some of the differences in behavior that you'll encounter when porting from one compiler to another.

Structure Size, Packing, and Alignment

The C struct aggregate data structure, along with C++'s class type, allows programmers to manage complex data sets in a convenient, easy-to-maintain format. However, there are subtle nuances regarding the size, packing, and alignment of these types.

Early computer systems often restricted the total size of a structure to some small number, such as 32 KB, due to addressing constraints or other limitations. These constraints would often manifest themselves only after a program had been ported to a new architecture, resulting in link errors or very hard-to-find run-time bugs.

The C and C++ standards do not mandate how members within a structure are aligned or packed. This means that two compilers for the same architecture may format the following structure differently:

```
struct foo
{
    int i;
    char c[ 2 ];
    short s;
};
```

Assuming that an int is 32 bits, a char is 8 bits, and a short is 16 bits, compilers that pack structures tightly would format this structure as follows:

Member	Byte Offset
i	0
	1
	2
	3
c	4
	5
s	6
	7

This is intuitively correct, since

```
sizeof(foo) == sizeof(foo.i)+sizeof(foo.c)+sizeof(foo.s)
```

However, on many architectures, it is faster (or even required, depending on the CPU design) to access "naturally aligned" data elements (as explained in the "Alignment" section of Chapter 5). On such systems, a compiler will pack the structure loosely, inserting unused padding bytes as necessary to maintain optimal alignment. So, foo would be formatted using four-byte natural alignment as follows:

Member	Byte
i	0
	1
	2
	3
c	4
	5
[padding]	6
	7
s	8
	9
[padding]	10
	11

Now we find that sizeof(foo) > sizeof(foo.i)+sizeof(foo.c)+sizeof(foo.s), leading many programmers into the dark forest of compiler-specific behavior.

These differences can hurt you in many ways. If you serialize data to disk one way, and then load it with a different executable built with a different compiler, the packing and sizes may be completely off, corrupting your data:

```
void read_foo( FILE *fp, struct foo *f )
{
   /* sizeof( foo ) may not be consistent across platforms! */
   fread( f, sizeof( foo ), 1, fp );
}
```

Assumptions about the layout through pointer arithmetic can also lead to much pain:

```
struct foo f;
/* WARNING: assumes tight packing, may fail unexpectedly! */
short *s = ( short * ) ( f->c + sizeof( f->c  ) );
```

Third-party libraries expect structures to be packed and aligned a certain way when passed to their APIs. This is why prebuilt libraries must either explicitly force alignment/packing assumptions (through compiler pragmas) or manually perform alignment by inserting dummy padding bytes as necessary—and even then, they must be diligent about ensuring that this works.

Many compilers offer an appropriate command-line or preprocessor function to enforce a specific alignment. For example, Microsoft Visual C++ offers the #pragma pack option:

```
/* This pragma may not work with all compilers */
#pragma pack(1)
struct foo
{
    int i;
    char c[ 2 ];
    short s;
};
```

You may also attempt to enforce the padding yourself by inserting the appropriate padding bytes:

```
struct foo
{
    int    i;
    char   c[ 2 ];
    char   pad1[ 2 ];
    short  s;
    char   pad2[ 2 ];
}
```

This will *try* to force objects of type foo into alignment and guarantee a size of at least 12 bytes, but although it's better than the previous version, it's still not foolproof. For example, some compilers may use eight-byte alignment, or the native types themselves may change in size (on some Cray platforms all types were eight bytes in size except for characters).

EXAMPLE: MOTOROLA 68000 AND POWERPC

The Motorola 68K series of processors allows 32-bit integers to appear on any even address boundaries, instead of requiring four-byte alignment. However, the Motorola PowerPC line of processors forces 32-bit integers to reside on four-byte boundaries, which requires padding to ensure compliance in some situations. When programmers migrated from the 68K (used in earlier Macintoshes) to the PowerPC (used in modern Macintoshes), they found that sometimes their old "portable" C software would crash unexpectedly due to alignment requirement differences between the two processors.

Do not make assumptions about the size, packing, or alignment of structures unless you have explicit control over these parameters by specifying the appropriate compiler flags.

Memory Management Idiosyncrasies

Memory management is another potential source of portability problems. Many machines have different ways to represent and manage memory, both in the heap and the stack. It's very easy to become accustomed to one platform's way of doing things, only to be bitten when moving to another platform. Two differences to watch out for are the treatment of freed pointers and aligned memory allocation.

Effect of free

A lot of older software assumed that a recently freed pointer could still be used "for a while" (that is, until another memory allocation call was made):

```
typedef struct node_struct
{
    struct node_struct *next, *prev;
    void *data;
} node;
void delete_node( node *n )
{
    free( n );
    n->prev->next = n->next; /* BAD! */
}
```

While this *might* work with some compilers, this technique is heavily frowned upon, since different heap management implementations may overwrite the freed pointer immediately for various bookkeeping purposes. Some compilers will clear out the memory pointed to during debug builds, so that any attempts to use that memory will result in a failure.

Aligned Memory Allocation

Both C's malloc function and C++'s new operator must return maximally aligned pointers, since the memory might be used for any type or size of object. For example, if you do this:

```
char *c = ( char * ) malloc( sizeof( char ) * 1 );
```

the pointer returned will be aligned on the minimum alignment size required to access any object, irrespective of the number of bytes requested. This way, you can never have a misaligned access when using a pointer acquired through dynamic memory allocation. (Of course, with sufficient pointer casting, you can still force an unaligned access.)

Pragmatically speaking, this puts a floor on the minimum granularity for allocations, so multiple small allocations will consume more space than a single allocation of the same combined size.

However, inevitably some compilers mess this up. At least one compiler I'm aware of will always provide data aligned on four-byte boundaries, even though some objects (double types) require eight-byte alignment.

If alignment is critical, or if your alignment needs exceed that of the default alignment, it probably pays to implement a wrapper around malloc and/or new to pad the requested bytes and return a pointer aligned to some size parameter.

The Stack

The C/C++ stack is a quirky little beast. Everyone uses it, and everyone knows what it is, but it often has a huge set of limitations that many programmers are not aware of.

Stack Size

Typically, a compiler and linker together will determine the available stack size statically, and once that stack is exceeded, things go downhill quickly. And, unfortunately, it is all too easy to blow through your stack when running on limited hardware, such as embedded and handheld platforms. For example, when developing for the early Palm OS, a developer could rarely count on having more than a few kilobytes of stack space. Wireless phone applications using the BREW API have only about 500 bytes of stack with which to work.

The stack is consumed every time a local (automatic) variable comes into scope. Programmers coming from desktop PC systems, where the available stack may be measured by the megabyte, often don't realize just how bad this can be. It's not uncommon for such a developer to casually declare a 1 KB array for some temporary storage, only to see her program explode ingloriously on a BREW platform or by using a couple levels of recursion on a Palm OS handheld.

Even desktop systems can run into stack exhaustion problems, especially with programs that use heavy recursion. For example, a few years ago, I was working with a team to develop an application we had to port from Windows to the Macintosh (Mac OS 9). We were finding a mysterious crash that seemed to occur only with our release builds. We tracked it down to a problem in the audio system—at least, that's where we thought the problem was. After over a week of desperate, hair-pulling bug hunting, we finally found that the problem was due to stack corruption. The compiler's default small stack size on the release build (64 KB) differed from that of the debug build (256 KB), and in one critical section of our code, we were using 65 KB of stack. This was enough to destroy some important internal data, a problem that manifested itself much later (in the audio subsystem).

Stack-related crashes are often mysterious and difficult to track down, since the damage can happen in a location far away from the location of the actual error.

Problems with alloca()

Related to the stack is the magical function `alloca()`, which is seductive in its power and simplicity, but extremely dangerous. `alloca()` is, for all intents and purposes, a `malloc()` for the stack. Instead of allocating data from the heap, `alloca()` allocates it from the stack if possible, automatically freeing it when the program exits the current scope.

Using `alloca()` is appealing for several reasons. For starters, it's simpler; if your function has a lot of different exit paths, you don't need to remember to call `free()`. That by itself is handy but not overwhelmingly compelling. However, another enticement is that it doesn't touch the heap, thereby possibly avoiding fragmentation. It gives you the convenience of allocating from the local stack frame and the power to make this allocation variable length (instead of relying on a hardcoded stack array).

But `alloca()` has a host of problems. For starters, it's not part of the ANSI standard, meaning that it doesn't work everywhere (although, wickedly enough, it's available on enough platforms that many people assume that it is portable). As with `malloc()`, it doesn't work with C++ classes correctly. If `alloca()` fails to find enough stack space, there's no guarantee it will simply return `NULL` (unlike `malloc()`), so it may just decide to give you the stack space anyway (if it's a simple stack pointer adjustment) or may throw a stack overflow exception. You just don't know.

`alloca()` also often confuses debuggers trying to keep track of the local stack frame for variable inspection. You may step over a call to `alloca()` and suddenly find you can't see your call stack or variables in a watch window.

The printf Routine

If there is a single function associated with the C programming language, it would have to be the ubiquitous `printf()` routine, in part due to many programmers' first exposure to a "Hello world!" program and also because it's an immensely powerful and useful function.

The C standard identifies a set of compatible and standard `printf()` format specifiers for values such as integers, floating-point numbers, hexadecimal values, and strings. However, there are subtle differences in behavior among implementations, such as how they handle illegal values and print compiler-specific data types.

Some compiler vendors silently support the proper handling of `NULL` parameters. Consider this example:

```
printf( "this is a string: %s\n", 0 );
```

This may crash on some systems, but on other systems, the run-time library will catch this condition and print "NULL" or "(null)" instead.

Since there are numerous compiler-specific type extensions, printing these values will differ from platform to platform. A common example is the treatment of 64-bit integers. With Microsoft Visual C++, the format specifier for a 64-bit integer is:

```
__int64 v = 0x0123456789ABCDEF;
printf( "this is a 64-bit int: %I64i\n", v );
```

However, `glibc` (the C run-time library used by most implementations of GCC) uses `ll` instead:

```
long long v = 0x0123456789ABCDEFLL;
printf( "this is a 64-bit int: %lli\n", v );
```

NOTE   *MinGW, a GCC derivative on the Windows system, actually uses the Microsoft run-time library* `MSVCRT.DLL` *instead of* `glibc`.

While very few modern commercial applications rely on `printf` due to the proliferation of graphical user interfaces (GUIs), these caveats still apply to its buffer-oriented variants—`sprintf()` and `vsprintf()`—which *are* heavily used by many programmers.

One way to work around this is to use a constant format specifier, such as the following:

```
#ifdef _MSC_VER
#define PRINTF_SPEC_64BIT "%I64i"
#elif defined __GNUC__
#define PRINTF_SPEC_64BIT "%lli"
#endif
printf("this is a 64-bit int: "PRINTF_SPEC_64BIT"\n", v );
```

The ANSI C99 specification has introduced a set of constants specifically to handle this situation, as described in the next section.

Type Sizes and Behavior

Many portability problems arise from the compiler's implementations of types. These include handling of 64-bit types, as well as sizes and treatments of basic types.

The 64-Bit Integer Types

The original ANSI C specification was written prior to the proliferation of 64-bit CPU architectures. The revised C99 specification has incorporated support for 64-bit integers through the use of the `<stdint.h>` header file and the associated `int64_t`, `uint64_t`, `long long`, and `unsigned long long` types.

Prior the C99 standard, however, compiler vendors provided different implementations of 64-bit integers. Under DOS and Microsoft Windows, the type was called `__int64` (Microsoft, Borland, and Watcom compilers all used this type). Compilers with a Unix heritage, however, preferred the `long long` type. Of course, on native 64-bit compilers that support the LP64 model, it's also possible that the standard long integer type will be 64 bits, with int remaining 32 bits. (See Chapter 5 for details on programming models.)

Portable code that uses 64-bit integers frequently should either abstract the name of the 64-bit type (using typedef) or stick to the definitions defined in <stdint.h> or <inttypes.h> if C99 compliance can be assumed. The C99 standard provides for the following:

- long long and official 64-bit types, such as int64_t and uint64_t
- The 64-bit constant macros INT64_C() and UINT64_C()
- The 64-bit printf format specifiers PRIi64 and PRId64

Note that the standardized 64-bit types are a part of C99 and are not available with C++. (At the time of this writing, I am not aware of any available compilers that are fully compliant with the C99 specification.)

Along with different ways of specifying the type, there are also different ways of specifying the constant. Compilers that use the __int64 type will usually require a cast:

```
__int64 x = ( __int64 ) 0xFEDCBA9876543210;
```

Compilers that use the long long type usually use the LL suffix:

```
long long x = 0xFEDCBA9876543210LL;
```

Of course, compilers that possess 64-bit native long integers can use a constant with no suffix.

Sizes of Basic Types

Every compiler implements its own ideas of the sizes of basic types and user-defined structures. The C standard does not specify the sizes of specific types; it guarantees only certain ranges. The standard header file <limits.h> includes the predefined constants shown in Table 8-1.

Table 8-1: Sizes of Types Defined in the C Standard Header File

Constant	Definition	Value
CHAR_BIT	Number of bits for a char	>= 8
SCHAR_MIN	Minimum value for a signed char	<= -127
SCHAR_MAX	Maximum value for a signed char	>= 127
UCHAR_MAX	Maximum value for an unsigned char	>= 255 (should equal $2^{CHAR\_BIT}-1$)
CHAR_MIN	Minimum value for a char	If char is signed, then must be the same as SCHAR_MIN; else 0

Table 8-1: Sizes of Types Defined in the C Standard Header File (continued)

Constant	Definition	Value
CHAR_MAX	Maximum value for a char	If char is signed, then must the same as SCHAR_MAX; else UCHAR_MAX
SHRT_MIN	Minimum value for a short int	<= –32767
SHRT_MAX	Maximum value for a short int	>= +32767
USHRT_MAX	Maximum value for an unsigned short int	>= 65535
INT_MIN	Minimum value for an int	<= –32767
INT_MAX	Maximum value for an int	>= +32767
UINT_MAX	Maximum value for an unsigned int	>= 65535
LONG_MIN	Minimum value for a long int	<= –2147483647, or –$(2^{31}-1)$
LONG_MAX	Maximum value for a long int	>= +2147483647 $(2^{31}-1)$
ULONG_MAX	Maximum value for an unsigned long int	>= 4294967295 $(2^{32}-1)$
LLONG_MIN (C99)	Minimum value for a long long int	<= –9223372036854775807 or –$(2^{63}-1)$
LLONG_MAX (C99)	Maximum value for a long long int	>= 9223372036854775807 or $(2^{63}-1)$
ULLONG_MAX (C99)	Maximum value for an unsigned long long int	>= 18446744073709551615 or $(2^{64}-1)$

The values shown in Table 8-1 allow you to infer some size parameters:

```
sizeof( char ) <= sizeof( short int ) <= sizeof( int ) <= sizeof( long )
<= sizeof( long long)
```

In addition, the magnitude limits define the minimum sizes shown in Table 8-2.

Table 8-2: Minimum Type Sizes

Type	Minimum Size
char	8 bits
short	16 bits
int	16 bits
long	32 bits
long long	64 bits

EXAMPLE: POSH AND 64-BIT INTEGER SUPPORT

POSH provides a set of portable 64-bit abstractions encompassing type definition, constant specification, and the printf format specifier.

```
#if defined ( __LP64__ ) || defined ( __powerpc64__ ) || \
defined POSH_CPU_SPARC64
#   define POSH_64BIT_INTEGER 1
typedef long posh_i64_t;
typedef unsigned long posh_u64_t;
#   define POSH_I64( x ) ((posh_i64_t)x)
#   define POSH_U64( x ) ((posh_u64_t)x)
#   define POSH_I64_PRINTF_PREFIX "l"
#elif defined _MSC_VER || defined __BORLANDC__ || \
defined __WATCOMC__ || ( defined __alpha && defined __DECC )
#   define POSH_64BIT_INTEGER 1
typedef __int64 posh_i64_t;
typedef unsigned __int64 posh_u64_t;
#   define POSH_I64( x ) ((posh_i64_t)x)
#   define POSH_U64( x ) ((posh_u64_t)x)
#   define POSH_I64_PRINTF_PREFIX "I64"
#elif defined __GNUC__ || defined __MWERKS__ || defined __SUNPRO_C \
|| defined __SUNPRO_CC || defined __APPLE_CC__ || defined \
POSH_OS_IRIX || defined _LONG_LONG || defined _CRAYC
#   define POSH_64BIT_INTEGER 1
typedef long long posh_i64_t;
typedef unsigned long long posh_u64_t;
#   define POSH_U64( x ) ((posh_u64_t)(x##LL))
#   define POSH_I64( x ) ((posh_i64_t)(x##LL))
#   define POSH_I64_PRINTF_PREFIX "ll"
#endif

/* hack for MinGW */
#ifdef __MINGW32__
#undef POSH_I64
#undef POSH_U64
#undef POSH_I64_PRINTF_PREFIX
#define POSH_I64( x ) ((posh_i64_t)x)
#define POSH_U64( x ) ((posh_u64_t)x)
#define POSH_I64_PRINTF_PREFIX "I64"
#endif
```

Using POSH's macros, you can portably specify and use 64-bit values:

```
posh_i64_t x = POSH_I64(0x1234567890ABCDEF);
printf( "64-bit value = %"POSH_I64_PRINTF_PREFIX"d", x );
```

There is nothing that states that all sizes cannot be, say, 64 bits in length. In fact, some architectures have been known to be particularly aggressive with sizes (for example, some Cray variants had 32-bit shorts and 64-bit ints, without any 16-bit types at all). A huge number of programs assume, for example, that shorts are 16 bits and longs are 32 bits, which is not guaranteed (but very likely, which is why the assumption exists).

For these reasons, you should never make hardcoded assumptions about sizes, like so:

```
int *foo = ( int * ) malloc( 4 ); /* will fail if int is 8-bytes! */
```

Instead, always uses sizeof:

```
int *foo = ( int * ) malloc( sizeof( int ) );
```

or

```
int *foo = ( int * ) malloc( sizeof( *foo ) );
```

If you require concrete sizes, use appropriate type definitions based on the underlying platform and verify these assumptions using compile-time assertions. C99 provides a set of guaranteed size types in <stdint.h>, and POSH provides the same in <posh.h> (see also the "Abstract Data Types (typedef)" section in Chapter 3).

Signed versus Unsigned char Types

The ANSI C standard does not dictate whether a char is signed or unsigned by default. This can lead to some extremely confusing behavior due to implicit promotion rules. Consider the following example:

```
char c; /* indetermine sign since it was not stated explicitly */
c = 0xFF;
if ( c == 0xFF )  /* note: 'c' is promoted to int for the comparison */
{
    /* sometimes this is never reached, depending on compiler */
    printf( "Hello!" );
}
```

This fragment may or may not work the way you expect, depending on the compiler's choice of default signedness for characters. If char is implicitly signed, then C promotion rules will expand it to a signed integer value of 0xFFFFFFFF for the comparison (on a system with 32-bit integers). The resulting comparison is thus between 0xFF and 0xFFFFFFFF, which will fail.

However, if characters are unsigned by default, then c retains the value 0xFF, and the test will succeed.

A common location to encounter this particular problem is the standard library getchar() function.

```
char c;
while ( ( c = getchar() ) != EOF )
   processCharacter( c );
```

EOF is defined as −1 by default, so on a system where char values default to nonnegative quantities, the while loop will never exit.

For obvious reasons, this isn't particularly intuitive and can be the source of some very hard-to-understand bugs. Either make no assumptions about the signedness of char, or enforce this through global compiler options (most compilers allow you to set the default sign for char) in conjunction with a global compile-time assertion:

```
/* this ensures that characters are signed */
CASSERT( (char)0xFF == (int)~0, char_signed );
/* this ensures that characters are unsigned */
CASSERT( (unsigned char)0xFF == (int)0xFF, uchar_unsigned );
```

enums as ints

The enum data type is a very handy tool when you are creating large sets of constants and want to generate new values automatically. However, the ANSI C specification does not dictate the size of an enum, allowing the compiler to select an optimal size based on the actual enumerated values. For example, suppose you have this:

```
enum Color
{
   RED, GREEN, BLUE
};
```

One compiler may deduce that the range of legal values is [0,2] and decide that an 8-bit character is a better representation than an integer since it consumes less space. Another compiler will instead decide that an optimal implementation will be 32 bits, since that may align better on the target platform.

Differences in the perceived size of an enum can lead to many different and subtle errors. Structure packing, discussed at the beginning of this chapter, becomes an immediate concern since:

```
enum Color { RED, GREEN, BLUE };
struct foo
{
   enum Color a, b, c, d;
};
```

may result in a structure of 4 bytes or 16 bytes in size, depending on the underlying size of the Color enum as chosen by the compiler.

Even something as simple as passing a parameter might run into problems:

```
void set_color( enum Color c );
```

On most modern computer systems, parameters passed on the stack are aligned and padded to 32 bits, so the opportunity for error is reduced. However, simple platforms such as 8-bit microcontrollers can present an opportunity for unexpected behavior. Using the previous example, if the caller assumes that `enum Color` is 1 byte, but the called function expects 4 bytes, then bad things can happen.

Most compilers have an optional switch to treat `enum` values as `int` values, which forces all `enum` values to be at least the size of an integer. Failing that, you can force an `enum` to some minimum number of bits by using a dummy constant:

```
enum Color
{
    RED,
    GREEN,
    BLUE,
    FORCE_INTEGER = 0xFFFFFFFF /* force Color to be at least 32-bits */
};
```

Numeric Constants

Do not assume that certain numeric constants will share the same representation across all platforms. Programmers often assume that −1 is the same as 0xFFFFFFFF, but this is true only if integers are two's-complement, 32-bit quantities. 0xFFFFFFFF is simply a very large positive value on a system with 64-bit integers.

Another common problem hot spot involves bit masks. If you want to mask off the low 4 bits of a value, it is common to see something like this:

```
unsigned long x = some_value;
x = x & 0xFFFFFFF0;
```

This is correct only on systems with 32-bit integers. Instead of hard-coding the mask as in the preceding example, the following use of the complement operator will ensure all one bits, except for the portion you wish to mask:

```
unsigned long x = some_value;
x = x & (~0xF);
```

Likewise, avoid using −1 when you really want ~0 (all bits on).

Signed and Unsigned Right Shifts

The C standard allows an implementation to arbitrarily choose whether to propagate *(sign extend)* the sign bit when right-shifting a signed integer:

```
int32_t x = 0x80000000;
x >>= 31; /* depending on implementation, x may be 1 or 0xFFFFFFFF */
```

If you want an unsigned shift (for example, because you're working on a bit mask), you should cast the value to an unsigned quantity before executing the shift. If you're trying to achieve a fast division by power of two using a right-shift, you should use an arithmetic division and hope that the compiler will generate an optimized machine-level shift instruction.

Calling Conventions

Function calls, while conceptually very simple to a programmer, are surprisingly complex operations. The caller and the called function must agree on a protocol that defines the following:

- How parameters are passed
- How return values are returned
- What state, if any, must be preserved

This is collectively known as the *calling convention*. Different platforms will have varying calling conventions, and sometimes a single architecture may have multiple calling conventions, depending on the compiler and/or operating system.

For example, Microsoft's PASCAL calling convention had the following characteristics:

- Passed arguments from left to right
- Required the called function to clean up the stack
- Required the called function to preserve the direction flag and the EBX, ES, FS, GS, EBP, ESI, and EDI registers

In addition, a PASCAL function had its name converted to uppercase, since the Pascal language was not case-sensitive.

On most platforms, the compiler and linker adhere to one rigid calling convention, which is often defined by the operating system as part of its *application binary interface (ABI)*. A single, agreed-upon protocol avoids a lot of unnecessary complexity that can arise when different calling conventions coexist. For example, if the calling convention for a program is different than that of a library it calls, there will be errors (either at link time or run time, depending on the nature of the incompatibility).

Unfortunately, the Intel x86 and other Complex Instruction Set Computer (CISC) architectures such as the Motorola 68K, suffer from an overabundance of calling conventions invented to solve different problems. Some calling conventions are required for languages such as C (which supports variable argument lists); other conventions were designed to minimize space or maximize performance. Since neither C nor C++ standards address the issue of calling conventions, a compiler writer may freely offer different calling conventions.

The Intel x86 architecture has at least three common calling conventions:

- cdecl is the default calling convention since it is very flexible and allows for variable argument lists (variable argument lists require the caller to clean up the stack, since the called routine may not know how many parameters were passed). However, there is a slight performance penalty.

- The stdcall convention is reasonably fast and general. The Windows ABI uses stdcall (in the form of the WINAPI macro) for most of its API entry points.

- The register or fastcall convention passes some implementation-dependent number of parameters in registers (usually two), with the remainder spilling over onto the stack. This is theoretically the fastest calling convention; however, in practice there are enough mitigating factors that often there is little or no speed benefit. As the number of parameters increases, the performance advantage over other conventions decreases.

The characteristics of these conventions are summarized in Table 8-3.

Table 8-3: Intel x86 Common Calling Conventions

Convention	Parameter Location	Parameter Order	Stack Responsibility
cdecl	Stack	Right to left	Caller
stdcall	Stack	Right to left	Called
fastcall/ register	Registers and stack	Right to left	Called

While these are common labels, keep in mind that different compilers may still have slightly different interpretations of these conventions. The register calling convention may be different from one compiler to another, and sometimes even between different revisions of the same compiler. That said, compiler vendors recognize the importance of interoperability, so you will often find calling conventions implemented identically on multiple architectures. In addition, operating systems promote their own standard ABIs, so if Windows says stdcall means something, you can bet that compiler vendors will use that definition.

Name Decoration

Because of the potential catastrophe that can arise if a program compiled with one calling convention tries to link to a library that was compiled with a different one, most tool chains will *decorate* function names differently depending on the calling convention.

Microsoft Visual C++ will generate the following symbol names for a function int test(int x):

Convention	Decorated Name
cdecl	_test
stdcall	_test@4
fastcall	@test@4

If a vendor builds a library assuming the cdecl convention and an application is built with the stdcall calling function, calls to the vendor's API will fail to link. This is far better than linking successfully, only to collapse at run time due to incompatibilities between their respective calling conventions.

Function Pointers and Callbacks

The calling convention doesn't just affect static linkage; it can also become a problem if you use function pointers. If you present an API to an application that accepts a function pointer (such as to register a callback), you will need to specify its calling convention:

```
/* NOTE: use a CDECL macro of some type so that it works on
multiple compilers/platforms */
void register_callback( void (CDECL *func)( int a, int b, int c ) );
```

Portability

Portable software should avoid making any assumptions about calling conventions. Never, ever assume anything about the format of parameters on the stack, as the following example illustrates:

```
void func( int a, int b )
{
    int *pa = &a; /* what if a is in a register?! */
    /* no guarantee that they're contiguous! */
    int *pb = (int*)(((char*)&a) + sizeof( int ));
}
```

If you are developing a library that is distributed in binary form, you will likely need to deal with calling conventions unless you're working on a platform with only a single convention. Very often, you will either need to distribute multiple binaries compiled with the different calling conventions or enforce a particular calling convention using the compiler's proprietary function signature modifiers, like this:

```
#ifdef _MSC_VER
#define API_TYPE __cdecl
```

```
#else
#define API_TYPE
#endif
void API_TYPE MyFunction( void );
```

EXAMPLE:

SAL'S HANDLING OF CALLING CONVENTIONS

SAL uses whatever calling convention is in effect when it is compiled, which is fine since it is integrated as source into another project. If a binary version of the library were distributed, then whoever packaged the library would need to note the specific calling convention in use when it was compiled and linked.

SAL explicitly sets the calling convention of its user-defined callbacks:

```
typedef struct SAL_Callbacks
{
    sal_i32_t cb_size;
    void * (POSH_CDECL *alloc)( sal_u32_t sz );
    void   (POSH_CDECL *free)( void *p );

    void   (POSH_CDECL *warning)( const char *msg );
void   (POSH_CDECL *error)( const char *msg );
} SAL_Callbacks;
```

SAL is dependent on POSH, which defines POSH_CDECL appropriately depending on the compiler and platform:

```
#if defined POSH_CPU_X86 && !defined POSH_CPU_X86_64
#  if defined __GNUC__
#     define POSH_CDECL __attribute__((cdecl))
#     define POSH_STDCALL __attribute__((stdcall))
#     define POSH_FASTCALL __attribute__((fastcall))
#  elif defined _MSC_VER || defined __WATCOMC__ || defined \
__BORLANDC__ || defined __MWERKS__
#     define POSH_CDECL    __cdecl
#     define POSH_STDCALL  __stdcall
#     define POSH_FASTCALL __fastcall
#  endif
#else
/* This will likely have to be expanded if running on a system with
   varying calling conventions and which was not x86 based, such as
   68K Macintosh systems which had C, Pascal, and
   OS calling conventions */
#  define POSH_CDECL
#  define POSH_STDCALL
#  define POSH_FASTCALL
#endif
```

Returning Structures

Compilers vary as to how they return aggregate data types such as struct, class, and union objects. Small objects are often returned in a single register, but some compilers may always return any large objects on the stack.

Things get a bit more confusing returning large (greater than the size of a register) structures by value. Some implementations pass a hidden pointer to a local stack variable; others return the address of a static variable (this is not multithread-safe, but was fine on single-threaded operating systems such as MS-DOS or Mac OS). There is no standard for this, which is why it is a good idea for the caller to pass a pointer to a local variable, instead of attempting to get a copy by value:

```
struct thingy get_a_thingy_by_value( void )
{
    struct thingy result;
    /* do some stuff */
    return result; /* how is this returned?  Implementation dependent */
}
void get_a_thingy_by_copy( struct thingy *t )
{
    struct thingy s;
    /* do some stuff */
    *t = s;
}
```

Bitfields

C and C++ provide the ability to identify specific bits inside a structure by name using a construct known as a *bitfield*:

```
struct OpCode
{
    int code: 4;
    int operand0: 4;
    int operand1: 4;
    int flags : 8;
}
```

There are so many problems with bitfields that I'm not sure where to start. First of all, the language standards do not dictate whether the bitfields are signed or unsigned by default, so confusion reigns if you attempt to retrieve a value of 15 but find that the real range is +/− 7 due to a specific implementation's choice of bitfield sign.

In addition, the order and packing of bits is up to each implementation. It is possible that unnamed bits are automatically inserted into a structure by a compiler to maintain alignment:

```
/* This is very unlikely to be 64-bits in size except with
   systems using 64-bit native integers */
struct RegisterBits
{
    int a : 31;
    int b: 31;
    int c: 2;
};
```

A common use of bitfields is to allow easy access to specific bit ranges inside a register definition for a hardware device, often inside a union with an integer the size of the register:

```
/* This will not give you the expected results on most 32-bit systems */
union RegisterSpec
{
    struct RegisterBits register_bits;
    int64_t register_direct;
};
```

Bitfields may sound neat, but they are rife with portability problems. Don't use them—they really aren't *that* convenient.

Comments

Surprisingly, even simple comments can be the source of portability problems. Nested comments, C++-style single-line comments (//) inside C source files, and assumptions regarding the transformation of comments to white space all contribute to errors.

The C and C++ specifications do not state whether nested multiline (/*) comments are allowed. So this bit of code may work on one compiler, but fail on another:

```
/* I have commented this out but the following /* may cause problems */
```

If a compiler supports nested comments, this comment will cause a compiler error, since two comment open tokens (/*) exist, but only one closing token (*/) is present. This can be the source of immense confusion when previously functional code suddenly stops compiling on one platform (with a cryptic error such as "unexpected end of file found inside comment") but works normally on another.

Some have only half-jokingly argued that the single greatest contribution of the C++ language is the single-line comment:

```
// This line is commented out
```

It's a small but very convenient feature that many other languages possessed, yet C lacked. For this reason, many C compiler vendors added support for single-line comments as a nonstandard extension. In fact, this became so popular that many developers did not realize that it was non-standard (most of the major compilers supported this even before its ratification as part of the C99 standard).

The ANSI C99 specification formally added single-line comments to the language. However, it's possible that there are some compilers out there that have not added this ability to their implementations (and maybe never will). If you have an extensive base of source code that uses single-line comments, and you find yourself needing to strip them, you'll be in for a long night with a good text processor.

Of course, you can happily ignore this if you program strictly in C++.

One final comment about comments. Under early C, an empty comment was often used as a hack for token pasting:

```
/* this doesn't do what you want under ANSI C! */
#define combine( a, b ) a/**/b
```

The intent is to substitute ab wherever combine(a,b) is encountered.

ANSI C provides a better way of accomplishing this by using its token concatenation operator:

```
/* this works with ANSI C, but not under K&R C */
#define combine( a, b ) a##b
```

If you insist on supporting old-style token pasting, you can always use a __STDC__ guard:

```
#ifdef __STDC__
#define combine( a, b ) a##b
#else
#define combine( a, b ) a/**/b
#endif
```

Summary

As rigorous as the C and C++ standards may seem, compiler authors have a great amount of leeway when it comes to the interpretation of the standard and the implementation of features. Dealing with different compiler implementations can be an adventure unto itself when developing portable software, but with the proper knowledge, planning, and preparation much of the pain can be mitigated.

9

USER INTERACTION

One of the key components of any modern software application is the face it presents to the user, usually through the assistance of the operating system's *graphical user interface (GUI)*, if one exists. Examples of these include the Microsoft Windows GDI, the Commodore Amiga Intuition, the Atari ST GEM, Linux X11 with an optional desktop manager such as GNOME or KDE, and Palm OS.

While very basic command-line programs such as filters and batch processors can get by with minimal facilities such as `printf()` and `fgets()`, modern applications have sophisticated user interfaces that are inherently system-dependent. Abstracting user interaction is a key architectural concern for software developers.

The Evolution of User Interfaces

Before the popularization of glitzy user interfaces (1985 and 1990, depending on whether you were a Mac or PC user, respectively), users were expected to interact with their computer systems through the command line or command prompt. The next step in the evolution of user interfaces was to move away from the text-driven command line and into the world of the mouse-driven GUI that nearly every computer user today knows.

Command Line

With the command-line interfaces, you typed in commands and then watched the output scroll by on your display (or, if you're old enough to remember, on a teleprinter). No mice, no windows, no dialog boxes—just a bunch of text. Radical concepts like "responding immediately to key presses" were not well supported and definitely not portable. Applications such as FTP and Telnet embodied this approach.

While crude and simple, text-driven command-line user interfaces are also, by their nature, reasonably portable, since they leverage the C standard library's standard I/O functions, such as fputs(), printf(), and fgets(). It is much easier to write a portable program when you can factor out the entire concept of graphics and display systems.

For primitive or simple programs, a command-line interface may be acceptable, but as a general rule, commercial applications require visually pleasing and intuitive GUIs.

Window Systems

Originally developed in Xerox's Palo Alto Research Center (PARC) research group, the mouse-driven GUI was commercialized by Apple with the introduction of the Macintosh computer in 1984—a milestone event in the history of personal computing. Over the ensuing two decades, the GUI has pushed the command line to the brink of extinction.

GUIs were considered proprietary by nature. Even discarding the various patent and copyright protection actions undertaken by companies such as Apple to protect what they considered unique concepts (for example, overlapping windows in a workspace), many companies were still loath to overtly copy a competitor's user interface (no one likes to seem like a follower instead of a leader).

The result was that in the late 1980s, there were an incalculable number of competing (and proprietary) GUI systems:

- Apple's Mac OS (up through System 9)
- Apple's Mac OS X/Cocoa (based on NeXT Computing's NeXTStep)
- GEOS for C64 and the Apple II
- GeoWorks for the PC
- Digital Research's GEM for the Atari ST and (in a limited fashion) on the PC

- Commodore's Amiga Intuition
- Microsoft Windows (which has evolved numerous times)
- X Window–based window managers such as Motif, Sun's OpenLook/ OpenWindows, GNOME, and KDE
- IBM's Presentation Manager for OS/2
- Adobe PostScript-based display systems like NeXT's NeXTStep and Sun's NEWS

And that's just on the desktop! The PDA/handheld market introduces its own set of user interface factions.

When we speak of GUIs, we may actually be referring to one or more components of a GUI implementation. GUIs can include as many as three different and distinct layers:

- The windowing toolkit, which provides the raw rendering and event management capabilities
- The window manager, which presents a common look and feel
- The desktop manager, which handles filesystem navigation and management

Some operating systems, such as Apple Mac OS and Microsoft Windows, have a single monolithic user interface that integrates all three layers into the operating system. Other operating systems, specifically Unix and its derivatives, keep the operating system independent of the GUI, and the GUI itself may be stratified into independent layers. For example, a typical Linux desktop might use the X Window System as its window system, Sawfish for its window manager, and GNOME as its desktop manager.

As with most burgeoning industries, the early user interface competitors fought hard and killed each other, leaving a few survivors to emerge from the rubble. Today, the predominant user interfaces for desktop computers are Microsoft Windows and, to a much lesser extent, Apple's Macintosh (both the older Mac OS Classic look and the newer Cocoa). The various X Window derivatives running on Unix and Unix-like operating systems (Sun Solaris, IBM AIX, Linux, and so on) make up the remainder, forming a very small niche on the desktop.

While a GUI is often intertwined with the operating system, such as with Microsoft Windows, in some cases, the user interface is independent of the operating system. The most common example of the latter is MIT's X Window System GUI toolkit, which can be layered on just about any operating system, but is traditionally seen on Unix-like workstations (and is the default interface library for most Linux distributions).

Native GUI or Application GUI?

Even though an operating system can provide a graphical interface, sometimes an application may wish to present its own. This requires a lot of redundant work and has a lot of downsides, especially when it comes to presenting a consistent look and feel with the rest of the applications on a particular system. So when users engage your program with its custom interface, they'll often struggle or become aggravated due to its nonstandard behavior.

On the positive side, by decoupling your application from the specifics of an operating system's user interface, you enhance your software's portability. At the very least, you can ensure a consistency between your own applications across platforms. If you have loyal users, they may appreciate that your application works and looks the same, no matter which system they're running it on.

Low-Level Graphics

Even ignoring user interface needs, modern computer applications often have a need to display high-quality graphics. Early computer systems allowed direct access to the video card's memory (the *frame buffer*); however, most modern operating systems will deny a user-level process access to any of the hardware at such a low level.

Instead, most special APIs provide access to the frame buffer indirectly by managing in-memory "surfaces" that the application writes to, and then "blits" to the back buffer using a special system call. Microsoft Windows supports this with *device-independent bitmaps (DIBs)* in GDI and, at a lower level, DirectDrawSurfaces (as part of the DirectX gaming API). Macintosh and Linux systems offer similar functionality.

Conveniently enough, the basic concept of "draw to surface, then copy to the video card" is constant across most operating systems, so porting from one to another requires only a straightforward abstraction.

Even so, raw access to the video memory is sometimes possible, either on an unprotected operating system or through the cooperation of a low-level hardware access device driver. An application might request a pointer to a back buffer, perform its operations on that buffer, and then when done, flip it to the front buffer. This "flipping" consists of updating a pointer used by the display refresh hardware. Updating this pointer is extremely fast, and by flipping buffers you avoid the cost of an extra copy.

Today's computer programs have graphics requirements that far outstrip the ability of most programmers to code themselves, so accessing the frame buffer directly is no longer as necessary as it was even a decade ago. Popular 3D libraries such as OpenGL and DirectX perform high-level, complex rendering, using the full extent of the underlying hardware's features, thereby reducing the need to access the frame buffer at all.

Digital Audio

Sound has slowly become a more integral part of the computing experience. As recently as 1998, digital audio was an optional component for PCs (although Macintoshes and many other home computer systems such as the Amiga and Atari ST had integrated digital audio support much earlier).

Each operating system has one or more mechanisms to take a raw waveform, usually encoded as pulse code modulated (PCM) sample data, and send it to the speaker. Sometimes there is a hierarchy of APIs that provide increasingly lower-level access to the sound subsystem. For example, Microsoft Windows has the high-level PlaySound API, the medium-level waveOut APIs, and the very low-level DirectSound buffer manipulation APIs. An application can select the appropriate API based on its own requirements of convenience and control.

Other operating systems usually have similar splits in functionality. For example, the Cocoa API under Mac OS X has the NSSound class for basic sound loading and playback. Beneath this is the medium-level (now deprecated) CarbonSound/SoundManager APIs. The lowest-level sound interface is known as CoreAudio, which provides very raw, high-performance access to the digital audio subsystem.

Most modern operating systems seem to adhere to this basic scheme. They provide high-level, easy-to-use sound routines suitable for simple functionality such as light sound effects or alert sounds, as well as low-level routines for complex audio processing by the application. Wrapping all these different libraries isn't particularly difficult, but it can be tedious, especially since sound is one of those areas that a lot of different implementations just mess up in subtle ways. For cross-platform sound, there are commercial libraries, such as Miles Audio and FMOD, and open-source libraries, like SDL, OpenAL, PortAudio, and, of course, SAL.

However, some operating systems and devices do not provide an API at all, requiring the programmer to access the hardware directly. In situations like this, you will need to roll your own sound access, mixing, and buffer management engine.

SAL EXAMPLE: HANDLING DIGITAL AUDIO

SAL does not abstract the capabilities of an underlying sound API, but instead *wraps* those capabilities with its own. It uses a sound API's low-level buffer management facilities to implement its own, higher-level, sample playback and mixing features.

Some sound APIs have their own mixing facilities built in, but their implementations are often tenuous and unreliable. SAL addresses this by implementing its own mixer and relying on the back end solely for buffer playback.

Input

Cross-platform applications must be acutely aware of the differences between input devices. Even though it seems like every computer has a keyboard and a mouse, minor differences between mouse and keyboard configurations impact portability.

Keyboard

You would think that a keyboard is a keyboard, but that's not the case when dealing with cross-platform software development. Keys can move around depending on the keyboard, even when those keyboards are for the same computer system. Laptop keyboard layouts often have a radically different design from their desktop counterparts, in order to minimize space. Many keys that exist on one system may not exist on others. Here are a few examples:

- Early Sun keyboards had 15 keys that were not present on PC keyboards.
- Early iMac keyboards did not have a numeric keypad.
- Early Macintoshes lacked the ESC and function keys common on PCs.
- The modern Apple Pro USB keyboard does not have NUM LOCK, PRT SCRN, or SCROLL LOCK keys.

You cannot rely on the placement or existence of many types of these keys, not to mention the issues with keyboards of different languages. (See also the discussion of internationalization in Chapter 16.)

Mouse

For the most part, mice operate the same way across many different platforms, but you still must deal with different configurations. At one extreme is the Apple Pro one-button mouse, with its single button. At the other extreme you have mice such as the Microsoft IntelliMouse Explorer, with five buttons and a scroll wheel. And there are devices, such as Wacom digitizing tablets or laptop touchpads, that act like mice to an application, even though they are not really mice at all.

Applications that wish to run on a wide variety of systems should not rely on the existence of more than one button and should support additional buttons (and wheels and thumb wheels) only when available.

A typical desktop operating system provides access to mouse and keyboard information through its GUI toolkit's event system. For example, in Windows, an application handles `WM_MOUSEMOVE`, `WM_KEYDOWN`, and `WM_KEYUP` messages in its message handler function. Cocoa/OS X applications override the appropriate `keyDown:`, `keyUp:`, `mouseDown:`, and `mouseUp:` methods (although it is possible to directly retrieve `NSEvent` events). And an X Window application system retrieves `XEvent` events using the `XPending()` and/or `XNextEvent()` APIs.

Joystick and Gamepad

While the mouse and keyboard may be the most popular input devices around, they're not the only ones. Many computer systems also support alternate input devices such as joysticks and gamepads. These devices are rarely integrated into an event system, since few window systems consider joysticks a high-priority input device.

For applications that must support alternate input devices, a plethora of system-specific is APIs available. Windows has a standard Win32 API, `GetJoyPosEx()`, and the entire DirectInput library. Linux treats joysticks as devices accessed with the standard Unix file metaphor (an application opens `/dev/js0` or something similar, and then performs `read()` operations).

The most cumbersome aspect of abstracting input is that each operating system has a different idea of when and how events are propagated to the application. In Windows, there is a standard message loop that an application may poll in addition to an application-specific message handling callback. Under the X Window System, an application may call the event system directly, or it may set up a separate thread to "pump" the event queue.

And on top of all of these, polling a joystick device often must be done outside the standard event loop.

Cross-platform Toolkits

Due to the difficulty and complexity inherent to managing the differences between user interfaces, there have been numerous cross-platform toolkits designed to abstract the differences. These include wxWindows, Qt, and GTK+ for C++, and packages such as SWT, AWT, and Swing for Java. This is discussed in more detail in Chapter 18.

Summary

While command-line programs that require no interactive user input still have their place today, the vast majority of applications must present point-and-click graphical interfaces, with sound, to their users. These interfaces vary greatly between and within operating systems, and portable software must be able to migrate between these GUIs.

10

NETWORKING

Computers have been networked together
for decades, but it wasn't until the popularity
of the Internet that networking became a
significant issue for cross-platform development.
Networked communication implies heterogeneity,
since two completely unalike systems may be connected.
When heterogeneous machines network with each other and exchange data
you're basically dealing with the same data storage and load problems that
you encounter when saving to disk. The topics covered in Chapter 15 apply
just as much to networked communication as they do to saving and loading
data. Writing software that can run on different networking layers and also
successfully communicate with different platforms is a tricky topic, which I
address in this chapter.

The Evolution of Networking Protocols

When networking first appeared, the landscape consisted primarily of high-powered, insular, and proprietary hardware, and software implementations, all vying for market share and control of local area network (LAN) and wide area network (WAN) standards. Digital Equipment Corporation had its DECnet protocol suite; IBM had NetBIOS Extended User Interface (NetBEUI); Apple had LocalTalk/AppleTalk and OpenTransport; Novell had Internetwork Packet Exchange (IPX) and Sequenced Packet Exchange (SPX); Banyan Systems provided VINES; and even DOS-based PCs had low-cost networked operating systems such as Artisoft LANtastic. However, most of these protocols were limited to LANs or proprietary WANs.

As you would guess, the sheer number of different protocols made writing portable networked applications tedious and difficult, at least if you wanted to support the different proprietary protocols directly. But since so few programs were designed to be portable or work across heterogenous architectures, this wasn't a large concern.

During the 1980s, the focus began to shift to interoperable networks, so a decision was made to declare the Transport Control Protocol/Internet Protocol (TCP/IP) standard as the official protocol for the ARPAnet (the predecessor to the Internet at the time). This standardization directly fueled the ensuing rapid growth of the Internet.

In today's environment, the only truly relevant networking protocol is TCP/IP. It's the standard networking implementation in use by the vast majority of computers today; any computer connected to the Internet is going to use TCP/IP. Proprietary protocols such as DECnet and IPX/SPX are becoming increasingly rare, as their support is often relegated to legacy applications and systems.

Programming Interfaces

In the early 1980s, the 4.1c Berkeley Software Distribution of Unix included the *BSD Sockets* API, which was to become the standard programming API for Unix-based network applications. The simplicity and ease of use of the sockets API led to its rapid propagation on other Unix variants, and even on microcomputer operating systems such as BeOS, Amiga, OS/2, and Windows.

If you are writing a portable networking application, odds are that you'll be using either the sockets API directly or, if your design allows it, a higher-level API layered on top of sockets, such as Remote Procedure Call (RPC), Java Remote Method Invocation (RMI), distributed objects (CORBA and COM/DCOM), or Simple Object Access Protocol (SOAP).

Sockets

The BSD Sockets API is the most ubiquitous low-level TCP/IP programming interface. It is available on every major platform that supports networked computer systems, and it presents a standard interface across all Unix-like implementations. Of course, this didn't prevent Microsoft from implementing its own version of the sockets API, *WinSock*. Abstracting between WinSock and BSD Sockets is pretty much all that's necessary if you're writing an application with low-level network communication.

But even with a relatively stable API and a standardized conceptual approach, different socket or TCP/IP stack implementations may exhibit radical changes in behavior across platforms. Since there are no hard-and-fast rules regarding the differences, they can often be very subtle (for example, the default values for certain configuration variables).

WinSock is maddeningly close to the BSD Sockets standard—identical in many respects, but just different enough that you still need to deal with it. It straddles the line between "different enough to warrant abstraction" and "close enough that a couple conditionals should make it all work."

Abstracting between the two can be done easily enough, since they share much the same concepts and syntax. Both WinSock and BSD Sockets are thin wrappers around basic TCP/IP functionality, specifically the UDP and TCP protocols. Both provide the ability to open and close connections, along with sending and receiving data, even using similar syntax.

WinSock and BSD Sockets are a great case study of small, irritating differences between otherwise similar APIs. For example, the fundamental socket handle type differs between the two platforms. BSD Sockets defines sockets as signed integers, which matches the Unix idiom of representing file descriptors as integers. WinSock uses the SOCKET type definition, defined in winsock.h or winsock2.h, which is an unsigned type. This means that the value for an invalid socket changes depending on the platform: –1 on BSD Sockets and 0xFFFFFFFF on Windows.

To fix this, you can incorporate the SOCKET type and INVALID_HANDLE definition on BSD Sockets, making both feel more like the Windows version and avoiding pollution of core code, as follows:

```
#if !defined POSH_OS_WIN32
#define INVALID_HANDLE -1
typedef int SOCKET;
#endif
```

This allows a single code path when allocating a socket on either system, meeting your goal of having as much shared source as possible, without relying on excessive conditional compilation directives. The following:

```
SOCKET s = socket( PF_INET, SOCK_STREAM, IPPROTO_TCP );
if ( s == INVALID_HANDLE )
   return -1;
.
/* the above code should compile and run identically on
   BSD Sockets and WinSock */
.
```

is much more pleasant than:

```
#ifdef POSH_OS_WIN32
SOCKET s;
#else
int s;
#endif
   s = socket( PF_INET, SOCK_STREAM, IPPROTO_TCP );
#ifdef POSH_OS_WIN32
   if ( s == 0xFFFFFFFF )
#else
   if ( s == -1 )
#endif
      return -1;
```

Another minor difference between WinSock and BSD Sockets is the handling of header files. Under Windows, the WinSock definitions are in either <winsock.h> or <winsock2.h>. BSD Sockets require a plethora of header files, including <sys/types.h>, <sys/socket.h>, <netinet/in.h>, <netdb.h>, <arpa/inet.h>, and <unistd.h>. If you have a lot of sockets-related files, having a single local header file that provides the appropriate headers can help keep your code clean.

```
#ifndef MYSOCKETS_H
#define MYSOCKETS_H
#ifdef POSH_OS_WIN32
#include <winsock2.h>
#else
#  include <sys/types.h>
#  include <sys/socket.h>
#  include <netinet/in.h>
#  include <arpa/inet.h>
#  include <netdb.h>
#  include <unistd.h>
#endif
#endif /* MYSOCKETS_H */
```

Other minor differences exist as well. For example, Unix has traditionally tried to unify device access using the file metaphor, so in keeping with this, BSD Sockets uses the close() function to close a socket. On Windows, however, sockets are not considered files, so you must call a special API called closesocket() to close a socket. Similarly, controlling some options such as blocking versus nonblocking behavior requires the Unix-centric fcntl() API for BSD Sockets and the Windows-specific ioctlsocket() API for WinSock.

Error handling between the two APIs also has its subtle differences. On Unix, the standard method to identify system errors is by examining the global identifier errno. This value will correspond to one of the standard error constants such as EWOULDBLOCK or EAGAIN. WinSock, however, requires that you call the WinSock-specific function WSAGetLastError(), which returns a constant *similar* to the standard Unix ones, such as WSAEWOULDBLOCK or WSAEAGAIN.

You could conceivably encapsulate all these differences by using macro substitution and type definitions, as in this example:

```
#if defined POSH_OS_WIN32
#define CLOSESOCKET(s) closesocket(s)
#define SOCKERR() WSAGetLastError()
/* etc. etc. */
#else
typedef int SOCKET;
#define INVALID_SOCKET -1
#define CLOSESOCKET(s) close(s)
#define SOCKERROR() errno
#define WSAEWOULDBLOCK EWOULDBLOCK
/* etc. etc. */
#endif
```

Scarily enough, you *can* just barely manage this with the preprocessor. The result may or may not be very clean, and is sometimes hard to debug, but it does work and leaves a minimal amount of platform-specific code to be written. If the differences were the tiniest bit more pronounced, moving to a larger-scale abstraction would be necessary.

RPC and RMI

RPC is a higher-level function call abstraction that sits on top of a lower-level transport layer such as BSD Sockets. Remote procedure calls are designed to be transparent, operating much the same way (to an application) as standard function calls.

Specific RPC implementations are available through the use of toolkits like Sun's rpcgen and the Open Software Foundation (OSF) Distributed Computing Environment (DCE). These toolkits are designed to handle most of the grunt work associated with implementing a particular RPC relationship. They accept an interface definition and then generate the appropriate "stubbed" (functional but essentially empty) client and server code, which handles marshaling/unmarshaling parameters and broadcasting them, and do the same with return values.

XML-RPC, a precursor to the more heavyweight and cumbersome SOAP, is an RPC specification that uses HTTP as its transport layer and XML for parameter encoding. The motivation behind XML-RPC was to have a human-readable encoding format (in this case, XML) carried over an industry standard protocol (HTTP), theoretically allowing for smoother interoperability between networked applications.

Many firewalls and routers block unexpected traffic on unknown ports, which is what "raw" RPC implementations often require. For example, a typical RPC implementation might require communication on TCP port 9822 (an arbitrary port number of no particular significance), but a firewall will routinely block traffic to any ports not explicitly opened by an administrator. However, since HTTP port 80 is used by web traffic throughout the world, traffic often flows through that port unimpeded. XML-RPC (and SOAP) ride that port, so it is often much faster and easier to get XML-RPC/SOAP-compliant programs up and running on a system, because they do not require reconfiguring the network.

Distributed Objects

RPC abstracts the concept of function calls, a procedural programming paradigm. A desire to provide an RPC-like capability that extends to object-oriented programming has given rise to *distributed objects*. The two primary distributed object implementations are the Distributed Common Object Model (DCOM), pushed by Microsoft, and the Object Management Group (OMG) Common Object Request Broker Architecture (CORBA), which is a more open industry standard than DCOM.

Like RPC implementations, distributed object implementations provide tools such as Interface Definition Language (IDL) compilers and code generators, which create the stub (client-side) and skeleton (server-side) code for a particular system.

Summary

The need for modern computer systems to communicate with each other is inescapable. Networked computer systems pose their own portability concerns, specifically with varying programming interfaces and even something as simple as exchanging raw data.

11

OPERATING SYSTEMS

The core software run by almost every modern computer system is the *operating system.* Since the operating system is the focal point for most computer systems, and also the central arbiter for access to limited system resources, it affects how software is written and operates at a fundamental level. In this chapter, I'll talk about both the functional aspects of an operating system and APIs as they relate to portability.

The Evolution of Operating Systems

Technically speaking, operating systems are optional. Embedded software running on specialized systems often consists of just a raw program programmed into EEPROM or flash memory, along with a minimal bootloader that begins execution on bootup.

One step beyond no operating system are the very simple older operating systems, such as Microsoft MS-DOS and Digital CP/M. MS-DOS was nothing more than a thin veneer over the hardware. Very often, an application would take over the entire machine and access many resources directly. MS-DOS did not allow multiple programs to execute simultaneously (multitasking) without the assistance of higher-level multitasking software such as Quarterdesk, Microsoft Windows, or DRI's GEM.

One step beyond DOS are operating systems that provide useful features such as simple multitasking, a GUI, and moderated access to low-level devices. Operating systems like early Apple Mac OS, Microsoft Windows 2.x (which was layered on MS-DOS), Commodore's AmigaDOS, and Atari's TOS/GEM fall into this category. However, they all share the same trait of still allowing an application to directly access any memory or devices desired.

Modern operating systems also incorporate important features, such as support for multiple users, protected memory, and security. Microsoft Windows XP, Linux, FreeBSD, and Apple Mac OS X share these features.

Among other things, the operating system may or may not do the following:

- Manage the system's resources such as memory, file descriptors, and hardware devices
- Implement security protocols
- Limit the ability of a process to consume resources and space
- Multitask different simultaneously executing applications
- Provide a simplified, centralized application programming interface to assist with memory management, input, output, process control, and other mundane tasks that are commonly required by applications

Hosted and Freestanding Environments

Not every computer has or requires an operating system. Those that do not are sometimes known as *freestanding* environments, where program startup and termination are implementation-defined. In addition, features that many programmers take for granted (like much of the C/C++ standard library) are often unavailable. Embedded systems—such as video game consoles, portable MP3 players, and vehicle control software—are common examples of freestanding environments.

On the other hand, a *hosted* environment, with which most users are familiar, has an operating system that is responsible for loading and executing programs, along with providing system services.

A system designer may opt for a freestanding environment when system resources are so scarce that the additional overhead of an operating system is not justifiable. As time marches on, however, even the lowliest of devices has become powerful enough to run a limited operating system. Not too long ago, PDAs and cellular phones were freestanding environments with a single-purpose built application. Now, even these simple devices run operating systems.

The Operating System Portability Paradox

One of the paradoxes of an operating system is that, like a portability library (see also Chapter 18), it is simultaneously a facilitator of and an impediment to application portability.

The first significant cross-platform operating system for microcomputers was Gary Kildall's Control Program/Monitor (CP/M) operating system, which gained its popularity due to its portability between the myriad microcomputers based on the Intel 8080 and Zilog Z80 microprocessors prevalent at the time.

The Intel 8080 microprocessor heralded the arrival of the microcomputer era. Numerous manufacturers used the 8080 as the core logic for their systems, which became a significant problem, since each system was slightly different architecturally. An application that ran on one 8080 system would not run on another similar system due to variances in the floppy drive controller or display circuitry.

The CP/M operating system was written to address this problem, creating a consistent environment for applications across multiple 8080-based microcomputer systems. The key to this innovation was the requirement of a BIOS supplied by each computer manufacturer. CP/M would interface to each BIOS in a consistent manner, creating a cross-platform API of sorts.

Applications would then, in turn, write to CP/M's standard API (by way of software interrupts), isolating themselves from the idiosyncrasies of any one particular computer's architectural nuances. This allowed the development of cross-platform killer applications such as WordStar and dBase II, which were now able to run on a wide variety of similar but still different microcomputers. Without an operating system like CP/M, these applications would have had a much harder time attaining critical mass. Instead of appealing to "anyone who has a CP/M compatible machine," they would have needed to target the myriad different manufacturers in the Balkanized world of personal computing.

The price for this portability was that writing for CP/M, well, required CP/M. So portability to a new operating system (such as the up-and-coming MS-DOS) was more difficult in some ways. In fact, MS-DOS borrowed many features from CP/M in order to make the migration from CP/M as painless as possible.

As operating systems become more all-encompassing, applications become more dependent on them for system services such as user interface, memory allocation and mapping, security and privilege access, sound, video, and networking. If an application is littered with direct operating system API calls, migrating to a new operating system will often necessitate a complete rewrite of the code.

Of course, one of the goals of this book is to show you how to avoid just this scenario.

Memory

As software packages become larger and more complex, their memory requirements often outstrip the available physical memory installed in typical computer systems. Applications can adopt one of two attitudes when it comes to memory: assume that it's scarce or assume that there's a near infinite amount limited only by the system's address space. This choice can have significant ramifications on program's portability. Other portability issues involve memory mapping and memory protection.

Memory Limitations

Embedded systems and early personal computers had very limited amounts of memory, and most of it was completely exposed to any running programs. If a program had a working set larger than the available memory, it would crash or fail to run, unless it implemented its own paging system.

Modern operating systems hide annoying memory limitations by giving each application its own address space, effectively convincing each program that it has a huge amount of memory all to itself. Behind the scenes, however, data is paged to and from disk on demand, allowing the application to storm ahead, blithely allocating massive data structures. A system with X amount of megabytes of memory might have total allocations among all programs exceed that amount, with little deleterious effect, as long as physical memory were not oversubscribed.

Memory Mapping

Memory-mapped files are another common portability hot spot. Memory mapping, as the name implies, maps the contents of a file into memory, avoiding explicit file operations altogether. This can have significant advantages, including better performance and lower overall memory churn compared to allocating a buffer and reading the contents of a file into it. In fact, with very large files, it may not be feasible to load the entire contents into memory.

For example, geographic information system height field data or medical visualization volume data can often be many gigabytes in size—beyond the capabilities of a typical desktop PC to load entirely.

There are different tacks to handling cross-platform development and memory mapping:

Require memory mapping
You might require it, and then abstract its implementation, which is reasonable if you're creating a medical visualization application that routinely operates on 16 GB files.

Assume memory mapping is available
You could assume memory mapping is there, build an abstraction, and then emulate the feature if it's not available. However, this is rarely feasible, since emulating memory mapping can be painfully slow and resource-intensive to the point of impracticality.

Prioritize portability

You can just say that while memory mapping is neat, portability is more important. So, you write your application from the outset without memory mapping, predicating your software on the assumption that file access is slow and cumbersome. This increases your software's complexity in exchange for portability to systems with memory management.

Protected Memory

Some of the most frequent errors of neophyte C and C++ programmers involve accessing out-of-bound memory locations, such as stepping off the end of an array or dereferencing freed points. Even experienced programmers are bitten by the occasional illegal memory accesses.

Early PC operating systems didn't offer any protection from illegal memory access errors, so a renegade bug could often bring down an entire system by trashing important systemwide data structures. Apple Mac OS, Commodore AmigaDOS, and Microsoft MS-DOS allowed applications to peek and poke the computer's memory willy-nilly with nary a slap on the wrist. The CPUs of the time did not have the necessary logic for memory protection, and it wasn't until the widespread adoption of on-chip memory management units (MMUs) that the idea of *protected mode* desktop operating systems became viable.

On these early operating systems, an application could poke and prod about to its heart's content, getting to interesting bits and pieces of information, without needing permission. For example, on MS-DOS-based PCs, an application could look at and even modify low memory, where important system variables were kept. Or, more commonly, if a program wanted to render graphics quickly, it would write directly to the video card's frame buffer at some magic memory location (0xA000:0000 for the VGA on 16-bit real-mode DOS).

Of course, well-behaved programs on these systems tried very hard not to muck about with memory that wasn't their own. Accessing video memory safely on these machines was done through the BIOS by way of the interrupt 10h interface, which was safe and efficient but very slow.

Commercial applications can't make up for poor performance by saying, "Hey, we might be slow, but we're accessing your computer's resources in a very polite manner," so hordes of programmers went about twiddling bits they didn't own in order to get as much performance as possible. As a result, rogue programs could destabilize or crash a computer system very easily by overwriting the stack or global memory locations.

On today's computers, this type of behavior isn't tolerated. Memory errors will usually result in a little pop-up box to let you know that something bad just happened—calling it a general protection fault, access protection violation, bus error, or some other name. But instead of shutting down the system or quietly corrupting data in memory, the offending program is terminated without prejudice, while the user's other programs continue on with their little digital lives unperturbed.

Protected memory access is a concern for portability if an application relies on it, such as the aforementioned direct video memory manipulation. This is rarely a consideration, however, since these types of access are simple to abstract.

Processes and Threads

The fundamental unit of work in an operating system is the *process*, which often corresponds to a running program (but not always). Each process encapsulates an entire state, consisting of code, data, stack, current instruction pointer, and registers. In a protected operating system, processes are logically separated from each other's memory spaces such that they do not affect each other's state (process A cannot directly modify the variables in process B).

Primitive operating systems support only the notion of a single process. For example, CP/M and DOS understand only the concept of the *current process*, and multiple processes may not run concurrently. Modern operating systems, however, allow for *multitasking*, or the ability to run multiple processes concurrently.

Process Control and Communication Functions

Most programmers don't have to think too much about the operating system's process model. Typically, they just know that they are running inside a process, and that exiting the process is achieved by returning from main() or calling an appropriate function such as exit(). However, there are still some process control and communication functions that some programs must perform, specifically process startup.

For example, a network server application may need to spawn a new process for every user who connects. Or an application might wish to launch another program, which would entail using something like the system() (available in ANSI C) or spawn*() (a common, but nonstandard, extension to the C and C++ standard libraries) functions. Unfortunately, those calls do not inherit the data and state of the spawning process; in which case, a system-specific process duplication *(forking)* API must be called. On Unix-like systems, this has traditionally been the fork() call. Windows does not have a direct analog to Unix fork(), but you can manually spawn a new process using CreateProcess().

Unfortunately, these techniques have pretty important implementation differences, specifically with how they inherit the parent process's state at the time of spawn. On Unix, it's a full duplication. On Windows, there is no duplication at all, so an important state must be passed to the child process manually.

Other process-related tasks—such as killing, switching, communication, and prioritization—also depend on nonportable system APIs.

Interprocess Communication (IPC)

Processes, either in a parent-child relationship or just multiple programs running simultaneously, occasionally need to communicate with each other. Depending on the underlying operating system, a developer can select any of numerous mechanisms for this: pipes, mailslots, shared files, shared memory, networking, remote procedure calls, or system events.

Unlike with networking, where the BSD Sockets API provides a de facto pseudo-standard, there is no unifying, lightweight, cross-platform IPC system. However, abstracting simple communication between two processes is not very difficult.

Multithreading

Threads are a subset of a process, consisting of the register set, stack, thread-specific data, and program counter—all the data necessary to represent a thread of execution. Multiple threads can run simultaneously, sharing the same address space, code, and operating system resources (such as window handles and file descriptors). A process is essentially at least one thread and these shared resources.

Early operating systems didn't have an explicit concept of threads. Instead, everything was tossed into the process model. The best you could hope for were *user threads*, also sometimes known as *coroutines*, which were a form of cooperative multitasking, where each thread would yield control during certain operations. Native operating system support for threads, called *kernel threads*, didn't become popular until their introduction in the late 1990s. Kernel threads, working the related *lightweight process* concept, first appeared in modern architectures such as the Mach kernel, IBM OS/2, and Microsoft Windows NT. The threads discussed here are of the kernel thread type implemented as lightweight processes.

As with so many other new technologies, when multithreading was first introduced to the computing world, every operating system vendor went off and designed a proprietary implementation. The following were introduced in rapid succession: Unix International (UI) threads (aka Solaris threads), DCE threads (based on early POSIX definitions), C-Threads, Mach threads, Win32 threads, OS/2 threads, Linux threads via clone(), and, finally, POSIX *pthreads*, an attempt to standardize the threading API on Unix-like systems. After the better part of a decade, we're left with pthreads and Microsoft Windows, although some pthread libraries for Windows are available.

By creating and supporting multiple threads of execution within a process, you gain several advantages:

- Since threads are often lighter in weight than processes, switching between threads is often significantly less taxing than switching between processes, reducing overhead.

- Threads share the address space of their parent process, meaning they can share and access the same data without relying on interprocess communications.

- When a thread is *blocked* on a resource (for example, waiting for bytes to be read from disk), another thread can resume execution, providing more responsiveness and efficiency.
- Multiple threads within the same program can run on multiple processors in a multiprocessor system, resulting in significantly faster performance if the program was designed with parallelism in mind.

Since threads are a platform-specific feature, the ANSI C and C++ languages do not treat threads as first-class entities. In fact, they don't treat threads as anything at all, since they're not addressed by the standards. C and C++ programmers must use either operating system native thread support or a thread library such as pthreads (the POSIX threads library). More modern languages such as Java and C# treat threads as a fundamental type, resulting in more robust and full-featured thread support.

The advantage of threads—concurrent threads of execution that can access the same data efficiently—is also their biggest disadvantage. Race conditions and deadlocks can arise when two threads vie for the same resource simultaneously. A *deadlock* occurs when one thread modifies data that another thread has just read, invalidating the latter thread's view. Deadlocks happen when two or more threads end up waiting on each other for more information and grind to a halt, unable to proceed since each thread is dependent on the next. Common data structures that address these problems include mutexes, critical sections, and semaphores. Each operating system or thread library implements these data structures differently, both syntactically and semantically.

Software developers must decide if multithreading is a net win. If you choose to support multithreading, you must put a lot of effort into properly abstracting the actions of thread creation, suspension, killing, prioritization, and synchronization. Additionally, software that is dependent on multiple threads is often difficult to port to single-threaded systems, whereas single-threaded applications can move to multithreaded platforms transparently (albeit with some potential inefficiency).

SAL EXAMPLE: THREAD HANDLING

SAL assumes that its core audio mix-and-send-to-hardware routine will be called asynchronously, either by another thread or through an interrupt service routine. (Actually, the interrupt service routine has not been implemented and would require some work to get running, but other implementations all use the thread-calling technique.) All implementations, except for OS X/CoreAudio, manually create a separate thread for the background mixer and buffer update function. The OS X/CoreAudio implementation registers a callback that is executed by a separate thread created by the operating system.

SAL requires a back end to implement thread creation (if necessary) and synchronization (via mutexes).

Creating a thread in SAL (which should be done by only SAL back-end implementations; the thread and mutex APIs are not exposed outside of SAL) is as simple as calling _SAL_create_thread(), which dispatches to the appropriate back-end function.

```
sal_error_e
_SAL_create_thread( SAL_Device *device, SAL_THREAD_FUNC fnc, void *targs )
{
    if ( device == 0 || fnc == 0 )
    {
        return SALERR_INVALIDPARAM;
    }
    return device->device_fnc_create_thread( device, fnc, targs );
}
```

SAL's threading implementation assumes that a thread is defined as SAL_THREAD_FUNC:

```
typedef void ( POSH_CDECL *SAL_THREAD_FUNC)( void *args );
```

Since this is an application/client-defined callback, you must specify the calling convention (POSH_CDECL) explicitly, because the application and client code might be compiled with a different default calling convention. In addition, a SAL_THREAD_FUNC accepts a single pointer to a void for any arguments (which are forwarded through _SAL_create_thread()). Each back-end implementation of SAL_Device::device_ fnc_create_thread must properly execute the SAL_THREAD_FUNC as a start thread function. This is a direct mapping in Windows:

```
static
sal_error_e
_SAL_create_thread_win32( SAL_Device *device,
                          SAL_THREAD_FUNC fnc, void *targs )
{
    HANDLE hThread;

    if ( device == 0 || fnc == 0 )
    {
        return SALERR_INVALIDPARAM;
    }

    if ( ( hThread = (HANDLE) _beginthread( fnc, 0, targs ) ) == (HANDLE)-1 )
    {
        return SALERR_SYSTEMFAILURE;
    }

    SetThreadPriority( hThread, THREAD_PRIORITY_HIGHEST );

    return SALERR_OK;
}
```

Under Linux and OS X, the thread start function is also a direct mapping with an appropriate cast. The thread start function passed to pthread_create() is expected to return a pointer to a void. Although a SAL_THREAD_FUNC returns nothing, it is harmless in this situation, since the returned value is never used.

```
sal_error_e
_SAL_create_thread_pthreads( SAL_Device *device,
                             SAL_THREAD_FUNC fnc, void *args )
{
    pthread_attr_t attr;
    pthread_t tid;
    int result;

    if ( device == 0 || fnc == 0 || args == 0 )
    {
        return SALERR_INVALIDPARAM;
    }

    pthread_attr_init(&attr);

    result = pthread_create( &tid, &attr, (void* (*)(void *))fnc, args );

    if ( result != 0 )
    {
        return SALERR_SYSTEMFAILURE;
    }

    return SALERR_OK;
}
```

Mutexes serialize access to a shared resource (in this case, the SAL_Device), preventing race conditions. SAL requires *recursive mutexes*, which may be locked multiple times by the same thread (nonrecursive mutexes will allow a thread to deadlock against itself, which is a pretty silly concept). Linux's pthreads support recursive mutexes as an extension; Win32's mutexes are recursive. OS X's pthreads are not recursive, so OS X uses a a higher-level implementation, NSRecursiveLock, instead.

SAL abstracts the mutex structure as a void pointer exported to the application.

```
typedef void *sal_mutex_t; /**< mutex used for interthread synchronization */
```

The contents of the mutex depend on the underlying implementation. The sal_mutex_t is a HANDLE under Windows, but it is a pointer to a pthread_mutex_t under Linux. As with much of SAL's back-end implementation, mutex management is handled through a handful of functions which, in turn, dispatch dynamically to a platform's underlying mutex implementation. The following is the dispatch to a specific thread-creation function:

```
sal_error_e
_SAL_create_mutex( SAL_Device *device, sal_mutex_t *p_mtx )
```

```
{
    if ( device == 0 || p_mtx == 0 )
    {
        return SALERR_INVALIDPARAM;
    }
    return device->device_fnc_create_mutex( device, p_mtx );
}
```

Here is the Windows implementation:

```
static
sal_error_e
_SAL_create_mutex_win32( SAL_Device *device, sal_mutex_t *p_mtx )
{
    if ( p_mtx == 0 || device == 0 )
    {
        return SALERR_INVALIDPARAM;
    }

    *p_mtx = CreateMutex( NULL, FALSE, NULL );

    if ( *p_mtx == 0 )
    {
        return SALERR_SYSTEMFAILURE;
    }

    return SALERR_OK;
}
```

And here is the Linux implementation:

```
sal_error_e
_SAL_create_mutex_pthreads( SAL_Device *device, sal_mutex_t *p_mtx )
{
    if ( p_mtx == 0 || device == 0 )
    {
        _SAL_warning( device, "Invalid parameters to SAL_create_mutex\n" );
        return SALERR_INVALIDPARAM;
    }

    *p_mtx = ( sal_mutex_t * )
device->device_callbacks.alloc( sizeof( pthread_mutex_t ) );

    if ( *p_mtx == 0 )
    {
        _SAL_error( device, "Out of memory allocating mutex\n" );
        return SALERR_OUTOFMEMORY;
    }

#if defined POSH_OS_LINUX
```

```
{
pthread_mutexattr_t attr;

        attr.__mutexkind = PTHREAD_MUTEX_RECURSIVE_NP;

        pthread_mutex_init( (pthread_mutex_t * ) (*p_mtx), &attr );
    }
#else
#error pthreads mutexes currently only supported on POSH_OS_LINUX
#endif

    return SALERR_OK;
}
```

Environment Variables

Operating systems often provide a handy static communication and configuration mechanism known as *environment variables*. By setting an environment variable, either on the command line or through some kind of control panel application, you can configure an application directly, without using external files or a user interface. And since an environment variable can be interactively queried by a running program, it's a convenient way to change a running program without halting it.

For example, a simple server application may listen for traffic on a particular port. Designing an entire user interface for it is overkill, but for whatever reason, restarting it to change some parameters is not acceptable. A simple compromise is to have the server periodically look at an environment variable and adjust its settings accordingly dynamically.

The need to set and retrieve environment variables is so common that the ANSI C standard provides the putenv and getenv APIs for just this purpose. The aforementioned server application might look like this:

```
int port = DEFAULT_PORT;
while ( 1 )
{

    const char *portenv = getenv( "MY_PORT" );
    if ( atoi( portenv ) != port )
    {
        port = atoi( portenv );
        update_port( port ); /* let the application update its port value */
    }
    /* do other stuff */
}
```

Additionally, some operating systems will pass an array of environment variables as the third parameter to main():

```
int main( int argc, char *argv[], char *envp[] )
{
}
```

However, this is not mandated by the ANSI specification. POSIX.1-compliant implementations also provide a global variable:

```
const char **environ;
```

But since the latter two have spotty implementations, getenv and putenv are the safer bets when accessing environment variables.

Exception Handling

During the course of program operation, certain "exceptional" situations (a euphemism for bugs and severe errors) may arise. These can be due to errors in the program (illegal memory access, divide-by-zero, floating-point exceptions, and so on), user input (CTRL-C pressed, for example), or possibly system errors external to the program. Different operating systems handle and broadcast such exceptions uniquely; however, the ANSI C language provides a limited but standardized method for trapping and handling such circumstances: the signal and raise APIs.

C Exception Handling

When an exceptional situation occurs, the operating system will look to see if your program has installed a special handler for just such an event. If so, it calls your handler and, in some cases, even allows it to attempt some kind of recovery.

An application installs an exception handler with the signal API, passing the type of signal to handle and the address of the handler. For example, if you wish to trap illegal memory accesses in your handler (or at least know when they might occur), you might code the following:

```
#include <signal.h>

/* this should get called when the *buf = 0xCC line is executed */
/* You can test this out by running it in a debugger and
    setting a breakpoint in the handler */
void handler( int x )
{
}

int main( int argc, char *argv[] )
{
```

```
char *buf = 0;

/* install SEGV handler */
signal( SIGSEGV, handler );

/* test it out!! */
*buf = 0xCC;
}
```

Even though ANSI C provides a standardized exception management system, there are still significant portability issues:

- Not all signals are catchable (SIGSEGV requires hardware-assisted memory management).

- The scope of operations available during an interrupt handler may vary (some implementations disallow the use of any C run-time library functions inside a signal handler).

- Some implementations may provide more handling mechanisms than the default set. For example, Microsoft Windows provides a comprehensive and powerful exception-handling system using its proprietary Structured Exception Handling (SEH) mechanism based around the _try, _except, and _finally keywords.

As a rule, portable programs should not rely on exception handlers to do "real" work. Your programs should instead concentrate their efforts on masking the effects of a signal handler as much as possible.

C++ Exception Handling

The C++ language has its own set of exception-handling mechanisms using the try, catch, and throw keywords, but these are designed to catch application-defined errors, not operating system exceptions. In fact, current C++ exception-handling implementations are completely unrelated to operating system–generated exceptions. To make matters worse, you cannot safely and portably throw exceptions from a signal handler.

User Data Storage

Many personal computer operating systems support multiple user accounts on the same computer. Businesses often have dedicated workstations or servers with multiple users, and even families are finding the need to share a single computer among different members. This means that application developers need to support per-user configuration and data.

For example, Betty and Dave may have drastically different preferences for the desktop background, application settings, and audio. Neither relishes the idea of resetting preferences every time he or she sits down at the computer. In the past, each application had to implement its own "multiuser" feature if it wanted to support user-specific customization, or users would be forced to fight over the system's configuration.

Unfortunately, there is no universal standard for storing per-user data; in fact, there's nothing even close, not even commonly used open-source libraries that hide these details. For global application data, a developer could store data in the application directory; however, this would fail if the application's directory were not writable or if multiple instances of the same application were installed.

Microsoft Windows Registry

Microsoft Windows uses a central database, called the *registry*, to store system-wide and per-user information. This was an attempt to address all the problems encountered with earlier versions of Windows, where configuration data spread randomly through myriad files on a user's system.

The registry stores and retrieves data by keys in a filesystem-like hierarchical structure. For example, a user's preference for the volume setting in your application might be stored at HKEY_CURRENT_USER\Software\ MyCompany\MyProduct\volume:

```
unsigned char get_volume()
{
    HKEY hKey;
    DWORD dwDisposition;
    unsigned char value;
    DWORD dwSize = sizeof( value );
    DWORD dwType;

    /* error checking omitted for brevity */
    RegCreateKeyEx( HKEY_CURRENT_USER,
                    "SOFTWARE\\MyCompany\\MyProduct",
                    OL,
                    "",
                    REG_OPTION_NON_VOLATILE,
                    KEY_ALL_ACCESS,
                    NULL,
                    &hKey,
                    &dwDisposition );

    RegQueryValueEx( hKey,
                     "volume",
                     NULL,
                     &dwType,
                     ( BYTE * ) &value,
                     &dwSize );

    RegCloseKey( hKey );

    return value;
}
```

Microsoft's registry system has proved to be very unpopular with both casual and power users alike. Since it's a centralized repository for system-wide information, any damage to it may result in an unusable system. In contrast, application- or user-specific configuration file corruption localizes the damage. Apart from this, the registry is difficult to navigate (it requires a custom tool, Regedit, for examination and modification) and transfer from machine to machine. Contrast this with a file-based configuration system, where individual preferences are easy to transport by merely moving that single file.

Linux User Data

Linux does not have a standard mechanism for supporting per-user preferences, but since it was designed as a multiuser operating system from the start, it is relatively easy for an application to store configuration data in a file such as ~/.MyApplication/preferences. This does require more work on the part of the application, and it prevents a user from using a unified preferences system, but since that's not an option on Linux, it's a moot concern.

OS X Preferences

Apple has gone a different route with its user data system, Preferences, in Mac OS X. Unlike the Microsoft Windows registry, Mac OS X uses an open text-file format based on XML, so anyone with a text editor can open and examine preferences files. In addition, instead of a single monolithic system preferences file, OS X has multiple, targeted preferences files that contain a limited amount of information. Systemwide preferences are stored in /System/Library/Preferences, and user-specific preferences are stored in ~/Library/Preferences.

Programming the preferences system is, unfortunately, a bit cumbersome:

```
unsigned char get_volume()
{
    unsigned char value;
    CFStringRef pref_name, value_name;
    CFPropertyListRef plref;

    /* error checking omitted for brevity */
    pref_name =
        CFStringCreateWithCString( NULL,
                                   "com.MyCompany.MyProduct",
                                   CFStringGetSystemEncoding() );
    value_name =
        CFStringCreateWithCString( NULL,
                                   "volume",
                                   CFStringGetSystemEncoding() );
```

```
    plref = CFPreferencesCopyAppValue( value_name, pref_name );

    CFDataGetBytes( ( CFDataRef ) plref,
                    CFRangeMake( 0, sizeof( value ) ), &value );

    CFRelease( pref_name );
    CFRelease( value_name );
    CFRelease( plref );

    return value;
}
```

Security and Permissions

The anarchistic technology buffet that defined computing throughout the 1980s and early 1990s slowly calmed down, giving rise to a handful of predominant standards. Microsoft Windows (operating system), Internet Explorer and Mozilla Firefox (web browsers), Microsoft Outlook (email client), Apache and Microsoft IIS (web servers), sendmail and Exchange Server (email servers), and JavaScript (client-side presentation for web browsers) have staked claims as the dominant entities in their domains. But with this homogeneity came an opportunity for exploitation by nefarious individuals and organizations.

If a virus author, spam sender, identity thief, or similar "cyberterrorist" wants to attack a large number of systems, targeting a vulnerability in a commonly used application will reap huge returns. The first cataclysmic Internet worm was distributed through an exploit in the ubiquitous sendmail server. The standardizations we see today have led to even more exploits, as worm and virus authors take advantage of security holes in popular applications such as Microsoft Outlook and Internet Explorer.

The rampant spread of spam, viruses, spyware, adware, worms, and other malware emphasizes the flaws and holes in applications and operating systems. The adoption of secure (compared to earlier incarnations) multiuser desktop operating systems has made the matter a primary consideration for cross-platform application developers, who must contend with security policies.

As noted in the previous section, multiuser operating systems allow different users to use the same computer, sometimes simultaneously. For obvious security and privacy reasons, it is undesirable to have a random user modify or even access files he does not "own," such as another user's documents or key operating system files.

Some of the issues associated with security and privileges on modern computer systems include application installation, data storage, and low-level access.

Application Installation

The first problem you may encounter is a relatively mundane one: simply installing your application. A lot of developers try to install their software into a global system directory—such as in `C:\Windows` or `/usr/bin`—by default. The problem is that on a secure multiuser operating system, this is not allowed without appropriate privileges or temporarily logging in as a superuser, an administrator, or root.

If new or updated system software must also be installed (for example, Windows games will often attempt to install the latest version of Microsoft's DirectX libraries by default), then the issue of privilege rears its head.

In many cases, this is just a temporary inconvenience for the user— she must obtain sufficient privileges (using an operating system–specific command)—but sometimes, this can stop the installation dead in its tracks if the user does not have sufficient rights. Instead of requiring a specific installation directory, allow the user to specify a location (possibly relative to their home directory) to which they have better access.

Privileged Directories and Data

Privilege and access aren't the only concerns during installation. How users access shared data or store their own data are issues that affect them after installation. Some applications prefer to place data in their own directories— for example, `C:\Application\Data`. However, many multiuser operating systems do not allow this, at least, not easily or without compromising security in some other fashion.

If it is feasible, data should be stored *per user*. That way, each user that uses your software will have his copy of data files without fear of other users inadvertently accessing or deleting those files. If data must be shared, make it an explicit action on the part of the users: require them to place shared data into special shared folders or directories. This way, there is no confusion as to whether or not a file will be private.

EXAMPLE:

MICROSOFT WINDOWS REGISTRY PERMISSIONS

Access to the global system registry key `HKEY_LOCAL_MACHINE` on Windows is restricted to users with administrator rights. With Windows 9x/Me, this wasn't a concern since all users, by default, had administrator rights. But when a lot of software was installed on Windows NT, 2000, or XP, problems arose. Many developers would store application global data in `HKEY_LOCAL_MACHINE`, instead of the more appropriate `HKEY_CURRENT_USER`, which sometimes prevented their application from running at all on multiuser Windows systems. Simply changing the application key from `HKEY_LOCAL_MACHINE` to `HKEY_CURRENT_USER` fixes the problem.

Other operating systems have analogous situations. For example Mac OS X separates preferences in `/System/Library/Preferences` and `~/System/Library/Preferences`.

Low-Level Access

Programmers of embedded or older operating systems are used to accessing or modifying global data or privileged CPU instructions directly. Early DOS applications routinely performed low-level access to hardware ports (parallel, joystick, serial, and VGA) using Intel 8086 instructions such as OUT and IN. Graphics were drawn by writing to certain constant addresses (0xA0000 for VGA frame buffer access). BIOS functions were called by setting registers and generating a software interrupt. Simple problems called for simple solutions.

A secure operating system will not allow these types of actions, since they could crash the system or subvert security policies. For example, file permissions are irrelevant if an industrial spy can program an IDE controller to read raw sectors from a hard drive.

A portable program should not be affected by these issues, as long as it properly abstracts low-level access.

Summary

The operating system is the face of a platform, where the heart and soul are the processor. Most software interacts with the operating system instead of the hardware directly, and for this reason the operating system is a major element of portable software development. In this chapter we've covered many of the features that operating systems support and how to abstract and move between different implementations of these features on different platforms.

12

DYNAMIC LIBRARIES

Traditionally, applications have been statically linked to any necessary libraries, incorporating all the code in the library into the program's executable. When enough applications started using the same libraries, developers wondered whether users were suffering from unnecessary code bloat. If ten different applications were all using the same string functions, each consuming space on disk or in memory, wouldn't it be great if all those libraries could share the same library, thereby reducing their collective footprint?

This dilemma generated shared objects on Unix/Linux, import/shared libraries on Mac OS, shared libraries on AmigaDOS, dynamic link libraries (DLLs) on Windows and OS/2, and frameworks on Mac OS X. In fact, it is the rare modern operating system that lacks shared library facilities.

Shared libraries also provide (in theory) the ability to fix bugs globally. If there is a bug in a system-installed shared library, then the operating system vendor can distribute a new version, and all applications that use that library will automatically receive the bug fix.

Dynamic libraries also allow the creation of *plug-ins*, or dynamically loadable pieces of code used to extend an application's features.

As you might expect, shared libraries operate differently between operating systems. In this chapter we'll cover the task of writing portable software that leverages the power of dynamic libraries.

Dynamic Linking

As the name implies, *dynamic linking* binds references from the application to external libraries at run time. When the program is built, it is linked either to an import library, which provides stubbed references so that the link process may proceed, or directly to the dynamic library, so that the linker can ascertain which functions need to be resolved dynamically and add appropriate startup code as necessary.

When the program is run, the operating system notes which external references must be resolved, loads the application and any dependent dynamic libraries (which are not already resident), and then patches a jump table (usually) so references to the dynamic library are properly resolved. If the dynamic library cannot be found or is possibly of the wrong version, the operating system will report an error at program startup.

Dynamic Loading

Dynamic loading is similar to dynamic linking, but the application does not explicitly link to imported functions and data. Instead, it loads a dynamic library explicitly and manually binds any references.

This approach has a couple major advantages:

- The application can run even if some dynamic libraries are missing, allowing the use of certain features only if present and ignoring them otherwise.

- Specific dynamic libraries may be selected at run time, providing configuration options and application extensibility.

An example of the latter case would be if an application wanted to select a math library based on the presence of different instruction sets of the host CPU. If the CPU supported AMD's 3DNow instruction set, then one library could be loaded; if Streaming SIMD Extensions (SSE) were present, then another could be loaded; and if SSE2 were present, yet another could be loaded instead. This is far better than requiring a different version of the program for each different optimized instruction set.

A very common and powerful use of dynamic loading is to acquire *application plug-ins*, which are optional components that can be loaded at run time. Spelling checkers, photo-editing filters, and file import/export routines are common examples of plug-ins.

Problems with Shared Libraries (aka DLL Hell)

While shared libraries are powerful and useful, they also create a whole new set of problems, some of which have made many programmers question their actual value. The main problems are associated with versioning and their proliferation in various locations.

Versioning Problems

As mentioned earlier, one of the theoretical advantages of dynamic libraries is that they can be updated to fix bugs and add new features. Any application that uses the upgraded dynamic library automatically inherits the improvements. Unfortunately, in practice, this can backfire.

As an example, suppose that your application Super Graphics Visualizer uses a popular third-party shared library, math3d, which provides system-optimized 3D mathematics facilities. Somewhere in your code, you initialize math3d:

```
unsigned int flags;
if ( M3D_Init( flags ) == 0 ) /* flags is uninitialized! */
{
  SGV_Error( "Could not initialize math3d!!!" );
}
```

The version of math3d that you've been using states, "The flags parameter to M3D_Init() is currently unused but must be zero in this version of Math3D." Of course, you don't notice this caveat, and even worse, the library doesn't enforce this requirement. So while your code works, it's not adhering to the letter of the law.

A user downloads your application and installs it. Part of the installation process is putting the ever-so-popular math3d library in a systemwide shared location to minimize redundancy. On Windows, you've probably installed math3d to C:\Windows\System32; on Linux, maybe it's in /usr/lib or /usr/lib/share; and on Mac OS X, it's in /System/Library/Frameworks.

Everything works fine for weeks. Then one day, the user installs another application, Math Formula Express, which also happens to use math3d. The installation program notices that there is an older version of math3d present and "conveniently" updates it to the latest version, which is faster, smaller, and less buggy.

After using Math Formula Express for a while, the user tries to run Super Graphics Visualizer, only to see it crash with a cryptic error message. She hasn't modified or changed Super Graphics Visualizer at all, so why would it suddenly stop working?! After calling tech support and spending a lot of time and energy tracking down the problem, the culprit is identified:

Super Graphics Visualizer is now failing the call to M3D_Init(). Previous versions of math3d did not enforce the edict of "the flags parameters must be zero." The new version does, resulting in this inexplicable failure. What used to work now stops working, even though the application itself has not been modified.

Applications become dependent on undefined or undocumented behavior, often without realizing it, and then unexpectedly break when the implicit underlying behavior changes.

Querying the dynamic library's compiled version, while not fixing the problem, at least identifies it quickly. The application can check its instance of a version constant against the constant compiled into the library:

```
if ( M3D_Version() != M3D_VERSION )
{
    SGV_Error( "Incorrect version of math3d found!" );
}
```

Proliferation

Shared libraries, like socks and loose change, have a habit of showing up in the oddest, least expected places. As helpful as it would be to have all shared libraries residing in the same location, users, installation programs, and application developers often put shared libraries in arbitrary places.

In a Windows environment, an attempt to load a DLL will search directories in the following order:

1. Application's directory
2. Windows system directory (for example, C:\Windows\System32)
3. Windows directory (for example, C:\Windows)
4. Entire path
5. Current directory

Accordingly, replacing a widely used shared library may or may not have the intended results. If a DLL in the system directory is updated, local copies stored in an application's directory may still get loaded inadvertently. Or, if a shared DLL is located in the path but not in the system or Windows directory, updating it may not have the intended effect if another application, which also has its own copy, is listed earlier in the path.

Linux uses a single search path defined by the environment variable `LD_SEARCH_PATH`. Each system may have a different search path, possibly with or without the current directory in it, so the behavior may change from system to system as well.

Gnu LGPL

One of the unexpected uses of shared libraries came to light with the promotion of the Gnu Library/Lesser General Public License (LGPL), which, unlike the general GPL license, allows the distribution of closed-source applications if they *dynamically* link to a library in question.

I'm not a lawyer, so you should read the full text of the LGPL license yourself if you're considering using or creating an LGPL-licensed work (http://www.gnu.org/copyleft/lesser.html). The gist is that if you use someone else's LGPL-licensed library in your own application, anyone must be able to modify the library and still use it with your application.

This forces the application developer to provide the source code to the application (so it can be recompiled and relinked to the LGPL-licensed library) or dynamically link to the library in question. For obvious reasons, most closed-source developers prefer the latter.

Windows DLLs

The Microsoft Windows operating system supports shared libraries through its DLLs. DLLs are built like any other library, with a few additional flags specified, either in the IDE or at the command line.

The DLL developer must specifically indicate which functions are to be exported (all other functions remain private to the DLL). Previously, this was done by creating a .def (module definition) file:

```
LIBRARY    MATH3D
DESCRIPTION "My simple math library"
EXPORTS
    M3D_Init @1
    M3D_Dot3 @2
    M3D_Cross3 @3
    M3D_Normalize3 @4
    M3D_Version @5
```

As you can imagine, this became pretty cumbersome as the number of exports continued to grow. Every time you added a new function, you had to remember to add it to the .def file to ensure that it was exported.

Later versions of Windows compilers from Borland, Microsoft, and Watcom simplified this by allowing the programmer to export a function with a function signature statement:

```
/* math3d.h */
float __declspec( export ) M3D_Dot3( const float a[3],
                                     const float b[3] );
void __declspec( export ) M3D_Cross3( const float a[3],
                                      const float b[3],
                                      float dst[3] );
float __declspec( export ) M3D_Normalize3( const float a[3],
                                           float dst[3] );
```

The __declspec(export) directive informs the compiler that that function must be exported from the DLL.

Compiling and linking the source code generates two libraries: the static import library (with an .lib extension) and the dynamic link library (with a .dll extension). In this example, the libraries would be math3d.lib and math3d.dll.

There is one unfortunate problem with __declspec(export): when an application uses a DLL function, it's not *exporting* that function, but trying to *import* that function, so the previous header file won't work. Instead, the application must use __declspec(import). Now, you can manage this with brute force and have two different header files—one for building the DLL and another for using the DLL—but this is clumsy and error-prone. Instead, most library developers predefine a symbol when building the DLL—something like BUILDING_LIBRARY or BUILDING_DLL—and set a shared predefined constant appropriately, so that they are properly exporting or importing a function, depending on the situation.

An application may then either dynamically link to the DLL or dynamically load it. The former requires linking to the DLL's import library (math3d.lib in this example), and the latter requires manually loading the library and searching for exported functions.

Dynamic loading is quite a bit more tedious than linking, but has the advantage of working even if a DLL is not present. Windows provides the LoadLibrary() and GetProcAddress() APIs for dynamic loading.

```
#include <windows.h>
float (*M3D_Dot3)( const float a[3], const float b[3] );
void  (*M3D_Cross3)( const float a[3], const float b[3], float dst[3] );
float (*M3D_Normalize3)( const float a[3], float dst[3] );
HINSTANCE hM3D;
int load_math_library( void )
{
   if ( ( hM3D = LoadLibrary( "math3d.dll" ) ) == 0 )
      return 0;
   M3D_Dot3 = (float (*)( const float a[3], const float b[3] ))
             GetProcAddress( hM3D, "M3D_Dot3" );
```

```
    M3D_Cross3 = (void  (*)( const float a[3], const float b[3], float dst[3] ))
            GetProcAddress( hM3D, "M3D_Cross3" );
    M3D_Normalize = ( void (*)(const float a[], float dst[]))
                GetProcAddress( hM3D, "M3D_Normalize3" );
    return 1;
}
void unload_math_library( void )
{
    FreeLibrary( hM3D );
}
```

POSH EXAMPLE: DLL EXPORT/IMPORT

POSH examines two symbols—POSH_BUILDING_LIB and POSH_DLL—and then sets another, POSH_IMPORTEXPORT, appropriately. If POSH_BUILDING_LIB is defined as 1, POSH knows that a library is being built. If POSH_DLL is defined, POSH knows that a DLL is either being built or used. Based on this matrix, it sets POSH_IMPORTEXPORT as follows:

POSH_BUILDING_LIB	POSH_DLL	POSH_IMPORTEXPORT
Not defined	Not defined	Empty
1	Not defined	Empty
Not defined	1	__declspec(import)
1	1	__declspec(export)

An application may then prefix its functions appropriately for export/import:

```
void POSH_IMPORTEXPORT foo( void );
```

Some compilers change the location of the declspec statement, so POSH wraps its usage inside another macro, POSH_PUBLIC_API:

```
POSH_PUBLIC_API( void ) foo( void );
```

Windows also provides DLL authors the ability to execute a specified function under certain special circumstances. Specifically, a DLL may provide a special function, DLLMain(), declared as follows:

```
BOOL WINAPI DllMain( HINSTANCE hinstDLL,
                DWORD dwReason,
                LPVOID lpvReserved );
```

That is automatically called whenever a process first attaches to a DLL, a process detaches from a DLL, or a thread in the current process is created or destroyed. This allows a DLL to perform initialization and cleanup functions without the assistance of any applications, and it also allows a DLL to remain thread-safe by giving it the opportunity to allocate thread local variables.

Linux Shared Objects

Linux and other Unix flavors provide *shared objects*, which are shared library files that have a .so extension and adhere to the convention of a lib prefix, such as libmath3d.so. Static libraries use the .a extension, as in libmath3d.a.

Building a library as a shared object requires passing special flags to the compiler:

```
$ gcc -shared -fPIC -o libmath3d.so math3d.c
```

This compiles math3d.c and creates a shared object libmath3d.so. The -shared flag tells the linker that a shared object is being created (so it won't attempt to build an executable), and the -fPIC option tells it to generate position-independent code that can be relocated (which is necessary since a shared object does not know at what address it will be loaded).

Unlike Windows, the compiler and linker do not need to generate or use a separate special import library. Instead, the appropriate library dependencies are specified when building the program. The program is linked to the .so file directly to resolve references and define dependencies:

```
$ gcc test.c -L. -lmath3d
```

This compiles test.c using the current directory (-L.) to search for libraries, including libmath3d (-lmath3d). The executable will dynamically link to libmath3d.so at run time. If the shared object can't be found, an error will result, usually something like this:

```
$ ./a.out: error while loading shared libraries: libmath3d.so:
 cannot open shared object file: No such file or directory
```

Dynamic loading can be implemented just as in Windows, but using the <dlfcn.h> API.

```
#include <dlfcn.h>
float (*M3D_Dot3)( const float a[3], const float b[3] );
void  (*M3D_Cross3)( const float a[3], const float b[3], float dst[3] );
float (*M3D_Normalize3)( const float a[3], float dst[3] );
void *hM3D;
int load_math_library( void )
{
   if ( ( hM3D = dlopen( "libmath3d.so", RTLD_NOW ) ) == 0 )
      return 0;
   M3D_Dot3 = (float (*)( const float a[3], const float b[3] ))
              dlsym( hM3D, "M3D_Dot3" );
   M3D_Cross3 = (void (*)( const float a[3], const float b[3], float dst[3] ))
```

```
                dlsym( hM3D, "M3D_Cross3" );
    M3D_Normalize = ( void (*)(const float a[], float dst[]))
                    dlsym( hM3D, "M3D_Normalize3" );
    return 1;
}
void unload_math_library( void )
{
    dlclose( hM3D );
}
```

And, like Windows, the Linux <dlfcn.h> API allows a shared object to execute code optionally when loaded and unloaded. Instead of DllMain, a shared object author implements the _init() and/or _fini() functions, which are called when the shared object is loaded and unloaded, respectively:

```
void _init( void )
{
    /* do startup code here */
}
void _fini( void )
{
    /* do shutdown code here */
}
```

Which functions to export are determined with a simple process: all nonstatic functions are exported, period. Development is easier, since header files do not need to be littered with __declspec(import) and __declspec(export), as on Windows, nor is there a need for a separate .def file. However, an unfortunate side effect is that it's difficult to keep a nonstatic function private to the shared object.

Mac OS X Frameworks, Plug-ins, and Bundles

The shared library and plug-in situation on Mac OS X is a bit more confusing than one would hope. Unlike with Linux or Windows, Mac OS X does not offer a single shared library type that can be used as a dynamically linked library or as a dynamically loaded piece of executable code. Instead, it uses a rather mind-numbing array of different technologies to provide these features, depending on the needs of the programmer. In fact, a dlfcn.h compatibility library for OS X has already been developed and is widely used, providing the dlsym style interface for OS X applications. We'll look at some the OS X specific technologies here.

Frameworks

Frameworks are versioned, hierarchical, dynamically linked shared libraries, with a .framework extension. For example, the math3D shared library would be called Math3D.framework.

Frameworks operate much like dynamically linked shared libraries on Windows and Linux (DLLs and shared objects, respectively); however, they contain more than just executable code. Frameworks may have header files, resources, localization information, and documentation—all located inside a standard folder hierarchy.

Frameworks may be installed in a systemwide directory (/System/Library/Frameworks), in a user directory (~/Library/Frameworks), or inside an *application bundle*, where they are private to the application. The latter minimizes conflicts between multiple versions of the same framework on the same system. Unfortunately, frameworks may not be dynamically loaded in the same manner as shared objects or DLLs.

Bundles

NSBundle is an Objective-C (the Apple standard language for Mac OS X development) wrapper around the CFBundle API. CFBundle is a middle-level layer for managing loadable code and resources. It hides a lot of implementation details from the programmer (such as the executable file format, which may be PEF or Mach-O), but is still low level enough that it doesn't dictate too much policy to the user.

Here is an example of using a bundle:

```
#include <Carbon/Carbon.h>

float (*M3D_Dot3)( const float a[3], const float b[3] );
void  (*M3D_Cross3)( const float a[3], const float b[3], float dst[3] );
float (*M3D_Normalize3)( const float a[3], float dst[3] );

CFBundleRef m3d;

int load_math_library( void )
{
    const char *bundlename = "math3d.bundle";
    CFURLRef ref = CFURLCreateFromFileSystemRepresentation(
                        NULL,
                        bundlename,
                        strlen( bundlename ),
                        FALSE );


    /* roughly equivalent to LoadLibrary/dlopen */
    if ( ( m3d = CFBundleCreate( NULL, ref ) ) == 0 )
    {
        printf( "Could not load bundle\n" );
        exit( 1 );
    }

    /* roughly equivalent to dlsym/GetProcAddress */
    M3D_Dot3 = (float (*)( const float a[3], const float b[3] ))
            CFBundleGetFunctionPointerForName( m3d,
```

```
                                        CFSTR( "M3D_Dot3" ) );
    M3D_Cross3 = (void  (*)( const float a[3], const float b[3], float dst[3] ))
             CFBundleGetFunctionPointerForName( m3d,
                                        CFSTR( "M3D_Cross3" ) );
    M3D_Normalize = ( void (*)(const float a[], float dst[]))
                 CFBundleGetFunctionPointerForName( m3d,
                                        CFSTR( "M3D_Normalize" )
);;
    return 0;
}


void unload_math_library( void )
{
    /* no equivalent! */
}
```

Although the preceding code is analogous to the Windows and Linux shared library functions, there are some notable differences and quirks. For starters, the Mac OS X Core Foundation libraries seem to have an abhorrence for just accepting raw pointers to characters for strings. Instead, you must use CFStringRef and CFURL. Additionally, there is no way to unload a bundle once it's loaded, nor is there a standard equivalent to DllMain(), _fini(), and _init().

Code Fragment Manager loads PEF files (an older style PowerPC binary format, compatible with both early Mac OS and Mac OS X).

Plug-ins

CFPlugIn is tied directly to the CFBundle, but it operates at a higher level of abstraction. For starters, it uses an interface query and factory system very similar to Microsoft's Component Object Model (COM). This has some theoretical advantages, but for many developers, it's overkill and extremely tedious dealing with all of the universally unique identifiers (UUIDs, also sometimes called IIDs or GUIDs), querying, and general hackery involved.

Simply loading a piece of executable code using the CFPlugIn API requires dozens of lines of code. While in the end you may gain something more robust, you definitely pay a price when it comes to usability.

dyld is the low-level Mach-O dynamic linker interface, which lacks the backward compatibility with PEF binaries that CFBundle and CFPlugIn provide.

```
#include <mach-o/dyld.h>
NSModule m3d;
NSObjectFileImage m3d_image;
int load_math_library( void )
{
    NSObjectFileImageReturnCode rc;
    NSSymbol symbol;

    rc = NSCreateObjectFileImageFromFile( "math3d", &m3d_image );
```

```
    if ( rc != NSObjectFileImageSuccess )
        return 0;

    m3d = NSLinkModule( m3d_image,
                        "math3d",
                        NSLINKMODULE_OPTION_RETURN_ON_ERROR );

    if ( m3d == 0 )
        return 0;

    symbol = NSLookupSymbolInModule( m3d, "_M3D_Dot3" );
    M3D_Dot3 = (float (*)( const float a[3], const float b[3] ))
            NSAddressOfSymbol( symbol );
    symbol = NSLookupSymbolInModule( m3d, "_M3D_Cross3" );
    M3D_Cross3 = (float (*)( const float a[3], const float b[3] ))
            NSAddressOfSymbol( symbol );
    symbol = NSLookupSymbolInModule( m3d, "_M3D_Normalize" );
    M3D_Normalize = (float (*)( const float a[3], float b[3] ))
                NSAddressOfSymbol( symbol );
}
void unload_math_library( void )
{
    NSUnLinkModule( m3d_image, NSUNLINKMODULE_OPTION_NONE );
    NSDestroyObjectFileImage( m3d_image );
}
```

Many operations that were previously one function call are now split into two calls. For example, LoadLibrary()/dlopen() on Windows and Linux both load a DLL and map it into the process's address space, but these are separate operations on OS X using NSCreateObjectFileImageFromFile() and NSLinkModule(). Likewise, looking up a symbol goes from a single call to GetProcAddress()/dlsym() to a two-step, find-symbol/get-symbol-address procedure using NSLookupSymbolInModule() and NSAddressOfSymbol(). The only other visible difference is that the Mach-O interfaces require the actual name of the symbol, post-mangling, which is why there are underscores prepended to the function names.

Believe it or not, there are still more ways of accomplishing related functionality on OS X, including weak-linking and loading dynamic libraries using the Mach-O image functions. Due to space and relevancy constraints, I won't go into those techniques here.

Summary

As you can see from this chapter, dynamic libraries are conceptually very similar across modern operating systems. Facilities must be present to load a binary image, find a symbol within that image, and then finally bind to that symbol. There are minor technical differences between the implementations, and fairly significant syntactic ones, but developing an abstraction for this is not that difficult.

13

FILESYSTEMS

Most computer systems today support the notion of a *file*—a chunk of data stored somewhere other than the computer's main memory, such as a floppy disk, CD-ROM, or CompactFlash RAM. Each operating system may support one or more types of *filesystems*, or formal specifications that define how to access and manage individual files. Some platforms, such as embedded systems that execute from ROM, may not have any filesystem present.

Due to the different ways each operating system presents files to the user, file access is one of the trickier points for portable software. Standard filesystems provide access through the C standard library's standard I/O routines, such as fopen(), fclose(), fread(), and fwrite(), but it is not uncommon to use special APIs to access special filesystems, such as networked or tape backup filesystems.

In this chapter, I'll go over some of the differences between filesystems and how to deal with them in your portable code.

Symbolic Links, Shortcuts, and Aliases

The hierarchical file folder system, seen on most modern consumer operating systems, is a conceptually simple but cumbersome way to manage large amounts of data. A lot of "up folder, up folder, up folder, down other folder, select file" type navigation occurs, which is often confusing and tedious for a user working on multiple files in different locations.

To alleviate this problem, filesystem designers introduced *symbolic links* (in Windows parlance, *shortcuts*), which are ways to link to a file in another directory. This allows you to access a file from a directory in which it may not be physically present, simplifying file management considerably. Not all filesystems support links, and even those that do often differ significantly in implementation. In fact, they're different enough to break portable software that might expect a certain type of behavior.

The best way to handle shortcuts and symbolic links depends greatly on the particular application. If your application doesn't open or manipulate files through the command line and can instead rely on the operating system's file open/query/selection dialog mechanisms, then you're probably in the clear. However, if you're writing a command-line application, you'll need to decide on a policy for links: ignore the issue and open a file however you want or, if you're feeling ambitious, handle links correctly depending on the filesystem.

Windows LNK Files

Windows has the most primitive form of file aliases. It creates special files with the .lnk extension that contain the name of the file to which they point. If you access the link file from a standard Windows file-open dialog box, things work the way you would expect. But if you try to process the link file from the command line, you're actually operating on the link itself, not on the file linked to. This means that if you do something like this:

```
C:\Documents and Settings\bhook\cd work
```

where work is actually a .lnk file that points to a directory elsewhere, you'll get an error message. If you use Notepad to open a file called Shortcut to todo.txt.lnk, you'll end up editing the .lnk file directly (which is ill-advised since .lnk files are in binary format and not amenable to editing with a text editor).

Unix Links

Many Unix-like systems have two different types of links:

Hard links
A *hard link* is a synonym for the file in question, and any operations, including deletion, will act on that file directly. A hard link is indistinguishable from a regular file.

Soft links

A *soft link* is a pointer to another file and, at the same time, is a file in and of itself. Soft links are identifiable as such, and some operations, such as deletion, operate only on the link itself, not its target.

This disparity may lead to unexpected and possibly dangerous consequences for the end user if your application expects one type of behavior and gets another.

Path Specification

Filesystems uniquely identify files with a fully qualified path name. Different filesystems provide different conventions for the layout of the path name, which can lead to significant portability problems when working with files.

Disk Drives and Volume Specifiers

Some operating systems allow or require specification of a particular logical or physical device in a qualified path name. This requirement and its implementation is not universal, so portable software should not rely on it.

Path Separators and Other Special Characters

Hierarchical filesystems use the notion of *directories* or *folders*, which are special files that contain other files. Early filesystems did not provide this structure, but it's been a long time since those particular dark ages. Without a hierarchical filesystem, all files inhabit the same location, making management a nightmare. Directory listings of hundreds or thousands of files are not pleasant.

Path separators distinguish between directories and are often different depending on the operating system. For example, DOS and Windows use the backslash (\) character; most Unix filesystems use the forward slash (/), and Mac OS uses the colon (:).

In addition, each filesystem has special characters, directories, or files that represent the root directory, the parent directory, and the current directory. Table 13-1 shows how these directories are represented on some common filesystems.

Table 13-1: Root, Current, and Parent Directory Representations

Operating Sysem	Root	Current Directory	Parent Directory
DOS/Windows	\ (of current disk)	.	..
Linux/Unix/OS X	/	.	..
Mac OS	Volume name	N/A	
VMS	Volume name	[]	[-]

As you can see, nonalphanumeric characters often have radically different meanings depending on the filesystem. For this reason, any files and directories you create for your own use should not contain anything but alphanumeric characters and possibly underscores (_). While it is tempting to use the space character or special characters (such as ., !, #, or $), doing so may create complications when moving between systems. The period character also may be used as part of a filename one time or many times, depending on the filesystem (FAT16 filesystems permit only a single period, to delineate between the filename and its extension).

Current Directory

When a program opens a file using a relative path name (that is, not fully qualified), as in the following example, there is an assumption that the file is located in the current directory:

```
fp = fopen( "myfile.txt", "r" );
```

As you can see in Table 13-1, most filesystem implementations support the notion of a *current directory*—the default directory in which to look for an unqualified filename. Where this directory is located is another matter altogether. When running from the command line, the current directory is clear; however, when running a program through the GUI, such as by double-clicking an icon, the current directory is vague. Sometimes you can specify the current directory as part of the program icon's properties; other times, it's assumed that the working directory will be the directory in which the program's executable is located.

Some platforms, such as gaming consoles and the Microsoft Windows CE/Pocket PC operating system, lack the concept of a current directory, and all unqualified path names are assumed to be in the root directory. Applications on this platform must infer or query their locations (GetModuleFileName()) in order to find their data files.

Path Length

Along with the constraints of name format, each filesystem also limits the maximum length of a path- or filename, from as low as 11 total characters to as high as several thousand. Here are some examples:

- The MS-DOS/Windows FAT32 and Win32 NTFS filesystems allow up to 256 characters.
- The MS-DOS FAT16 filesystem used the infamous 8.3 format (8 characters in the name and 3 characters in the extension).
- The Linux ReiserFS filesystem supports 4,032 characters.
- The Linux ext2 and ext3 filesystems support up to 255 characters.
- Mac OS, depending on the particular flavor and application support, usually supports 31 characters.

A portable application can either establish a baseline (the lowest reasonable common denominator) or attempt to maintain compatibility between all the different formats possible, but the latter can be very difficult if you're trying to move files between different platforms.

Case Sensitivity

Some filesystems are sensitive to case, others are not, and yet others will retain case for display but not for filename matching. Case-sensitive filesystems consider `Graphics.h`, `graphics.h`, and `GRAPHICS.H` different files; case-insensitive filesystems view those as the same files. Case-retentive (but insensitive) filesystems would consider those the same file, but retain case for display.

The moral here is that you should be rock-solid consistent about handling case, when dealing with files in your application or even just naming your source files. If you have a large project and you mistakenly name two files in the same directory `Globals.h` and `globals.h`, you'll run into an unpleasant surprise when you move your files to a case-insensitive filesystem.

Security and Access Privilege

Security is becoming an increasingly important part of computing in today's world. Historically, personal computers have been, well, personal. Developers did not place any real effort into providing security and privacy, leading to the plethora of problems encountered today: viruses, worms, spyware, and other ill-behaved denizens of the computing universe. Contrast this with business computer systems, where security and protection have been first-order priorities.

A lot of personal computer software has been written assuming that the user has unfettered access to any files on a system. That software, when migrated to a more secure system, will often fail to run.

The primary culprit is software assuming that it can read and write to systemwide locations, such as the operating system installation directory, application directory, or root directory. For example, a decompression program may blithely assume it may create a `temp` directory in the root directory of the current drive for its work, but this will fail on a secured operating system that prohibits arbitrary access to folders outside the user's home directory.

The only valid assumption that an application can make is that it should be safe and legal to access files in the current user's home directory. Access to globally accessed locations, such as temporary directories or the user's home directory, must be handled in a platform-specific manner. For more information about how to determine the user's home directory, see the "Special Directories" section later in this chapter.

PATH SPECIFICATION EXAMPLES

Under DOS and Windows, a fully qualified path name starts with a drive letter and colon and then has a series of directory names separated by backslashes, finally terminating with the filename and extension. Here's an example:

```
C:\Documents and Settings\brian\book\chapter.sxw
```

An application written for DOS or Windows would use this path when trying to open the file chapter.sxw on the C: drive, located in the directory \Documents and Settings\brian\book.

The proliferation of networked computers adds some complexity. Using the previous example, let's assume that the computer you're using is called PARROT and you're sharing the C: drive under the name C_DRIVE. From another computer, you could access the same file as follows:

```
\\PARROT\C_DRIVE\Documents and Settings\brian\book\chapter.sxw
```

Linux uses a different set of conventions. There are no drive letters, and the path separator is a forward slash. So a comparable path name might look like this:

```
/home/brian/book/chapter.sxw
```

where the home directory is attached to a disk drive partition (specified in a mount table, a detail mostly hidden from the application). Remotely networked computers are usually mounted in the same fashion as a disk drive, so the format for a networked file and a local file are identical.

Under Mac OS (prior to OS X), a fully qualified path consisted of the logical volume followed by directories separated by colons:

```
Hard Disk:Local Users:brian:book:chapter.sxw
```

To show a more esoteric example, under the DEC/COMPAQ VMS operating system, the same path might be as follows:

```
USERS$DISK0:[BRIAN.BOOK]chapter.sxw;8
```

Much like DOS and Windows, VMS allows you to specify a physical or logical device volume followed by a colon. The name of the directory path is enclosed by brackets, followed by the filename and an optional semicolon and version number. Networked computers are accessed by a DECnet prefix followed by two colons:

```
PARROT::USERS$DISK0:[BRIAN.BOOK]chapter.sxw;8
```

Macintosh Quirks

Until the arrival of the Macintosh in 1984, operating systems treated files as black boxes containing a chunk of bytes and nothing more. The contents of these files were inferred by extension, through attribute bits (to differentiate executable files from data files), or by searching the file's first few bytes for "magic cookies" indicating the file's type.

The Macintosh approached this from a very different direction. Instead of relying on—or even recognizing—file extensions, the Macintosh's user interface, Finder, relies on type and creator IDs stored in every file. When a user double-clicks a file, the Finder's desktop database is indexed by the file's *creator ID*, returning the appropriate application to open that file. The application is then launched, and it looks at the file's *type ID* to determine how to handle that particular file. While the type and creator IDs are stored in the files, the specific mapping of the type ID to the application is handled by the Finder.

In addition, Macintosh files are divided into two forks: the data fork and the resource fork. The data fork's contents are much like a file on any other operating system, consisting of raw data read and used by the application. The resource fork, however, is a structured database containing just about anything an application may want to store there, such as fonts, thumbnails, formatting information, or even program code. The intent was to separate pure data from application-specific data.

Transporting files from early Macintosh (pre–OS X) systems to nearly everything else became a severe headache. Macintosh users would need to "flatten" their files with special utilities before those files could be copied to a non-Macintosh system.

File Attributes

Files often have attributes assigned to them that control how they are interpreted by the filesystem. Under DOS, for example, a file can be marked as read-only, hidden, or system. Whether a file is considered a program or another type is determined solely by its extension.

Unix filesystems control a file's visibility based on whether it has a leading period in its filename, and a file's executability is determined by a specific attribute bit. In addition, Unix filesystems categorize attributes based on group, the world, and the owner. For example, the owner may have write access, but the world (everyone who is not the owner) might have only read access.

Cross-platform applications should not have to worry too much about filesystem permissions, as long as they do not try to modify or access files other than the current user's files.

Special Directories

Some operating systems have special directories, or folders, where certain files are expected to reside. Compliant applications must respect these locations and use them when possible instead of hardcoding their expectations. For example, the Microsoft Windows operating system recommends installing application files in the Program Files directory and storing user data in the Documents and Settings folder in the user's directory (for example, C:\Documents and Settings\bhook) or somewhere similar, depending on the specific Windows version.

Each operating system has a different way of querying these locations. Windows provides the SHGetFolderPath API. On Unix-like operating systems, the shell will typically expand a special character such as a tilde (~) to the user's home directory; however, this is shell-dependent and not viable in code. Instead, you'll need to call getpwent() to inspect a user's password file entry, from which you can derive the user's home directory.

Text Processing

Surprisingly enough, simple text files often have a bigger problem moving from platform to platform than binary files. There is no standard representation for text files across platforms (not even including the issues associated with internationalization), so something like representing end-of-file or end-of-line indicators can change from system to system.

On Unix systems, the standard for an end-of-file declaration is CTRL-D (0x04). On Windows, however, the end-of-file character is CTRL-Z (0x1A). Thankfully, this is not a major concern today, since most file APIs use the actual file's length to find its end instead of looking for special characters.

The end-of-line marker, however, is still a problem today. The three common ways to mark the end of a line in a text file are shown in Table 13-2.

Table 13-2: Common End-of-Line Markers

Operating System	End-of-Line Character(s)
DOS and Microsoft Windows	CR-LF '\r\n' (0x0A 0x0D)
Unix, Linux, and Mac OS X	LF '\n' (0x0A)
Mac OS	CR '\r' (0x0D)

An application that operates on text files will need to handle all of the different line-ending conventions. On DOS/Windows, the fopen() implementations will often accept a "text mode" flag, which automatically translates CR/LF pairs into LF on read and the reverse on write, along with watching for CTRL-Z as an end-of-file marker. If possible, this extension should be avoided to retain maximum portability.

Applications simply need to deal with supporting all line-ending conventions to remain as compatible as possible, especially if the program will need to edit a file that might use any of those three line-ending conventions.

The C Run-Time Library and Portable File Access

The C standard library provides a set of functions to access files declared in <stdio.h>, including fopen(), fclose(), fread(), fwrite(), ftell(), and fseek(). However, these functions, while portable across standard implementations, have their own limitations.

First, these functions provide only an API to interface to the filesystem; they do not dictate the path format. So while the semantics of these functions may be similar or even identical between platforms, the filename parameters will be system-dependent. Do not assume that fopen("/myfile.txt") will work on anything but a Unix-like filesystem.

Of greater concern—especially with today's hard drives that exceed a hundred gigabytes of storage on even an inexpensive consumer computer— is that functions such as fread(), fwrite(), and fseek() accept size_t parameters, which is analogous to an unsigned integer on most platforms, and thus are limited to how far they can seek. On Win32, for example, a size_t is 32 bits, meaning that a program can seek only up to 4 GB of a file. To breach this limit, you must use a nonportable 64-bit-compatible API, such as _lseeki64().

Summary

With all the confusion and opportunity for error that the different file-systems present, a consistent strategy is vital in order to make file operations manageable and safe. Aside from avoiding many of the invalid assumptions outlined in this chapter, it is helpful if you require the user (or operating system) to construct or specify filenames. The less manipulation of path names an application does, the more portable it will be.

14

SCALABILITY

Portability is more than just a case of "does it run correctly?" Users want the program to run *well*. Performance expectations and resource usage are major issues when developing software for a wide range of platforms. Designing software that is *scalable* across a wide range of different performance and feature profiles is a key element of portable software development.

In this chapter I'll cover how variations in performance can greatly affect a program's portability, and how to work around some of these issues.

Better Algorithms Equal Better Scalability

Computers have become so mind-numbingly fast that differences in performance may sometimes be perceived as academic for typical tasks. The tangible difference in speed between a 1.7 GHz Pentium 4 and a 3 GHz Pentium 4 is negligible for the vast bulk of applications, such as email and web browsing. In contrast to even five years ago, today's programmer can often get by with brute force or naive implementations of many tasks. The concept of optimization is almost as anachronistic as the floppy disk drive.

This can lull a developer into a false sense of security.

When you have more horsepower than you can reasonably harness, it is very easy to forget about efficiency. But when you need to migrate your software to a lower-performance platform, you may find that some of those assumptions are no longer valid.

To put this into numbers, say you need to search for duplicate entries in a 1,000-element database. Originally, you implement this as an $O(N^2)$ linear search, where each item must be compared against every other item. The total time for this operation is formulated as follows:

$$T = \frac{(N^{2C})}{2F}$$

where N is the number of entries, C is the cost per entry in clock cycles, and F is the clock speed of the processor. Suppose that each comparison takes 200 clock cycles, there are 10,000 items, and the CPU has a 2 GHz clock speed. Plugging these values into the equation gives you a run time of about 5 seconds. That's a reasonable length of time for an infrequent operation.

Now let's assume your software is running on a 16 MHz Palm Zire PDA. For argument's sake, let's assume 200 clock cycles as well (although it's very doubtful that the numbers would be even close to each other given the radically different nature of the two architectures). This operation now takes over *10 minutes*, which would make even the most patient user somewhat fidgety.

It's easy to just chalk this up to the hardware and say, "Well, that machine is much faster." However, suppose you switch to a more efficient search algorithm and data structure (in this case, a binary tree):

$$T = \frac{(N(\log N)C)}{F}$$

Now the numbers change dramatically for the average case. So, for the 2 GHz CPU, the time drops down to approximate 0.007 seconds, which is effectively intangible to the end user.

With the Palm Zire, the difference is far more dramatic: it drops to approximately 1.66 seconds, which is much more acceptable to a user than 10 minutes.

By switching to a more efficient data structure, you've made a program that was only theoretically portable become realistically portable. To a user with a 2 GHz CPU, both implementations are reasonably fast. On the slower machine, the change in performance is dramatic.

It's not just raw clock speed that can make a scalability difference. Assumptions about things such as the amount of available RAM can easily come back and bite a developer. It is completely reasonable to implement something that uses a 2 MB stack or a 32 MB temporary heap on a modern desktop PC, but that assumption will fall flat on its face on a handheld or embedded platform.

That said, scalability across an *arbitrary* range of hardware platforms is nearly impossible to achieve. An extreme case is a game meant to run on a wireless cellular phone and, say, an AMD Athlon 64 desktop system. How are you expected to reconcile the monumental differences between the architectures, where the total RAM in the cell phone is less than the level two cache in the Athlon 64? Algorithms that perform well on the high-end system may not be feasible on the low-end one, and practical choices made for the low end may be too limiting for the high end.

Scalability Has Its Limits

Because there are limits to scalability, you need to define *reasonable* baselines, as I suggested in Chapter 1. Code that *can* remain portable should probably remain so, especially library and shared code that is easy to factor out of the main code base, but entire programs are unlikely to port across completely disparate platforms. It's possible, but it's probably not worthwhile.

Some developers will make a big effort to abstract out every possible subsystem so that different, platform-appropriate modules can be plugged in. However, in the end, this approach often imposes an unnecessary level of indirection, where the abstraction interferes with implementation and doesn't buy the programmer any real benefits other than theoretical elegance.

For example, imagine a game developer making a new computer game, Tunnels of Destruction. He would like this game to run on his high-end desktop system and, ideally, on his Pocket PC, which has less memory than the video card in his other system! As powerful as the Microsoft Pocket PC platform has become these days, it is still a far cry even from PCs that are five years old today.

The developer has two choices: write the game twice, or write the game once and abstract it sufficiently so that an appropriate implementation for each subsystem is possible. In the latter case, the subsystems might include artificial intelligence, storage, input, display, sound, and networking—effectively, the entire game except for some very basic glue logic. A lot of engineering effort could be wasted trying to retain what ends up being a minimally useful level of portability.

Even so, some areas may still be portable, so you can't discount it altogether simply because two platforms are dissimilar. Certain subsystems such as ZIP file loading or networking (the WinSock layer on a Pocket PC is very similar to that of a PC) might be shared, but in that case, they should be moved into separate projects and shared by the main game. Trying to force a single source build is, in the long run, likely to cause more problems that it solves.

Summary

Portability must take practical considerations into account. The theoretical elegance of a single source build system is not reason enough to incur the extra complexity to achieve that goal if it doesn't buy you anything in the real world. Share code when it makes sense, but don't force the issue needlessly.

15

PORTABILITY AND DATA

Aside from code, applications rely on external resources such as images, sounds, and text (for internationalization). Developing resources that are easy to move between platforms is just as important as making sure that the code compiles and runs correctly. This chapter discusses the problems and techniques associated with portably sharing data between platforms.

Application Data and Resource Files

Most applications will have some kind of custom data or resource files, often with a custom file format. The first choice when specifying a resource file is whether to use binary or text format for storage.

Binary Files

Binary files are enticing since they are small, trivial to load and process, and provide at least one level of obfuscation from prying eyes. A binary resource file, if properly formatted, can often be loaded with a single file-read operation, along with associated adjustments for byte ordering. This will be significantly faster than loading and parsing even a simple text file.

For example, the AIFF/RIFF file format (used by WAV files) is a *chunked* format. All data can be loaded in one fell swoop and easily parsed in binary form once appropriate byte-ordering adjustments are made.

Text Files

Text files are often recommended as cross-platform proprietary file formats. There is some validity to this, but not as much as many people think. Granted, text files force the developer to avoid assumptions about byte order, size, structure packing, and alignment problems, since there is no option to read directly into an in-memory structure, but that's mostly an issue of discipline, not a fundamental advantage.

SAL EXAMPLE: PARSING A BINARY FILE

The following code snippet shows SAL parsing a binary buffer (presumably read with a single call to fread):

```
sal_error_e
SALx_create_sample_from_wave( SAL_Device *device,
                              SAL_Sample **pp_sample,
                              const void *kp_src,
                              int src_size )
{
    int i;
    int src_frame_size;
    int num_samples;
    SAL_DeviceInfo dinfo;
    _SAL_WaveHeader wh;
    _SAL_WaveChunk  wc;
    const sal_byte_t *kp_bytes = ( const sal_byte_t * ) kp_src;
    sal_byte_t *p_dst = 0;

    if ( device == 0 || pp_sample == 0 || kp_src == 0 ||
         src_size < sizeof( _SAL_WaveHeader ) )
    {
        return SALERR_INVALIDPARAM;
    }

    *pp_sample = 0;
```

```
        /* we can use memcpy() since it's four bytes */
        memcpy( wh.wh_riff, kp_bytes, 4 );
        kp_bytes += 4;
        wh.wh_size = POSH_ReadU32FromLittle( kp_bytes );
        kp_bytes += 4;
        memcpy( wh.wh_wave, kp_bytes, 4 );
        kp_bytes += 4;
        memcpy( wh.wh_fmt, kp_bytes, 4 );
        kp_bytes += 4;
        wh.wh_chunk_header_size = POSH_ReadU32FromLittle( kp_bytes );
        kp_bytes += 4;

        /* verify that this is a legit WAV file */
        if ( strncmp( wh.wh_riff, "RIFF", 4 ) ||
             strncmp( wh.wh_wave, "WAVE", 4 ) ||
             wh.wh_chunk_header_size != 16 )
        {
            return SALERR_INVALIDPARAM;
        }

        /* read in the chunk */
        wc.wc_tag = POSH_ReadI16FromLittle( kp_bytes ); kp_bytes += 2;
        wc.wc_num_channels = POSH_ReadI16FromLittle( kp_bytes ); kp_bytes += 2;
        wc.wc_sample_rate = POSH_ReadI32FromLittle( kp_bytes ); kp_bytes += 4;
        wc.wc_bytes_per_second = POSH_ReadI32FromLittle( kp_bytes ); kp_bytes += 4;
        wc.wc_alignment = POSH_ReadI16FromLittle( kp_bytes ); kp_bytes += 2;
        wc.wc_bits_per_sample = POSH_ReadI16FromLittle( kp_bytes ); kp_bytes += 2;
        memcpy( wc.wc_data, kp_bytes, 4 ); kp_bytes += 4;
        wc.wc_data_size  POSH_ReadI32FromLittle( kp_bytes ); kp_bytes += 4;
        /* etc. etc. */
}
```

Parsing the binary file is simplicity itself; bytes are processed sequentially and reassembled into appropriate values. The parser is careful not to assume anything about alignment, padding, byte order, or sizes, other than what is rigidly defined for the WAV file format. There is no need for an intermediate line or token buffer such as you would expect with a text parser. Of course, there is still a lot of room for error, especially if the file is malformed.

While blindly reading a file directly into a structure is very dangerous:

```
_SAL_WaveHeader wh;

    fread( &wh, sizeof( wh ), 1, fp );
```

sometimes it is reasonable; for example, on a fixed platform where you have complete control over the structure and packing of both data and code. The extra performance derived from this is sometimes worth it, and even though it's theoretically unsafe, remember that *portable programming is about converting implicit assumptions to explicit edicts.*

That said, text files are trivial to modify with easily available tools on most systems, such as vi on Linux, Notepad on Windows, and TextEdit on Mac OS X. This means that making configuration and last-minute changes is very easy. In addition, large numbers of text files can be efficiently edited, searched, and modified using standard tools such as Perl, sed, awk, head, tail, and grep. This property of text files is *very* powerful and should not be underestimated.

However, text files present their own set of problems. Since there is no universal standard for text file encoding (as discussed in Chapter 13), dealing with all the different text file formats can become complex. In addition, the developer must now write a text parser, which is a far more complex and error-prone task than reassembling values from a binary byte stream.

Finally, text files are usually significantly larger than their binary counterparts. A 32-bit value in binary form consumes 4 bytes in binary, and it may consume up to 10 bytes as decimal text. But text does compress well, so size might not be much of an issue, assuming the developer is willing to incorporate file decompression into his application.

XML

When people talk about text data files, the discussion invariably ends up at XML (eXtensible Markup Language), a more general version of the ubiquitous HTML used on the Web. XML enforces rigid, standardized file structures and has some advantages:

- Wide availability of XML parsing libraries and editing and inspection tools
- Well-understood, popular, and standardized syntax
- Support for structured and nested data formats

However, these advantages mostly just make up for the disadvantages of text file formats in general.

XML parsing libraries are often extremely large. In some cases, the XML library alone may be larger than your application (but their presence at least minimizes the problems associated with implementing a text file format). Also, if XML is manageable only through the use of an external library then, by definition, portability is reduced to the subset of platforms supported by the specific library.

The following is an example of an XML configuration file:

```
<MyAppConfig>
  <UserName>Brian Hook</UserName>
  <RegCode>8812BBC520DCF71C</RegCode>
  <SysConfig>
    <FullScreen>1</FullScreen>
    <MouseLock>1</MouseLock>
```

```
    <Volume>46</Volume>
  </SysConfig>
</MyAppConfig>
```

As you can see, that's quite a bit of verbiage for something simple. In many cases, XML is overkill when a simple, line-oriented text file format can be used instead. In the end, the right choice depends entirely on the needs of the application and development team.

Scripting Languages as Data Files

If you're already using an embedding scripting language such as Lua or Python, you have a text file format and parser for free. Instead of loading and parsing a data file, an application can load and execute a script, pushing the responsibility of parsing and validation into the scripting language implementation. By leveraging the existing implementation and any additional tools, instead of writing a parser from scratch, a developer can save a significant amount of time and effort. See Chapter 17 for more on scripting languages.

Creating Portable Graphics

When you're developing portable software, your bitmap images, icons, splash screens, and other graphics assets will need to move from platform to platform. Each target system will have its own preferred display sizes, aspect ratios, and color depth. Some may even prefer a specific file format. For example, Binary Run-time Environment for Wireless (BREW) and Windows both prefer the BMP format for bitmaps, whereas the Amiga used IFF/LBM.

Designing artwork so that it can be reformatted appropriately for a specific platform, either as a preprocess step or dynamically by the application, is a difficult task. The standard technique is to create art files at the highest resolution necessary, and then filter and quantize the images down depending on the requirements of a particular target system. Unfortunately, this doesn't always work, since the disparity between some platforms can be so great that making meaningful art for both extremes is nearly impossible. Some programs, such as Adobe Acrobat, work well across multiple platforms, but they operate within a limited domain (text with some moderate graphics) and limit themselves to scalable technologies such as PostScript to achieve this.

For example, the original Palm OS PDA is a 160-by-160 square screen with grayscale or 8-bit (256-color) paletted color graphics. A modern Macintosh may have high-resolution displays (1920-by-1200) with 32-bit color. Images created for the Palm will not look good on the Macintosh. Images created for the Macintosh will often turn to unidentifiable mush if resized and filtered down to meet the limitations of the Palm. So, when dealing with wildly disparate platforms, sometimes single-source (or, in this case, single-image) portability will not be practical.

Creating Portable Audio

As digital audio becomes standard on most computers—even lowly PDAs have modest sound capabilities these days—users increasingly expect audible cues while working. From something as simple as a beep notifying the user of an error, to full-featured sound while playing a game, audio is an important part of the computing experience today.

As with computer graphics, sound capabilities can range from incredibly primitive (monaural 4-bit PCM) to extremely advanced (Dolby Digital 5.1 surround sound). However, the feature difference isn't quite as dramatic as with graphics, so it's a bit more manageable.

At the high end, while Dolby Digital 5.1 is finding traction in higher-end personal computers, the bulk of users still use only a pair of speakers or headphones, so stereo or even monaural sound is often sufficient. You'll want to start with the highest-resolution files reasonable, such as uncompressed, stereo, 44.1 KHz, 16-bit PCM waveforms. From there, it's easy to use off-the-shelf tools to convert to lower-resolution, compressed formats appropriate for each of your target platforms. As with graphics, some audio assets do not convert down particularly well, so they may require manual adjustment or tweaking. Sounds with a lot of high-frequency content will often sound muddy or unintelligible when resampled, and quiet noises may have too much noise when quantized to a lower-resolution format.

Summary

As if writing code that runs between multiple platforms isn't enough of a task by itself, simply trying to share data between platforms can turn into a frustrating experience for developers and users alike. Files may have data stored in different formats and byte ordering, and in some cases the files themselves may be missing key data lost during the transition from one system to another. Using text files exclusively can mitigate these problems to some degree; however, this is at the cost of larger file size and increased time to load and parse.

16

INTERNATIONALIZATION AND LOCALIZATION

The rise of the Internet and the World Wide Web has created a global software market. The days of writing for just one market are ending, especially with the increased popularity of electronic software distribution (ESD) for delivery. If you sell your software on the Web, you won't know if your customer is down the street or in a different country. In this chapter we'll go over some of the issues involved when trying to expand your markets to cultures and locales outside your own.

The terms *internationalization* and *localization* are sometimes used interchangeably, although they are distinct (but related) processes. Internationalization consists of developing and preparing an application so that it can be localized easily. Localization is the process of taking an internationalized application and customizing it for a particular language, region, and/or culture (collectively known as a *locale*). Often, the application will be developed by one group, but the localization itself will be contracted out to another group that is familiar with a specific locale. So, internationalization and localization are two steps in the process of making software more accessible to a wider range of countries, cultures, and languages.

Internationalization and localization are very complex topics. Here, I'll touch on the important issues related to portability.

Strings and Unicode

The most obvious difference between regions is language—software written for English speakers will not be very friendly for French-speaking users. Much of the language-specific data is embedded as strings in an application. Here is an example:

```
void load_file( const char *filename )
{
   FILE *fp = fopen( filename, "r" );
   if ( fp == 0 )
   {
      /* this assumes that the error is displayed to an English-
      language user! */
      my_error( "Could not open file '%s'", filename )
      return;
   }
   . . .
}
```

Changing the error message in this code fragment requires manually altering the string and recompiling the executable. It's marginally better if you use a macro, like this:

```
#ifdef ENGLISH
#define COULD_NOT_OPEN "Could not open file '%s'"
#elif defined FRENCH
#define COULD_NOT_OPEN "n'a pas pu ouvrir le dossier '%s'"
#endif
void load_file( const char *filename )
{
   FILE *fp = fopen( filename, "r" );
   if ( fp == 0 )
   {
      my_error( COULD_NOT_OPEN, filename )
      return;
   }
   . . .
}
```

However, even though changing the message requires only setting a global macro, a new executable is necessary for each language, which is far from ideal.

Ideally, you could load the string dynamically based on the target system's locale setting. Microsoft Windows supports this through *string tables*, and Mac OS X supports this through *strings files* (for text embedded in the program) and .nib files (for the user interface).

Accessing a localized string is then performed with the appropriate API call, such as `LoadString()` on Windows or `NSLocalizedString()`/`CFCopyLocalizedString()` on OS X.

While platform-specific string-loading APIs do provide adequate solutions, they also decrease portability by introducing another abstraction layer and resource file to implement and manage. It's just as easy to create your own string table implementation that maps from one string to another based on the locale.

For example, you could make a file format that consists of key/value pairs, sectioned by language:

```
[English]
"Yes"= "Yes"
"No"="No"
[French]
"Yes"="Oui"
"No"="Non"
[Spanish]
"Yes"="Si"
"No"="No"
```

Localized strings can then be retrieved through a simple API that takes strings in the programmer's native language and returns locale-specific strings:

```
International_SetLocale( "French" );
my_message_box( International_GetString( "Do you wish to quit?" ),
                International_GetString( "Yes",
                International_GetString( "No" ) );
```

This has the advantage of working regardless of a particular operating system's underlying notion of string localization.

Currency

More than 180 currencies are in use throughout the world, many with different names and formatting conventions. Hardcoding a particular currency can lead to a cultural mismatch—not everyone understands what a dollar is.

In addition, different countries denote decimal portions of a value differently. For example, in the United States, it's common to write $1.23 for one dollar and twenty-three cents; in Europe, this amount might appear as 1,23. The former might confuse non-American users, and the latter could throw non-Europeans for a loop.

Date and Time

Like currency, time and date have many different representations. Certainly, every country agrees that time is divided into hours and minutes, but their individual notations vary quite a bit.

Americans use the *hour:minute* format, sometimes with a 24-hour clock, but often with a 12-hour clock, using AM or PM to denote morning versus night. For example, 13:30 and 1:30 PM both represent one hour and thirty minutes after noon. Some countries substitute a period for the colon (for example, Finland would use 13.30). There is a slow but steady move to support the ISO standard time format: a 24-hour time notation separated by colons (13:30:00.00).

Dates are a bit trickier because of the many different permutations for the order of month, day, and year. Separators also change, and, of course, the names of months depend on the local language.

One of the most frequent areas of confusion is the ordering month/day/year versus day/month/year. In the United States, the eleventh day of the eighth month (August) is represented as 8/11/2005 or 8-11-2005. In most other countries, this same date is formatted as 11/8/2005, 11-8-2005, or 11.8.2005. So a non-American reader who sees 8-11-2004 would assume November 8, 2005. This obviously affects Americans and non-Americans equally, depending on the nationality of the writer.

As with time, an ISO standard is intended to help alleviate any ambiguity. This standard dictates the form *YYYY-MM-DD*, as in 2005-08-11.

Portable software that is meant to run on international systems should track the date and time numerically and then use a locale-specific formatting function to convert from a canonical form to a locally compatible form.

This avoids all ambiguity. Conversely, code such as the following should be considered a relic of bygone ages:

```
void get_time_string( int h, int m, int s, char *buffer )
{
    /*
    For brevity I'm not checking for buffer safety here, but the
    point is that you should not hardcode the colons or make
    assumptions about the incoming range of values
    */
    sprintf( buffer, "%02d:%02d:%02d", h, m, s );
    return buffer;
}
```

Interface Elements

Localization issues aren't limited solely to text. Since modern applications depend more and more on graphical output to convey information, developers must contend with the localization of graphical content such as bitmaps and icons.

Icons familiar to one developer aren't necessarily relevant to someone from another culture. An open hand, facing palm outward, might mean "stop" to an American or European, but to someone from West Africa, this is considered an insulting gesture. The picture of a rural mailbox means "mail" to a lot of Americans, but in cultures where mail is delivered to centralized stations or through door slots, it's a meaningless reference. These types of elements should be set up so they are easily substituted during localization.

Keyboards

It is obvious that if a language has a different alphabet, then a different keyboard will be required. Yet, it's still quite common to see instructions that say something like "Please press the ~ key to open this menu" or "Pressing CTRL-$ performs this function," when many of the world's languages simply don't have a concept of the ~ or $ characters.

This problem is not limited to radically dissimilar languages such as English and Tamil. There are notable differences, such as currency, between keyboards in the United States and the United Kingdom, even though the languages are extremely similar.

Even relying on the physical location of a key instead of the key's assumed meaning doesn't always work. Scan codes (the raw value generated by a key, prior to any translation to a character value) often move around on a keyboard depending on the language, manufacturer, and form factor (desktop, notebook, or phone). The most common example is scan code 0x2B, the backslash key on English language keyboards. This key is above the ENTER/RETURN key on most United States keyboards, but to the left of the ENTER/RETURN key on non–United States English keyboards.

Summary

The increasing accessibility to international markets has allowed software developers to reach more and more distant (and foreign) customers. Small software organizations often don't have the expertise necessary to understand and create localization procedures, and thus their software suffers from cultural selfishness, because it's designed to interact with users of the same cultural and language background as the developers.

To avoid confusing and discouraging foreign users, software developers should move as much locale-specific information out of their executables and into data files that can be selected by the end user via a localization menu (or, better yet, automatically by querying the system for its locale information). Avoid hardcoded assumptions or dependencies on particular keyboard, date, and time formats. Design bitmaps and other interface elements to be as culturally neutral as possible, since some common idioms may be more culturally biased than many developers realize.

17

SCRIPTING LANGUAGES

ANSI C and C++ suffer from many portability problems, primarily because they are low-level languages specifically designed to allow, or even encourage, binding tightly to a particular system. System-level APIs and in-memory object layouts are exposed directly to the developer, so when an application is written entirely in one of these languages, it is often implicitly tied to the underlying platform.

If, instead, you write your application using a much higher-level language—one that doesn't truck in concepts such as memory layout, pointers, packing, alignment, or low-level system APIs—many portability problems vanish. Of course, many of the advantages of C and C++—such as higher performance and access to the very facilities that make portability difficult—are also lost.

A good compromise is to code in C/C++ only those parts of the program that need maximum performance and/or low-level access, and then develop the rest of the application using a portable high-level scripting language, such as Ruby, Python, or Lua. Languages such as these tend to be robust, system-agnostic, and embeddable (easy to integrate with another code base), while still retaining acceptable performance.

Hundreds of different high-level languages are in use today. Some are application-specific scripting languages, such as Autodesk AutoCAD's Alisp, GNU Emacs's Elisp, Alias|Wavefront Maya's MEL, and Discreet 3ds Max's MaxScript. Others, including Java, LISP, OCaml, and C#, are more general and suitable for high-level application development. The ones we're interested in are a subset known as *embeddable scripting languages*, specifically designed to integrate easily with a larger application. They have well-defined interfaces to low-level languages and often provide extensive support for utility packages. In this chapter, we'll take a look at a few of the more popular languages: Lua, Ruby, Python, and ECMAScript/JavaScript. Visit the Great Computer Language Shootout website (http://shootout.alioth.debian.org/great/index.php?sort=fullcpu) to compare the performance of various programming languages.

Some Scripting Language Disadvantages

By converting large swaths of code to a portable scripting language, an application can isolate itself from platform-specific idiosyncrasies. Why deal with low-level details if low-level access is not a requirement?

But you won't be surprised to hear that there are some downsides to using a scripting language. The first is performance. Most scripting languages are either interpreted or compiled to a generic bytecode, which is then executed by a *virtual machine*. Script interpretation or virtual machine execution is much slower than executing native instructions generated by a compiler. However, many applications don't need this level of performance except in a few core places, which may be written in a traditional compiled language. So, the difference in performance is often more of a theoretical concern than a practical one.

A much greater problem is the lack of high-quality tools for many scripting languages. Debuggers, profilers, and syntax checkers are often unavailable for scripting languages, and even when they are, they're often crude. The tools for scripting languages are not nearly as mature or popular as tools for more prevalent languages such as C, C++, and Java. This means that while you might save a lot of time by avoiding portability problems, some of that time is lost again due to the inefficiencies of using a less mature development environment.

Finally, by their very nature, scripting languages are "above the metal," which means that if you do need to do some low-level operation—such as execute a system API or simply twiddle some bits—you'll need to implement some circuitous hacks or find a package that provides the necessary low-level features. For example, the Lua language does not offer low-level features such as bit manipulation. As a result, this feature must be emulated clumsily in the scripting language or implemented through a helper library written in a lower-level language.

JavaScript/ECMAScript

JavaScript is a lightweight, embeddable scripting language originally developed by Netscape in the mid-1990s. Originally intended to act as a hook for Java applets, it quickly became used (abused?) as a way to make web pages dynamic and animated. Many developers don't realize that JavaScript is a language on its own, capable of standing apart from the Web, browsers, and HTML. Granted, these are the applications for which JavaScript is most famous, but they are not required environments for a JavaScript program.

The name JavaScript was a political/marketing invention. The language was originally called LiveScript, but because of Netscape's close relationship with Sun, and to capitalize on the hype generated over Java, LiveScript became JavaScript.

Microsoft, loath to let a perceived threat develop a standard without Microsoft's input, implemented its own variant, called JScript, which was a lot like JavaScript but different enough to annoy and irritate users and developers alike. Since then, there has been a constant struggle among various factions, as the different dialects slowly converge and drift apart between browser revisions.

Netscape submitted JavaScript to the European Computer Manufacturers Association (ECMA) for standardization, and both Netscape and Microsoft have agreed to adhere to ECMA's standards (ECMA-262). The language name changed again, this time to ECMAScript.

Thankfully, much of the fuss associated with JavaScript can be ignored by application developers who want to embed its functionality inside their applications.

JavaScript is easy to embed into larger programs if you use the open-source SpiderMonkey Engine, available at http://www.mozilla.org/js/spidermonkey. It is a well-tested and documented, 100 percent C implementation of the JavaScript language, and it has a very friendly license (the Mozilla Public License).

So, as a language, how does JavaScript stack up? First off, it's not blazingly fast. It's completely interpreted, so it lacks even the basic compilation-to-bytecode performance optimization that other languages possess. I would not recommend writing performance-sensitive modules in JavaScript. However, it is sufficient for higher-level application control.

JavaScript is also a fairly primitive language in terms of features. It is loosely typed, has automatic memory management, and supports exceptions. It is also *prototype-based*, which means that a programmer does not define new types (as in C, C++, or Java), but instead clones another object (the prototype) and modifies the new object. Variables are typeless and do not need to be explicitly declared.

The language has intrinsic support for *hash tables* (also known as *associative arrays* or *dictionaries*), which is a pretty powerful feature. In fact, all objects are basically just name/value pairs stored in hash table format. JavaScript has all the standard control flow features: if/else statements, switches, for, do/while, and while. In most respects, the syntax should be very familiar to a C, C++, or Java programmer.

JavaScript also has another major advantage: monumental amounts of documentation. Dozens of books and websites are devoted to the language, so finding sample source code for JavaScript is never difficult. There is also an abundance of JavaScript programmers as well, so finding experienced JavaScript programmers is not that difficult. (Most JavaScript programmers are actually web designers who have little formal training with programming, so the numbers can be misleading.)

Python

Python is one of the most popular dedicated scripting languages available today. This popularity is due in large part to its comprehensive feature set, robustness, and mind-boggling number of support libraries available for almost every purpose. The user community's size guarantees that the language is well documented, both on the Web and in print.

Python is a fairly modern language and provides many of the features a programmer would expect from a compiled language: classes, multiple inheritance, exception handling, native data types for dictionaries and lists, lambda functions, modules/packages, strong typing, garbage collection, and generators/list comprehensions. Python is easy to embed in an application, but it also operates effectively as a stand-alone application language.

The biggest complaint with Python is that many consider it bloated—the language's power comes at a price in terms of memory footprint. Also, the sheer complexity of the language can make it somewhat daunting for first-time programmers, but numerous tutorials are specifically aimed at the novice programmer.

For more information about Python, visit http://www.python.org.

Lua

Lua is a relatively new scripting language rapidly gaining popularity, particularly with game programmers. The authors of the language are staunch minimalists, and one of Lua's greatest strengths is its diminutive footprint. In many ways, Lua is similar to JavaScript in terms of features, although it is much smaller and faster than JavaScript. Like SpiderMonkey, Lua uses a very friendly license (the MIT License—more information at http://www.opensource.org/licenses/mit-license.php).

Lua programs are compiled from source code into bytecodes, which are then executed by the Lua virtual machine, providing a considerable speed boost. Lua is particularly adept at table operations. Its core data structure is the hash table (much like JavaScript). In fact, Lua has only seven data types: threads, user data, functions, booleans, numbers, strings, and tables. Lua is also a garbage-collected language, so memory management is automatically handled by the implementation.

Lua lacks many of the features that are provided by larger languages—such as classes, inheritance, and exception handling—but it does possess the capability to emulate these properties. You can find a growing number of support packages for tasks such as debugging, math, networking, database interfacing input/output, and operating system calls. There is also a very active (if small) user community. More information on Lua can be found at http://www.lua.org.

Ruby

Ruby shares many of the same properties as Python. It has a very large, dedicated user base, can be embedded, and provides many of the same features. Philosophically, Ruby comes from the Smalltalk "everything is an object" school of thought. In some ways, Ruby is the bastard child of Smalltalk and Perl, supporting the latter's strong text-processing and pattern-matching abilities with the former's object hierarchy.

Unlike Python, Ruby supports only single inheritance, which simplifies large portions of the language. Ruby is more object-oriented than Python and has a slightly cleaner syntax. It is considered a bit more modern, but it has significantly slower performance than Python.

The Ruby website is http://www.ruby-lang.org.

Summary

The use of higher-level scripting languages is a great way to reduce portability problems when migrating an application between platforms. The downside is reduced performance and a dependency on the makers of the scripting languages to support each platform that you will target.

18

CROSS-PLATFORM LIBRARIES AND TOOLKITS

After reading this book, you may be thinking, "Hey, portable software development can be pretty complicated stuff, but it's not impossible—so how come it's not a solved problem?" To some degree, it has been solved, with the move to higher-level languages that isolate the programmer from system-specific information. But when you must use a lower-level language, the issues described in this book still rear their heads with alarming frequency.

To alleviate some portability problems, various entities have developed numerous cross-platform libraries and frameworks, which are available either commercially or for free. In this chapter, we'll look at using libraries and application frameworks to develop portable code.

Libraries

Libraries are packages of related code and data designed to address a particular problem. Cross-platform libraries typically provide a universal interface to an abstraction, which, in turn, is implemented on each target system transparently. Many cross-platform libraries, both commercial and open source, are available today. Some have gained almost universal adoption due to their portability, robustness, and usefulness. For any conceivable task, there is probably an existing library to make it easier to implement that task on a wide range of platforms.

NOTE   *In fact, in many cases, the operating system itself was developed as a portability library. CP/M was designed in the late 1970s as an aid to portability for developers targeting Zilog Z80-based microcomputers (see Chapter 11), and Microsoft's original Windows NT operating system was envisioned to run across a wide range of microprocessors (MIPS R4000, Intel 386, and DEC Alpha), largely isolating the developer from the system choice of an end user.*

The hardest part is integrating the various libraries, since each library has a tendency to redefine many of the same types and symbols, or has particular expectations about how it will be built and integrated with an application.

Application Frameworks

Beyond libraries are *application frameworks* (not to be confused with Mac OS X's frameworks), whose key difference from libraries is that they are meant to subsume the entire application in their architecture. Developers don't call an application framework the way they might a library; instead, their code is absorbed by the framework. There is a much larger commitment when choosing to use an application framework.

Numerous application frameworks have been developed to bridge the differences between the various flavors of Unix, Windows, Macintosh, and other operating systems. For the most part, they attempt to abstract and unify access to the window system (widgets, gadgets, controls, windows, and so on), input, event handling, multithreading, file I/O, networking, and 2D/3D graphics. Some are commercial, but a good bulk of them are open source. Here, we'll look at a few examples.

Qt

Trolltech's Qt is a C++ cross-platform operating system abstraction library that allows developers to make a single-source application that can easily retarget Windows, Linux, HP-UX, and Solaris.

One of the nice things about Qt is that, while it is a commercial library, it is also open source and free for noncommercial use. If you plan on developing a commercial application that is closed source, you need to pay for a license. For more information, visit http://www.trolltech.com.

GTK+

GTK is a C library that was originally developed as a cross-platform user-interface library for GIMP, the GNU Image Manipulation Program, but has since grown into a separate library outside GIMP. It supports Linux, Windows, BeOS, and Mac OS X.

GTK+ is licensed under the GNU LGPL (http://www.opensource.org/licenses/lgpl-license.php), which makes it palatable for most commercial, closed-source development. You can find GTK+ documentation and source code at http://www.gtk.org.

FLTK

FLTK (Fast Lightweight Toolkit) is a cross-platform library written in C++ that supports Microsoft Windows, Unix/Linux (X Windows), and Mac OS X. As the name indicates, it is intended to be very lightweight, so that linking it into an application has minimal impact on its footprint.

FLTK is released under the FLTK License, which is basically the GNU GPL with an exception stating that you can statically link to FLTK without needing to distribute the source code to your own programs or libraries. The FLTK website is www.fltk.org.

wxWidgets

Formerly known as wxWindows, wxWidgets is one of the most popular cross-platform toolkits. It's a C++ application framework that has been around since 1992. wxWidgets is available for Windows and Linux, and it even supports sitting on top of GTK+. OS/2 and WinCE versions are also available in various states of completion.

The wxWidgets license is one of the more commercial friendly ones, effectively allowing developers to use it with very few restrictions. You can read more about wxWidgets at http://www.wxwidgets.org.

Summary

Libraries and frameworks present an interesting dilemma to developers: are the short-term gains of these tools greater than the long-term risk of losing control over an important part of your code base?

For example, the Qt library by Trolltech allows you to write an application that almost transparently compiles and runs on Mac OS X, Linux, and Microsoft Windows. Programmers who don't have the resources or experience to perform three native ports may find something like Qt a lifesaver. However, these same developers are now tied to a particular API, for better or for worse. If they find themselves with an urgent need to target an unsupported platform, they might be out of luck.

Relying on a third-party toolkit is not an action to be taken lightly. You must ensure the following:

- The library is available for platforms that you must support.
- Source code is available, so in the event you must support a new platform, you may do so.

You must take great care when committing to something that will give you "instant" cross-platform support, since such ease often comes with the cost of limited future portability.

POSH

A lot of work goes into writing a cross-platform code. However, every project seems to repeat the same effort when it comes to abstracting fundamental types, function signatures, and utilities to swap bytes; determining byte ordering; and performing the other mundane tasks associated with cross-platform development.

To avoid this, I've developed a completely free library, the Portable Open Source Harness (POSH) that automatically detects (within reason) the host and target platforms at compile time and provides appropriate types, macros, and functions as necessary.

POSH consists of a single header file (posh.h) and an optional source file (posh.c). Documentation and source code can be found at http://www.poshlib.org. I would have liked to include the source code for posh.h and posh.c here, but combined, they are about 2,000 lines. That would consume a lot of printed pages—a waste of paper and space. I think it's fairly reasonable to assume that anyone reading this book can access the website to download the most recent versions of those files.

POSH examines the compilation environment (predefined symbols) through a chain of #ifdefs to infer the host and target specifications. It's fairly robust, although still quite a bit of hackery (but that's the life of a portable software developer).

In this appendix, I'll provide an overview of POSH, including its exported and imported symbols, fixed-size types, and helper macros and functions.

POSH Predefined Symbols

The primary goal of POSH is to export its own symbols and types for programs that wish to be portable but don't have the luxury of relying on the C99 header files stdint.h and inttypes.h.

After posh.h has been included, the symbols listed in Table A-1 are defined.

Table A-1: POSH Exported Symbols

Preprocessor Symbol	Meaning
POSH_OS_STRING	Textual description of the target operating system
POSH_CPU_STRING	Textual description of the target CPU
POSH_CDECL	Synonym for appropriate function name decoration indicating C-style argument passing (x86-specific)
POSH_STDCALL	Synonym for appropriate function name decoration indicating stdcall-style argument passing (x86-specific)
POSH_FASTCALL	Synonym for appropriate function name decoration indicating fastcall-style argument passing (x86-specific)
POSH_IMPORTEXPORT	Function signature decoration to determine import or export for use of a DLL/shared library
POSH_BIG_ENDIAN	Set to 1 if target is big-endian
POSH_LITTLE_ENDIAN	Set to 1 if target is little-endian
POSH_ENDIAN_STRING	Textual description that should match the POSH_BIG_ENDIAN or POSH_LITTLE_ENDIAN setting
POSH_64BIT_INTEGER	Set to 1 if target supports 64-bit integers (not necessarily natively, but at least as a data type)
POSH_64BIT_POINTER	Set to 1 if target supports 64-bit integers (but not necessarily addressing)

In some instances, POSH may require the programmer's assistance when configuring the compile-time environment. Table A-2 lists the macros that should be defined.

Table A-2: POSH Imported Symbols

Macro	Purpose
POSH_BUILDING_LIB	Should be defined when building any libraries. Controls the definition of POSH_IMPORTEXPORT when building a DLL/shared library.
POSH_DLL	Should be defined when building or using a DLL/shared library.
POSH_NO_FLOAT	Disables floating-point support if set to 1.

POSH Fixed-Size Types

In addition to predefined symbols, POSH provides global exact-sized type identifiers, as listed in Table A-3.

Table A-3: POSH Exact-Sized Type Identifiers

Type Definition	Meaning
posh_i64_t	64-bit signed integer
posh_u64_t	64-bit unsigned integer
posh_i32_t	32-bit signed integer
posh_u32_t	32-bit unsigned integer
posh_i16_t	16-bit signed integer
posh_u16_t	16-bit unsigned integer
posh_i8_t	8-bit signed integer
posh_u8_t	8-bit unsigned integer
posh_byte_t	8-bit unsigned integer

POSH Utility Functions and Macros

Not all cross-platform work can be abstracted into a few symbols and types. POSH includes some optional helper macros and functions that streamline operations such as serialization, deserialization, and byte swapping. The only nonvital function is POSH_GetArchString(), which returns a pointer to a const string describing the current platform (after performing a basic sanity check on the run-time environment, such as ensuring that the run-time determination of byte ordering matches the compile-time assumption). This is handy when debugging code on a new system.

Table A-4 lists the POSH helper macros.

Table A-4: POSH Helper Macros

Macro	Purpose	Requires posh.c?
POSH_COMPILE_TIME_ASSERT(name,exp)	Compile-time assertion macro	No
POSH_I64(x)	Defines x as a 64-bit signed constant	No
POSH_U64(x)	Defines x as a 64-bit unsigned constant	No
POSH_LittleU16(x)	Converts unsigned x to little-endian form	Yes
POSH_LittleU32(x)	Converts unsigned x to little-endian form	Yes
POSH_LittleU64(x)	Converts unsigned x to little-endian form	Yes
POSH_LittleI16(x)	Converts signed x to little-endian form	Yes
POSH_LittleI32(x)	Converts signed x to little-endian form	Yes
POSH_LittleI64(x)	Converts signed x to little-endian form	Yes
POSH_BigU16(x)	Converts unsigned x to big-endian form	Yes
POSH_BigU32(x)	Converts unsigned x to big-endian form	Yes
POSH_BigU64(x)	Converts unsigned x to big-endian form	Yes
POSH_BigI16(x)	Converts signed x to big-endian form	Yes
POSH_BigI32(x)	Converts signed x to big-endian form	Yes
POSH_BigI64(x)	Converts signed x to big-endian form	Yes

Table A-5 lists the floating-point helper functions. All of these functions require posh.c and may be selectively disabled (for example, for systems that lack floating point) by defining POSH_NO_FLOAT.

Table A-5: POSH Floating-Point Helper Functions

Function	Purpose
POSH_LittleFloatBits	Extracts 32-bit floating-point representation as little-endian integer bits*
POSH_BigFloatBits	Extracts 32-bit floating-point representation as big-endian integer bits*
POSH_FloatFromLittleBits	Converts a 32-bit little-endian integer pattern to a floating-point value*
POSH_FloatFromBigBits	Converts a 32-bit big-endian integer pattern to a floating-point value*
POSH_DoubleBits	Converts a 64-bit double to a sequence of 8 bytes*
POSH_DoubleFromBits	Converts a sequence of 8 bytes to a double-precision floating-point value*
POSH_WriteFloatToLittle	Writes a floating-point value in little-endian form to a byte stream

Table A-5: POSH Floating-Point Helper Functions (continued)

Function	Purpose
POSH_WriteFloatToBig	Writes a floating-point value in big-endian form to a byte stream
POSH_ReadFloatFromLittle	Reads a floating-point value from a little-endian byte stream
POSH_ReadFloatFromBig	Reads a floating-point value from a big-endian byte stream
POSH_WriteDoubleToLittle	Writes a double-precision floating-point value to a little-endian byte stream
POSH_WriteDoubleToBig	Writes a double-precision floating-point value to a big-endian byte stream
POSH_ReadDoubleFromLittle	Reads a double-precision floating-point value from a little-endian byte stream
POSH_ReadDoubleFromBig	Reads a double-precision floating-point value from a big-endian byte stream

* Present only if 64-bit computing is available

Table A-6 lists the serialization and deserialization functions implemented in posh.c.

Table A-6: POSH Serialization and Deserialization Functions

Function	Purpose
POSH_SwapU16	Byte-swaps an unsigned 16-bit value
POSH_SwapI16	Byte-swaps a signed 16-bit value
POSH_SwapU32	Byte-swaps an unsigned 32-bit value
POSH_SwapI32	Byte-swaps a signed 32-bit value
POSH_WriteU16ToLittle	Writes an unsigned 16-bit quantity to a little-endian buffer
POSH_WriteU32ToLittle	Writes an unsigned 32-bit quantity to a little-endian buffer
POSH_WriteU64ToLittle	Writes an unsigned 64-bit quantity to a little-endian buffer
POSH_WriteI16ToLittle	Writes a signed 16-bit quantity to a little-endian buffer
POSH_WriteI32ToLittle	Writes a signed 32-bit quantity to a little-endian buffer
POSH_WriteI64ToLittle	Writes a signed 64-bit quantity to a little-endian buffer
POSH_WriteU16ToBig	Writes an unsigned 16-bit quantity to a big-endian buffer
POSH_WriteU32ToBig	Writes an unsigned 32-bit quantity to a big-endian buffer
POSH_WriteU64ToBig	Writes an unsigned 64-bit quantity to a big-endian buffer
POSH_WriteI16ToBig	Writes a signed 16-bit quantity to a big-endian buffer
POSH_WriteI32ToBig	Writes a signed 32-bit quantity to a big-endian buffer
POSH_WriteI64ToBig	Writes a signed 64-bit quantity to a big-endian buffer
POSH_ReadU16FromLittle	Reads an unsigned 16-bit quantity from a little-endian buffer

Table A-6: POSH Serialization and Deserialization Functions (continued)

Function	Purpose
POSH_ReadU32FromLittle	Reads an unsigned 32-bit quantity from a little-endian buffer
POSH_ReadU64FromLittle	Reads an unsigned 64-bit quantity from a little-endian buffer
POSH_ReadI16FromLittle	Reads a signed 16-bit quantity from a little-endian buffer
POSH_ReadI32FromLittle	Reads a signed 32-bit quantity from a little-endian buffer
POSH_ReadI64FromLittle	Reads a signed 64-bit quantity from a little-endian buffer
POSH_ReadU16FromBig	Reads an unsigned 16-bit quantity from a big-endian buffer
POSH_ReadU32FromBig	Reads an unsigned 32-bit quantity from a big-endian buffer
POSH_ReadU64FromBig	Reads an unsigned 64-bit quantity from a big-endian buffer
POSH_ReadI16FromBig	Reads a signed 16-bit quantity from a big-endian buffer
POSH_ReadI32FromBig	Reads a signed 32-bit quantity from a big-endian buffer
POSH_ReadI64FromBig	Reads a signed 64-bit quantity from a big-endian buffer

B

THE RULES FOR PORTABILITY

1. **Never assume anything.** Convert implicit assumptions to explicit require-
    ments by using appropriate run-time and compile-time checks.
2. **Portability is a means to an end, not an end unto itself.** Write portable
    software because it provides tangible benefits: larger markets, higher-
    quality software, and more flexibility. Avoid the portability-as-dogma
    mindset, since programs in the real world need to have nonportable
    elements in order to run effectively.
3. **Establish a reasonable baseline.** Don't try to make an application porta-
    ble across a ridiculous range of platforms. It is rare that meaningful
    software can run unchanged from a handheld system to a powerful
    supercomputer, yet for some reason, obsessive portability geeks will try
    to do this. To make the process palatable define a sane set of minimum
    requirements ("32-bit integers, virtual memory, and multithreading"
    and so on) and just accept that you will not be able to port your soft-
    ware easily to systems that don't meet that baseline.
4. **Never read or write structures monolithically from or to memory.** Always
    read and write structures one element at a time, so that endian, align-
    ment, and size differences are factored out.
5. **Never cast raw bytes to a structure.** This relates to rule 2, but due to byte
    ordering, alignment, and size differences, casting a raw set of bytes to a
    structure will often cause difficulties when migrating to new platforms.

6. **Always convert to or from a canonical format when moving data in or out of memory.** Applications that must compile, run, and share data between disparate platforms must deal with the different native data type differences. Converting to a known size and byte-ordering transferring to and from memory ensures this.

7. **Good habits trump specific knowledge of bugs and standards.** All the esoteric portability knowledge in the world isn't relevant if the tools or platforms don't cooperate. And the only way to ensure that the platforms cooperate (or are at least functional) is to adhere to strong practices and habits that root out problems as soon as possible.

8. **Avoid new language or library features.** Whenever a new language feature is ratified or accepted by the development community, it still takes a long time for that feature to propagate successfully, limiting portability.

9. **Integrate testing.** The easiest way to catch bugs is by installing "bug traps" designed to find failure cases and exceptional situations. This is doubly important when working on cross-platform software, where a piece of code may work fine on one system but fail inexplicably on another.

10. **Use compile-time assertions.** Finding invalid assumptions during compilation is preferable to finding those invalid assumptions at run time. The earlier you can find an error, the better.

11. **Use strict compilation.** Use the tools available to you when looking for portability problems. One of the best tools is the compiler. Most compilers have switches you can enable that tell them to generate errors or warnings when they encounter nonstandard constructs or compile-specific extensions.

12. **Write straightforward code.** The cleaner, more concise, and easier to read your code, the easier it is to identify any invalid assumptions and for programmers working on other platforms to understand what you're doing.

13. **Do not expect floating-point code to operate the same way on different platforms.** Floating point is a compatibility and standards nightmare, and the probability is very high that a set of floating-point operations on one system will not generate the same results on a different system. Expecting this type of consistency can lead to a lot of difficult-to-find bugs.

14. **Avoid excessive conditional compilation statements.** The C/C++ preprocessor is a wonderfully simple yet powerful tool, but it is far too easy to abuse its features, creating code that is difficult to read and maintain. If you find your code riddled with conditional compilation statements, that's probably a good sign that you need to refactor and abstract your implementation.

15. **Understand that almost anything can change between compilers.** Basic things like the size of basic types; size, alignment, and packing of structures; availability and size of stack; and so on can change unexpectedly.

16. **Leverage portable third-party libraries, but be careful.** Third-party libraries can do a lot of the work necessary when writing a cross-platform library, but they put your project in a very vulnerable position. Be careful that including such libraries is the right choice.

17. **Performance and resource usage must be as portable as your features.** It's relatively easy to get something working on two different platforms, but guaranteeing that the performance will be adequate across a wide range is a lot more difficult. An algorithm that is fine on a dual-processor desktop machine might need to be rethought when porting to a cell phone.

18. **Portability means supporting other cultures, regions, and languages.** Software development isn't just about code and processors and APIs anymore. Programmers and software developers are expected to understand that their software may be used by residents of other countries. You must consider simple things like languages and keyboard layouts, along with far more subtle issues, such as the appropriateness and meaning of icon graphics and sounds.

19. **Consider using a language more suited to the task.** A lot of programmers today use C and C++ simply due to familiarity. However, the performance of modern computers has made higher-level languages such as Java, Python, C#, and Ruby appropriate for many kinds of development tasks. Consider investigating these languages if you do not need the low-level access and performance of C and C++.

20. **Systems are becoming more secure.** Don't assume that you can install files anywhere, take over a user's system at will, or access all parts of the filesystem. Many users don't have administrative access to their own machines, so applications must be cognizant of limitations when accessing privileged areas or files outside the current user's control.

REFERENCES

ANSI. "ISO/IEC 14882: Programming Languages—C++." ANSI, 1989. The first draft ANSI standard for the C++ programming language.

ANSI. "ISO/IEC 9899:1990: Programming Languages—C." ANSI, 1990. The first ANSI standard for the C programming language.

ANSI. "ISO/IEC 9899:1999: Programming Languages—C." ANSI, 1999. The second ANSI standard for the C programming language.

Ellis, Margaret A. and Bjarne Stroustrup. *The Annotated C++ Reference Manual.* Addison-Wesley Professional, 1990. Before the C++ standard, there was the ARM. Interesting primarily for its historical value; much of the book's content is obsolete by today's standards.

Giencke, Patricia. *Portable C++.* McGraw-Hill, 1996. A decent but short overview of portability issues specifically as they apply to the C++ language.

Harbison, Samuel P. and Guy L. Steele. *C: A Reference Manual (5th Edition).* Prentice Hall, 2002. A good, straightforward reference on the C programming language.

Horton, Mark R. *Portable C Software.* Prentice Hall, 1990. An early attempt to talk about portable software development with the C programming language. Horton's book looks at portability from a more implementation-specific point of view, specifically restricting much of his discussion to porting software between Unix variants.

Kernighan, Brian W. and Dennis M. Ritchie. *The C Programming Language, Second Edition.* Prentice Hall, 1988. The definitive classic text on the C programming language.

Prasad, Shashi. *Multithreading Programming Techniques.* McGraw-Hill Osborne Media, 1997. A concise, well-rounded discussion of multithreading programming techniques across a wide range of platforms. Several of the platforms and APIs discussed are not relevant today, but the bulk of the book is still valuable and interesting.

Ritchie, Dennis M. "Development of the C Language." http://cm.bell-labs.com/cm/cs/who/dmr/chist.htm. Originally presented at the Second History of Programming Languages conference, Cambridge, MA, 1993. A fascinating look at the evolution of the C language.

Stroustrup, Bjarne. *The C++ Programming Language (Special 3rd Edition).* Addison-Wesley Professional, 2000. The C++ equivalent of Kernighan and Ritchie's classic text on the C language.

Stroustrup, Bjarne. *The Design and Evolution of C++.* Addison-Wesley Professional, 1994. An interesting historical perspective on the early design of C++. It's largely out-of-date, since the language has changed dramatically in the past decade.

Tribble, David R. "Incompatibilities Between ISO C and ISO C++." http://david.tribble.com/text/cdiffs.htm, 2001. A very good summary of the differences between C and C++ as per the latest standards for each.

Van Der Linden, Peter. *Expert C Programming: Deep C Secrets.* Prentice Hall, 1994. Thorough coverage of a lot of the trickier and more confusing parts of the C programming language.

INDEX

user thread, 161
USHRT_MAX, 128
utility functions, POSH, 225–28

V

variables, scoping of, 6–7
versioning problems, 177–78
VINES, 150
virtual functions, 45–46
virtual machine, 214
viruses, 171
void * type, 99–100
void feclearexcept(), 105
void fegetenv(), 106
void fegetexceptflag(), 105
void feraiseexcept(), 105
void fesetenv(), 106
void fesetexceptflag(), 105
void feupdateenv(), 106
volume specifiers, 189
vsprintf(), 126

W

WAN (wide area network), 150
WAV file format, 202
wchar.h, 112
wctype.h, 112
wide area network (WAN), 150
Win32 NTFS filesystem, 190
WINAPI, 134
Window systems, evolution of user
        interfaces, 142–43
WinSock API, 151
<winsock2.h>, 151
<winsock.h>, 151
WordStar, 157
worms, 171
WSAEAGAIN, 153
WSAEWOULDBLOCK, 153
WSAGetLastError(), 153
wxWidgets, 221–22

X

X Windows, 143
XML, 154, 204–5
XSI (X/Open System Interface), 23

Electronic Frontier Foundation
Defending Freedom in the Digital World

Free Speech. Privacy. Innovation. Fair Use. Reverse Engineering. If you care about these rights in the digital world, then you should join the Electronic Frontier Foundation (EFF). EFF was founded in 1990 to protect the rights of users and developers of technology. EFF is the first to identify threats to basic rights online and to advocate on behalf of free expression in the digital age.

The Electronic Frontier Foundation Defends Your Rights!
Become a Member Today!
http://www.eff.org/support/

Current EFF projects include:

Protecting your fundamental right to vote. Widely publicized security flaws in computerized voting machines show that, though filled with potential, this technology is far from perfect. EFF is defending the open discussion of e-voting problems and is coordinating a national litigation strategy addressing issues arising from use of poorly developed and tested computerized voting machines.

Ensuring that you are not traceable through your things. Libraries, schools, the government and private sector businesses are adopting radio frequency identification tags, or RFIDs – a technology capable of pinpointing the physical location of whatever item the tags are embedded in. While this may seem like a convenient way to track items, it's also a convenient way to do something less benign: track people and their activities through their belongings. EFF is working to ensure that embrace of this technology does not erode your right to privacy.

Stopping the FBI from creating surveillance backdoors on the Internet. EFF is part of a coalition opposing the FBI's expansion of the Communications Assistance for Law Enforcement Act (CALEA), which would require that the wiretap capabilities built into the phone system be extended to the Internet, forcing ISPs to build backdoors for law enforcement.

Providing you with a means by which you can contact key decision-makers on cyber-liberties issues. EFF maintains an action center that provides alerts on technology, civil liberties issues and pending legislation to more than 50,000 subscribers. EFF also generates a weekly online newsletter, EFFector, and a blog that provides up-to-the minute information and commentary.

Defending your right to listen to and copy digital music and movies. The entertainment industry has been overzealous in trying to protect its copyrights, often decimating fair use rights in the process. EFF is standing up to the movie and music industries on several fronts.

Check out all of the things we're working on at http://www.eff.org and join today or make a donation to support the fight to defend freedom online.

ELECTRONIC FRONTIER FOUNDATION · 454 SHOTWELL STREET · SAN FRANCISCO, CA 94110 · 415.436.9333

WRITE GREAT CODE, VOLUME 1
Understanding the Machine

by RANDALL HYDE

Many of today's programmers lack a formal education in computer science. The Write Great Code series is here to fill those gaps in education. Volume 1 of this series teaches machine organization, including numeric representation, binary arithmetic and bit operations, floating point representation, system and memory organization, character representation, constants and types, digital design, CPU instruction set and memory architecture, input and output, and how compilers work.

NOVEMBER 2004, 464 PP., $39.95 ($55.95 CAN)
ISBN 1-59327-003-8

WRITE GREAT CODE, VOLUME 2
Thinking Low-Level, Writing High-Level

by RANDALL HYDE

Today's computer science students aren't always taught how to carefully choose their high-level language statements to produce efficient code. *Write Great Code, Volume 2: Thinking Low-Level, Writing High-Level* shows software engineers what too many college and university courses don't: how compilers translate high-level language statements and data structures into machine code. Armed with this knowledge, they will be better able to make informed choices concerning the use of those high-level structures, which will help the compiler produce far better machine code, all without having to give up the productivity and portability benefits of using a high-level language.

SEPTEMBER 2005, 752 PP., $44.95 ($60.95 CAN)
ISBN 1-59327-065-8

HOW NOT TO PROGRAM IN C++
111 Broken Programs and 3 Working Ones, or Why Does 2+2=5986?

by STEVE OUALLINE

Based on real-world errors, the 101 fun and challenging C++ puzzles in *How Not to Program in C++* range from easy (one wrong character) to mind twisting (errors with multiple threads). Match your wits against the author's and polish your language skills as you try to fix broken programs. Clues help along the way, and answers are provided at the back of the book.

APRIL 2003, 280 PP., $24.95 ($37.95 CAN)
ISBN 1-886411-95-6

SILENCE ON THE WIRE
A Field Guide to Passive Reconnaissance and Indirect Attacks

by MICHAL ZALEWSKI

Author Michal Zalewski has long been known and respected in the hacking and security communities for his intelligence, curiosity, and creativity, and this book is truly unlike anything else out there. *Silence on the Wire* is no humdrum technical white paper or how-to manual for protecting one's network. Rather, Zalewski's book is a fascinating narrative that explores a variety of unique, uncommon, and often quite elegant security challenges that defy classification and eschew the traditional attacker-victim model.

FEBRUARY 2005, 312 PP., $39.95 ($53.95 CAN)
ISBN 1-59327-046-1

HACKING
The Art of Exploitation

by JON ERICKSON

Hacking: The Art of Exploitation is for both technical and non-technical people who are interested in computer security. Unlike many so-called hacking books, this book explains the technical aspects of hacking, including stack based overflows, heap based overflows, string exploits, return-into-libc, shellcode, and cryptographic attacks on 802.11b. Erickson's goal is to instruct—not to promote any illegal activity. If you're serious about hacking, this book is for you.

OCTOBER 2003, 264 PP., $39.95 ($59.95 CAN)
ISBN 1-59327-007-0

PHONE:
800.420.7240 OR
415.863.9900
MONDAY THROUGH FRIDAY,
9 A.M. TO 5 P.M. (PST)

FAX:
415.863.9950
24 HOURS A DAY,
7 DAYS A WEEK

EMAIL:
SALES@NOSTARCH.COM

WEB:
HTTP://WWW.NOSTARCH.COM

MAIL:
NO STARCH PRESS
555 DE HARO ST, SUITE 250
SAN FRANCISCO, CA 94107
USA

UPDATES

Visit **http://www.nostarch.com/wpc.htm** for updates, errata, and other information.

COLOPHON

Write Portable Code was written using OpenOffice.org Writer and laid out in Adobe FrameMaker. The font families used are New Baskerville for body text, TheSansMono Condensed for code text, Futura for headings and tables, and Dogma for titles.

The book was printed and bound at Malloy Incorporated in Ann Arbor, Michigan. The paper is Glatfelter Thor 60# Antique, which is made from 50 percent recycled materials, including 30 percent postconsumer content. The book uses a RepKover binding, which allows it to lay flat when open.